T0289905

ROUTLEDGE LIBRARY EDITIONS: MANAGEMENT

Volume 27

MANAGING THE MULTINATIONAL SUBSIDIARY

MANAGING THE MULTINATIONAL SUBSIDIARY

Response to Environmental Changes and to Host Nation R&D Policies

Edited by
HAMID ETEMAD AND
LOUISE SÉGUIN DULUDE

LONDON AND NEW YORK

First published in 1986 by Croom Helm Ltd

This edition first published in 2018
by Routledge
2 Park Square, Milton Park, Abingdon, Oxon OX14 4RN

and by Routledge
711 Third Avenue, New York, NY 10017

Routledge is an imprint of the Taylor & Francis Group, an informa business

British Library Cataloguing in Publication Data
A catalogue record for this book is available from the British Library

ISBN: 978-1-138-55938-7 (Set)
ISBN: 978-1-351-05538-3 (Set) (ebk)
ISBN: 978-0-8153-9319-1 (Volume 27) (hbk)
ISBN: 978-1-351-18919-4 (Volume 27) (ebk)

Publisher's Note
The publisher has gone to great lengths to ensure the quality of this reprint but points out that some imperfections in the original copies may be apparent.

Disclaimer
The publisher has made every effort to trace copyright holders and would welcome correspondence from those they have been unable to trace.

MANAGING THE MULTINATIONAL SUBSIDIARY

Response to Environmental Changes and to
Host Nation R&D Policies

Edited by HAMID ETEMAD AND LOUISE SÉGUIN DULUDE

CROOM HELM
London & Sydney

© 1986 Hamid Etemad and Louise Séguin Dulude
Croom Helm Ltd, Provident House, Burrell Row,
Beckenham, Kent BR3 1AT
Croom Helm Australia Pty Ltd, Suite 4, 6th Floor,
64–76 Kippax Street, Surry Hills, NSW 2010, Australia

British Library Cataloguing in Publication Data

Managing the multinational subsidiary. Response to environmental changes and to
host nation R&D policies —
   (Croom Helm series in international business)
   1. International business enterprises — Management. 2. Subsidiary corporations
   — Management
   I. Etemad, Hamid, II. Dulude, Louise Séguin.
   658'.049   HD62.4

ISBN 0-7099-0968-3

Filmset by Mayhew Typesetting, Bristol, England
Printed and bound in Great Britain

CONTENTS

FIGURES

TABLES

PREFACE

The subtitle, 'Response to Environmental Changes and to Host Nation R&D Policies', captures the focus of this book. In the past 25 years, multinational enterprises have constantly assumed greater importance in the economic life of host nations and account for a larger share than ever before of international business transactions. The interplay of a set of strong forces in favour of the future liberalisation of trade, above and beyond the system envisioned by the GATT's Tokyo Round, combined with the quickening introduction and integration of computers into communication, production, distribution and management resulting in massive productivity gains, are rapidly rendering obsolete the 'old ways' and challenging scholars, managers, and authorities to devise newer, more efficient ways. In this quest, host nations are forced to reformulate their science and R&D policies. Multinational enterprises, in turn, are responding to these waves of environmental and policy changes and examining their strategic options. Within such a highly charged environment, the management of subsidiaries has assumed certain delicacies of its own. This book is designed to address some of these concerns.

A number of notable individuals and institutions played a crucial role in the process that resulted in the current book. The Social Science and Humanities Research Council of Canada (SSHRC) provided us with a 'Strategic Grant' for organising a conference which brought interested academics, business leaders and governmental authorities to consider jointly various aspects of the topic and examine its possible strategic implications. This conference turned out to be an invaluable experience, as it exposed participants to the immediate concerns of managers of subsidiaries, the business community, governmental authorities, and academic researchers. Without such a rich and open forum of exchange, the views and directions of some of the papers would have been very different. We would like to express our sincere thanks and appreciation to the SSHRC for making the opportunity available.

The Centre for International Business Studies at the Ecole des Hautes Etudes Commerciales (HEC), Montreal, agreed to underwrite the additional costs of the conference and provided a wide range of support services that contributed tremendously to the success of local arrangements, and the conference as a whole. Additionally, our two institutions, the HEC and the Faculty of Management of McGill University, sponsored the conference and, in their own way, greatly contributed to the success of the conference, the ensuing research, and finally, the current book.

Without the generous financial support of the HEC, the task of copy editing this book into its existing form would have probably been unbearable. We deeply appreciate this support and remain indebted not only for this vital support but, more importantly, for their dedication to our research and trust in our work.

Professor Alan M. Rugman, the Editor of the Croom Helm International Business Series, provided encouragement from the beginning of the project and became a stimulating force in the publication stage. Mr Peter Sowden of Croom Helm was of no less importance. He also provided guidance and encouragement in all stages. We are thankful and appreciative of these sentiments.

Miss Kathleen Deslauriers took up the unenviable task of copy editing and bringing a consistent style to a collection of very different contributions in a rather short period of time. Miss Michèle Lessard and Miss Wendy Smith typed and retyped the edited manuscript. We feel greatly indebted to these individuals who accomplished the task in a graceful and efficient manner.

Finally, this book, in a sense, is the result of a joint venture of a large number of individuals and institutions based primarily on enthusiasm, commitment, and extreme cooperation, without which this final result would have been seriously in doubt. We would like to express a sincere word of thanks as a token of our appreciation to all of them for their contribution.

H. Etemad
L. Séguin Dulude

1 INTRODUCTION: MANAGING THE SUBSIDIARY

Hamid Etemad and Louise Séguin Dulude

The environment of international business has been going through a turbulent period of change that has greatly intensified during the past decade. These are not isolated or short-run fluctuations in an otherwise stable long-run trend that can be easily weathered. They are, rather, so radical as to have fundamentally challenged some basic understandings and standard assumptions about the nature of environment and the international business practices compatible with it.

This book is designed to enhance the understanding of these newly emerging patterns. It is not, therefore, concerned with the historic past and what it has entailed or implied, but with the new strategic responses that international business players are devising to cope with a fluid environment and a conflicting array of demands made on them. This changing array of demands and fluidity of environment are vivid manifestations of a fundamental and dynamic set of forces in the environment of international business that must be seriously considered. These forceful new currents of change are affecting various facets of multinational enterprises' (MNEs) working environment, impinging upon the state of technology, institutional arrangements, governmental expectations, consumer demands and, above all, international competition. In response to the forces and demands of change MNEs have adopted, and continue to try, various postures. This book will cover some of these response patterns and their ramifications.

MNEs and their subsidiaries are important players in the international business game. But MNEs are not the only players that are subject to change; home and host countries are also affected. The governments of these countries have begun to take an active role. By changing the rules, host countries have made unprecedented and successful bids to control and shape their own domestic environment and, in turn, that of the international environment. In so doing, they are further changing the situation, which imposes a new set of demands.

Intense competition among MNEs, combined with an improved state of information and information processing, is forcing a similar degree of competitiveness on the host and home countries. One clear result of this intensified multilateral rivalry is that the successful practices and strategies of the past are being rendered obsolete, and the potency of

1

newly emerging strategies is further heightening these changing patterns. There is a genuine need to study the emerging changes, to examine the possible options, and to contain the threat of potential harm to home, host and MNEs alike.

This book in fact deals with some of the pressures and forces that have been changing the environment and are challenging the efficiency, and hence the viability, of the old arrangements. For example, the familiar truncated subsidiary operations and the tariff factories of the past are being replaced by a range of new strategic arrangements which include, but are not limited to, rationalised but integrated operations, specialised but widely distributed products, and internally autonomous but still highly dependent MNE-subsidiary relationships. These were not among the desired features of the old types of arrangement. Except for those who are directly involved, the managerial, operational and policy implications of this new set of complex relationships have remained off-limits and, to a great extent, unexplored.

The complexity and the potency of new arrangements are changing past comparative advantages, rearranging old competitive forces and, more importantly, requiring new managerial practices and challenging almost everyone involved. This involvement includes, among others, the students of international business, managers who will eventually encounter them, and even the members of regulating agencies who are trying to increase the efficiency of particular operations. This book attempts to respond to the informational needs of these groups. It also aims to stimulate a process by which the widening gap between the newly emerging host country policies and corporate strategies and those of the past can be narrowed or closed altogether.

The Changing Environment of International Business

As just stated, the profound changes in international business within the past five years have reached a turbulent state. This turbulence has shaken the foundations of almost all of the accepted and standard rules. Past practices and established operating procedures have come under exceedingly increasing pressures, face radical attacks and require extensive modification. Consider, for example, the following states contributing to this turbulence.

Global Communication, and Shrinking Time and Distance

The rapid spread of the electronic age, especially in the area of communication, is encompassing every corner of the world in a trend toward a more homogenous world market and away from the heterogenous national and regional markets of the past. This trend, in turn, is increasing the acceptance rate of world products and reducing the need to produce locally adapted products. The old notion of distinct local product/market characteristics is disappearing; and, in a sense, time and distance are shrinking. Despite all the remaining differences, the concept of a global village is closer to reality than ever before. This has begun to pave the way for homogeneous product offerings and therefore points toward efficient world-scale production facilities and away from inefficient, small-scale, national and local production. In the absence of such development, national, commercial or industrial policies notwithstanding, the world product's risk of being rejected would make the massive ongoing global rationalisation logically and economically untenable.

Computer Revolution in Manufacturing

There has been a revolution in manufacturing. Computer aided design and manufacturing have increased the possibility of incorporating variety (or options) into the original concept so as to meet more accurately the needs of end-users without greatly increasing incremental costs or incurring losses in the scale economies of production. The old industrial technology offered scale economies and lower unit costs through longer production runs. Unfortunately, it also entailed certain rigidities which made variety costly or impracticable in some particular cases.

The North American automobile industry offers a prime example of this phenomenon. For decades, it dominated both the North American and worldwide markets through mass production and low costs. The industry suffered, however, from a low rate of significant innovation. Thus, only cosmetic changes and minor improvements or options could be introduced without adding tremendously to costs. By contrast, in Japan and some European countries, a switch to robotics and computer aided production introduced certain flexibilities into the production line that not only allowed for a real satisfaction of consumer needs, but also provided a worldwide competitive edge in their favour.

Massive Investment Requirements

The viability of fragmented and local manufacturing of the past and its associated relatively low investments have also changed. The investment requirements for world-scale or highly advanced production are massive, and are having a radical impact on the way related strategic decisions are made. For example, without the rich and lucrative markets of North America and Europe, the Japanese and Europeans could not possibly justify the huge investment outlays required for building world-scale plants and bringing the new technologies on line. Regardless of the investment criteria and expected returns, these massive commitments would not have been commercially viable, had worldwide marketing not been guaranteed. This dictated equally massive efforts in marketing. Conversely, once the markets were secured the investments were justified. The subsequent economies of scale, enhanced by the economies of scope because of the new technological innovation, facilitated sustained access and entry, reinforced consumer loyalty and created entry barriers for others. Should these developments be permitted to continue unchecked and unchallenged, a large share of world production would be supplied by these world-scale operations and their associates. But world markets cannot sustain a plethora of world-scale products or finance ever increasing waves of new technology or technological innovations. This trend is bound to disappear. Then the few lucky pioneers can expect to have the territory for themselves for some time. Soon, there may not be much choice left, because it may no longer be possible to establish a new world-scale operation or join an existing one, regardless of the cost or choice of strategy. This brings a sense of urgency to strategic options, as stakes are being raised all the time. This sense of urgency is further shortening the life of ineffi- cient and small facilities, accelerating the actual rate of transformation and curtailing the transitional period from current arrangements to those suitable for future operations. In so far as the range of options is concerned, MNEs face a wide choice from rationalised-integrated arrangements at one extreme, to the world product mandate (WPM) at the other. Unfortunately, indigenous firms and, for that matter, their governments, do not seem to have much choice — at least not yet. Owing to this lack of choice, discussion and examination of the situation are gaining in importance and urgency in government circles as never before.

Increased Global Rationalisation

Armed with the competitive powers of new technologies, world-scale production and lower labour costs, producers from the newly industrialised countries (NIC) of Asia and Latin America have begun to march into the large and rich markets of older industrialised countries. These producers leave no market unexplored, nor are they stopped by tariff and nontariff barriers. They can easily outcompete relatively high cost producers by simply offering a much better range of prices, quality and choice.

Faced with these difficult realities, MNEs' subsidiaries can no longer take any refuge in old truncated or tariff factories. They are forced to respond accordingly and recognise the need for rethinking, redesigning and reconstructing the past arrangements. Certain subsidiaries of US based MNEs seem to face a more urgent problem, as they can no longer rely on their parents' more advanced technologies to come to their rescue. To their dismay, the technological lead has already shifted to others (i.e. in Europe and Japan). In some cases, the shift is more pervasive. Not only have these MNEs lost their technological lead, they are also on the verge of slipping from their once commanding position. This latter subject is cause for extreme concern. For those host governments or businesses (including subsidiaries) that rely on, or are already attached to these particular US based MNEs, a reexamination and reformulation of the technological strategy and environment are in order. For other host governments and businesses not so directly attached or technologically aligned, the question of technological alignment is becoming a more crucial issue. Some of these leading-edge technologies are not compatible with each other, and the cost of shifting from one to the other at a later stage may prove to be very high — if not completely unaffordable.

Intensification of Research and Development and Investment Incentives System

Faced with new developments in production technology and the resulting invasion of their markets, host countries have also started to reassess their technological requirements, reexamine their policies with respect to technology, and reformulate their research and development (R&D) infrastructure and environment to resist and arrest any further erosion of their subsidiaries' viability. Although the range of choices (and their associated research commitment) is rather clear (e.g. from fully rationalised-integrated subsidiary with no R&D to a WPM with its own fully developed R&D), the MNE's response to the host country signals for change has, for the most part, been mixed and, at times, non-committal. In taking this stance, MNEs heighten the state of competition and raise the level of local support for such undertakings amongst the contending nations. This, in turn, forces the national government to apply an unprecedented level of scrutiny to the comparison of potential choices and/or candidates. As a result, the tables are turned. MNEs as suppliers of technology are induced to disclose and make commitments for larger undertakings than they initially foresaw. Thus, MNEs in concert with the host, and potential host, countries justify and pave the road for further rationalisation and globalisation of production, international trade and investment.

Emergence of NICs

The impressive success of NICs combined with ever mounting pressures from rather efficient low cost NIC producers have also started to play an influential role in the process. NICs' relative success in solving most of their own economic problems serves as a model, and, hence, justifies other host countries' demands for more potent technologies and highly favourable arrangements in order to catch up with these NICs. As a result, the push is on for better deals and for the transfer of more advanced technologies to combat the ongoing trade pressures, to improve the balance of payment crises that most developing nations face and, optimistically, to reserve these negative trends through future exports.

To enhance the future technological, and hence economic, viabilities, most host country governments have reformulated their new science, technology and R&D policies. These policies are not only quite progressive in terms of expectations and requirements, but also very competitive in terms of tax breaks, exemptions, grants and other financial and nonfinancial incentives. Therefore market pressures on the one hand and governmental pressures and incentives on the other are forcing new arrangements. MNEs, in turn, have come to realise that cooperation and a positive response to these signals may lead to access with favourable terms, and to an increase in their overall competitiveness, not only in the local markets but also in wealthy and lucrative markets elsewhere. Conversely, rejection or a negative response may not only shut them out of local markets, but also enhance their competitors' overall state of viability and competitiveness. In sum, the MNE-host country's once seemingly simple game of international business has recently begun to take on the complexity of multi-player and multipurpose games in which stakes and risks are high, but payoffs considerably higher. However, a real loss can still spell potential economic ruin.

The Fall of Trade Barriers and the Rise of Trade Intermediaries

Dramatic lowering of tariff barriers as a result of the Tokyo Round of the GATT is eliminating a substantial number of tariffs and reducing others. The average reduction is of 30 to 40 per cent. This has begun to threaten small and locally oriented producers. These producers must make a choice between increasing their scale to raise their efficiency to compete in the international market, or risk elimination. Their inexperience in international markets has given rise to the demand for international marketing related services. In response to these demands, a large group of small and medium sized intermediaries and trade agents have become rather active.

Parallel developments in the area of worldwide distribution through the advent of large-scale national and international trading companies are also changing the nature and composition of world trade in other ways. Through the facilities of these trading intermediaries, small but specialised companies are entering the international markets with a vengeance. These smaller companies are taking advantage of their market niches to reach their potential worldwide market segments in support of their ongoing quest for growth. This is done through further improvements in quality and variety, combined with product line expansion and further market penetration and expansion. There is strong evidence to suggest that this type of planned incremental and gradual growth has resulted in an increasing world market share for its practitioners, thereby changing the nature of competitiveness and source of competition, and intensifying the rate of change well beyond the reaches of past expectations.

Introduction of Nonconventional Procedures

The severe debt crises of developing countries, combined with the mismanagement or shortages of foreign exchange, is creating opportunities for innovative or nonconventional procedures. Some of these procedures have revived past practices. Countertrade is certainly one of these. Within the past five years, countertrade has started to assume an important place in international trade and transactions. Countertrade, or 'offset' transaction, as it is popularly called, was limited to the Eastern European and Communist countries for a long time. Shortages of foreign exchange and inconvertibility of their local currencies forced these countries to enter into a variety of 'counterpurchase' and 'barter' agreements when dealing with the rest of the world. The recurrence of similar problems, combined with a traditional lack of international marketing expertise, in the less developed and even developed countries, has revived barter agreements and is giving countertrade a new life. A large number of international transactions are reported to include an 'offset' component. Through countertrade, the seller of goods and services or the supplier of technology agrees to receive the other's goods and services as partial payment instead of an outright monetary payment. Under such arrangements, even the simplest monetary transactions of the past take on a degree of complexity that most conventional subsidiaries are not equipped to handle. Consider, for example, the fact that Pepsi

Cola was forced to accept foodstuffs and alcoholic beverages as partial payment, and thus became the supplier of these goods to international markets. Even more dramatic are the cases where lumber, coffee beans and primary metals are offered as partial payment for highly sophisticated products such as jet engines or aviation electronics. Countertrade has therefore introduced new opportunities and impediments. Although it is helping certain producers to enter international markets it is also adding new dimensions and complexities to international transactions. Simply, it is complicating the management of subsidiaries in general, and that of the headquarters in particular. The mastery of these complexities, however, creates market opportunities that would otherwise be considered closed or not viable.

The Scope and Coverage of the Book

Managing a subsidiary has never been an isolated affair. The additional interdependencies resulting from the above environmental changes have increased the need for a better understanding of the context within which subsidiary management is to be conducted. This context is not simple, nor is it set or controlled by an entity. In fact, there are many formal and informal entities exerting a multitude of influences which individually and collectively shape the environmental context. The interests of MNEs and home and host countries are factors of foremost and determining influence but a variety of other international institutions (e.g. international regulatory agencies, UN agencies, etc.) and nongovernmental organisations make their presence felt and also play a role in shaping and reshaping the overall environment and the subsidiary's immediate operational context.

Growing competition between MNEs for a larger piece of the action in international markets intensifies the need for efficiency. The quest for ever more efficient operations makes it imperative that MNEs find ways within their own organisations to achieve such required efficiencies. Thus, headquarters pressure operating subsidiaries to find innovative and more efficient procedures, or else face the inevitable consequences. Subsidiaries convey the same message to their own workers and suppliers; before long, the entire operating context in a host country is involved and forced to respond. In a reactive mode, home and host countries do indeed respond, and take policy actions to better protect their interest or at least to minimise the impact upon them of such adverse movements. In a proactive mode, however, the host and home countries may take the initiative and set the entire process in motion causing a whole wave of corresponding responses and changes. Regardless of the original cause and the force of the impact, it is important to recognise the continuing role of home and host countries in forming and reforming the environmental context. It is this context that increases the opportunity or the cost of certain actions at the expense of certain others; and hence sets the actual operating mode under which the potency of some strategies is increased and that of others reduced or invalidated.

Therefore the subject of operational context — popularly referred to by a variety of names, such as policy setting, policy context, industrial orientation or direction of policy — developed in the first three chapters constitutes a major theme and key part of this book. This part begins with a chapter by Carl E. Beigie and James K. Stewart. After an extensive review of new developments, embracing a wide range of topics such as the rising influence of NICs and Japan in international markets, the widening technological gap between local firms and foreign producers, the decline of tariffs under GATT's Tokyo Round, and the increasing demands for voluntary export restraints, these authors propose and then examine four policy options which Canada might use in confronting competitive threats and challenges posed by emerging developments. Their detailed examination covers the role and impact of specific policy tools used to shape policy context. The chapter comes to a series of distinct and related conclusions. It is suggested that a comprehensive Canada-US trade agreement would be a significant advantage for the subsidiaries. The much improved access to the rich North American markets, the resulting competitive pressures, and positive spillover to other areas would substantially improve the chances of specialised subsidiaries. Short of a comprehensive trade agreement, the authors still believe that there is 'tremendous scope' for better domestic policy management, especially in terms of indirect policy measures favouring WPM type arrangements. Yet these arrangements are subject to the countervailing measures of the US government and other trading nations. In their view, the final salvation lies in a combination of 'Canada-US trade with far-reaching initiative in competition, R&D and other policy spheres'. While the specificity of US-Canada relationships may have somewhat narrowed the scope of this chapter, the richness of the analytical framework in setting a formal policy context within which concrete options or questions can be examined contributes to developing insights in equally complex situations elsewhere.

The second chapter of this part adds a historical and a public policy perspective. In this chapter A.J. Sarna traces the direction of public policy on WPMs, and gives a vivid portrayal of the evolutionary path which has led to the current policy context. Sarna, for example, explains that 'prior to the Second World War, many US owned firms were established in Canada's manufacturing sector with exclusive mandates to take advantage of the country's privileged export market access to Britain, the West Indies, South Africa, Australia, New Zealand, and India under Imperial tariff preferences'. But as Canada's external trade started to gravitate away from the Commonwealth countries and toward the US and other countries, previous arrangements lost their viability and began to change. With the demise of the Commonwealth arrangements, US based parents began to limit their Canadian subsidiaries' power to export to the rest of the world and thereby altered their prevailing operational context. In response, Canada issued explicit policies concerning the behaviour of foreign owned operations.

Beginning with this early birth of the policy (or operational) context, in the 1950s, the chapter traces the highlights of change over the next 30 years to document its progression from earlier voluntary guidelines to the harsh and mandatory provisions of the now defunct Foreign Investment Review Act and its implementing agency popularly known as FIRA. While the voluntary guidelines encouraged foreign owned firms to develop the technological, research and design capacity 'necessary to take a full advantage of market opportunities domestically and abroad' and to strive progressively toward 'achieving appropriate specialisation of productive operations within the internationally affiliated group of companies', FIRA demanded concrete commitment for specific undertakings. It is interesting to note that the earlier voluntary guidelines 'encouraged' specialisation and after some 30 years the subsidiaries are now obliged to specialise because of market forces. In fact market forces have brought about a full circle.

The chapter then goes on to show that FIRA's demands for specialisation (e.g. WPM) and R&D undertakings were not an isolated act. Instead, they seem to have been a part of a well integrated public policy, with most ministries of the federal government in their own subtle ways lending support to WPM type operations. In some cases the application of the policy set a clearly stimulating context in a variety of ways ranging from government procurement to outright assistance in the form of subsidies and grants.

In terms of countervailing forces affecting the context adversely, the United States lodged a formal complaint under GATT Article XVII: 1 (C) and Article III: 5 was in direct challenge to such a policy. Although the 'US complaints against both types of FIRA related requirements were not upheld by the GATT panel, the US did win against FIRA elicited undertakings to purchase goods from Canadian sources'. Government procurement clearly falls within the latter category, and as Sarna speculates, the US is bound to raise the issue of 'national treatment' again in another forum and at other times, thereby reshaping and remoulding the existing operational context to its advantage. These two chapters as a whole are vivid examples of how home and host countries (and at times MNEs) individually and/or collectively have set about redefining the policy and operational context from which subsequent changes have emerged.

In the third chapter of this part David P. Rutenberg moves the operational context to the international scene and provides a still broader perspective. This chapter briefly reports the results of the author's extensive research in several countries in Asia and the European Community while on sabbatical leave with the National Defence College. This research was primarily motivated by the persistence of widespread calls for a comprehensive industrial strategy within which specific policies (e.g. ones towards WPMs) could be formulated. After a brief but comprehensive review of the role of national governments in supporting R&D, and the effects of such supportive policies on actual and potential WPM operations, the chapter presents the results of the survey of public policy and governmental attitudes in the countries studied. The findings point to a highly diverse set of national goals, policy tools and implementation procedures. They show, for example, that Japan has centralised basic research in its national research laboratories, while applied R&D is concentrated in corporate laboratories. The important thing in the Japanese system is the way in which new projects are mounted, new research teams are formed, old teams broken up and their members diffused into the corporate world to pursue further development of their work. In contrast to this, the chapter documents the German R&D system in which theoretical research is carried out in a series of 'Max Planck' government institutes, while applied research is done by German corporations. A set of hybrid research laboratories is designed and expected to provide the necessary interface. But, as Rutenberg states, 'their existence has reduced communication and coordination'.

Although not reviewed in this chapter, the Canadian system is much closer to the German system than to the Japanese one. Canada's National Research Council laboratories are mandated to conduct basic research in a variety of areas, while applied research is supposed to be done primarily in the corporate R&D laboratories. There are no 'interface laboratories', and as a result communication and coordination are less than optimal.

The chapter then focuses on the EC's efforts to set an agenda and to coordinate R&D efforts within the community. There is a striking similarity between the EC's efforts and those of Britain's Alvey Committee of British Industries. As reported in the chapter, they appear to be badly underfunded and can at best be expected to provide a forum and a means of social liaison.

This chapter comes to the general conclusion that nations have seriously begun to formulate their commercial and industrial strategies within which the generation of, access to, and control of certain technologies seem to hold a central place. Within this context, the chapter proposes a 'weighted assignment' procedure so that corporate planners can start to explore various mandating possibilities and begin to ask a variety of 'what if' questions. The implicit result of the proposed procedure is that countries which have developed high demands coupled with low projected benefit/cost ratios, including low profits, are likely to be left out of consideration for mandates. Similarly, those countries in which the development of industrial policy is not in congruity with associated rules and procedures are also likely to be left out, regardless of their level of support and sophistication. Simply, these countries project puzzling images to corporate planners and hence they will not be seriously considered as natural, and competitive candidates for receiving a mandate.

From Rutenberg's vantage point, a mandate can hardly be viewed as a monopoly right; it is only a 'right to be the most serious bidder in the ongoing progression of the product's evolution'. This chapter's critical review of some of the misconceptions of WPMs and their related operational features sets the stage for the book's next major theme.

This theme is concerned with the implications and operational effects of the above policy context with respect to the actual management of a subsidiary. Specifically, it examines the complexities or constraints that such a changing environment imposes, and the requirements or expectations that it demands. Five chapters address various facets of this subject and collectively constitute the second part of the book.

This part begins with a chapter on strategic management of the subsidiary. In this chapter, Joseph R. D'Cruz develops a framework for evaluating the subsidiary's potential strategic response to various policy or environmental changes emanating from the actions of MNEs, home and host countries, individually or collectively. D'Cruz states that 'similar considerations apply to multinational subsidiaries in other developed countries'. The findings of the chapter are based on the author's personal interview survey of a sample of 50 subsidiaries of US based multinational firms which were on both the *Fortune* 500 list of leading US corporations and the *Financial Post*'s list of the top 500 companies operating in Canada. After a brief review of strategic planning the chapter presents the four distinct phases of planning in a typical subsidiary setting. At one extreme, no significant formal planning is used, while at the other extreme not only does the subsidiary engage in formal strategic planning at the subsidiary level, but also participates at the parent's level in the planning and implementation of key strategic decisions affecting it.

Examination of various strategic facets of a subsidiary operation and the typical pattern by which it evolves from a simple importing outfit to a fully-fledged manufacturing and exporting firm in its own right, leads to an inevitable conclusion: managing a subsidiary based on strategic principles permits the subsidiary to achieve its goals, as strategically managed subsidiaries (Type IV) are found to be fully capable of weathering various policy changes and of taking the necessary steps to become a successful WPM operation.

D'Cruz finally concludes that 'WPMs are not granted as a gift from corporate parents to the subsidiaries: they have to be earned by the subsidiary on the basis of superior competence and resources'. Thus, Type IV subsidiaries seem to be the only viable candidates. This relates directly to the next chapter.

The strategic management of a subsidiary, however, is not carried out in vacuo. In addition to the external policy context, the strategic choice and management of the parent MNE create their own opportunities and constraints within which a subsidiary must operate. The relation of the foregoing facts to WPMs is the subject of a chapter by Alan M. Rugman and Sheila Douglas. In this chapter, the authors argue that, in formulating policies for subsidiaries, host countries cannot ignore the realities of corporate organisations if they expect their policies to yield positive results. Besides providing a rich discussion of several related topics, this chapter vividly demonstrates that a national science policy which reserves R&D grants for the Canadian WPM subsidiaries is doomed to fail if it runs counter to the parent MNE's policies regarding R&D and other innovative activities. For reasons well explained in the chapter, the authors state that multinationals are unable or unwilling to delegate full responsibility for a new product line to a subsidiary. Even when parent MNEs are willing to assign such functional responsibilities, most subsidiaries appear to lack sufficient managerial expertise to make a reasonable transition from a narrower to the much wider scope of their new mandate. This lack of pertinent expertise hinders the subsidiary from achieving the mandate's stated objectives and impairs the parent MNE in terms of loss of market share, global competitiveness and profitability. The third chapter of this part is concerned with the role of specialisation in international competitiveness, and is written by Harold Crookell. This chapter is based on a large study completed for the federal Department of Finance. It argues convincingly that the corporate strategies of MNEs have begun to reflect the impact of outside forces, ranging from the 40 per cent tariff reduction resulting from the Tokyo Round of the GATT, to the movement of technological leadership away from the United States. Most of these strategies, as the author explains, show a strong tendency toward 'specialisation'. As a result, the inherently inefficient 'miniature replica' operations are changing. By specialising, they are becoming better equipped to withstand the competitive pressures and attacks from the Far East and Europe, especially when their parents cannot bail them out with their superior technology. As a result, the past strategies of branch plant operations under tariff protection are being replaced by competitive and globally oriented strategies based on efficient world-scale factories. Although there are exceptions (mostly in the developing and Third World countries), the forms of specialisation in the developed and industrialised world have started to take a logical shape. This chapter distinguishes between two specific ones:

(1) Rationalisation-integration, and
(2) WPMs.

Both options result in improved productivity and export performance, and require extensive worker retraining, organisational restructuring and, above all, massive R&D support to sustain their specialised activities. Crookell explains that the differences between the two may seem subtle to outsiders, but from the subsidiary executive's viewpoint they are very real. Rationalisation-integration results in the mass production of a component or subassembly under assignment from the parent or one its major divisions for marketing worldwide, or in relevant markets. It involves a massive transformation from multiproduct output for the Canadian market to 'focused production' as a part of the multinational's highly integrated operations. Integration affects most aspects of operations, especially that of management and decision-making autonomy. While subsidiary management loses some of its autonomy, some R&D may still go on — but its nature will be different. It will mostly involve process oriented R&D to improve production and cut costs.

On the WPM side, the chapter explains that the subsidiary may become like a division of an MNE with great managerial autonomy. The R&D and innovative work is expected to be product oriented to support and reinforce its ongoing mandates or to obtain future mandates. The WPM option 'sounds like a cost free Canadianisation of foreign owned subsidiary', but as Crookell points out, massive costs are involved in the conversion from branch plant to a WPM. This requires a substantial change in the corporate culture, from the 'safety of protection to the risk of competition, from importer to exporter', and from Canadian to international marketing and orientation.

In making the choice between rationalised-integrated and WPMs, the corporate headquarters and the subsidiary appear to have adopted a pragmatic approach. They have chosen the mandate option where they have felt they had sufficient in-house expertise and have opted for other structures in other divisions to make the transition more manageable.

From a public policy viewpoint, each of the options comes with its own features and constraints. Rationalisation-integration requires massive worker retraining to achieve the necessary productivity gains, while the WPM's long-range survival is dependent upon management development and product innovation. Although potential problems in the areas of transfer pricing and lack of autonomy (especially in the case of rationalised-integrated operations) are bound to emerge with time, public concerns over subsidisation of WPM subsidiary's R&D from public sources are expected to fade away along with the fears related to Canadian supported R&D resulting in economic activities elsewhere.

Some of the issues raised by the above chapter are taken up in the chapter written by Hamid Etemad. Etemad's chapter is primarily concerned with a country's industrial policy orientation, the inherent effects of such orientation on the choice between various patterns of potential technological development, and the vehicles by which the industrial strategy and its subsequent technological capabilities are to be implemented. After a review and comparison of inwardly and outwardly oriented industrial strategies, Etemad contends that the overall benefits of outward orientation and its related strategies outweigh other rival alternatives. Specifically, the proactive nature of outwardly oriented strategies adds to their potency, especially when it comes to making strategic decisions among alternative technologies which could in turn pave the road for further competitiveness in international markets.

The author explains that the successful and timely development or transfer of new technology or new products gives a country a market position which is close to quasi-monopolistic, and hence leads to increased competitiveness in the international markets. Such a market position provides the country with a lead time advantage. Deeper penetration into existing markets or rapid expansion into as many international markets as possible can capture most of the advantages of this lead time. In turn, the country's initial outward orientation is reinforced, and the commitment to its international markets is strengthened.

However, an active linkage to international markets seems to be the prerequisite for the long-run success of outwardly oriented strategies. As alternatives for establishing such a linkage, WPMs and international trading companies are examined, and they are shown to be complementary and necessary for successful technological and industrial development, and both reinforce outward development. While the WPM is better suited for foreign owned subsidiaries, international trading companies can be of more potential use to indigenous firms.

In contrast to the discussion of industrial orientation at the country level in the preceding chapter, the next chapter of this part deals with managerial orientation at the subsidiary level. This chapter is coauthored by Norman W. McGuinness and H. Allan Conway. The main thesis of McGuinness and Conway is that an entrepreneurial spirit is a necessary ingredient for the success of any firm in general, and that of the WPM subsidiaries in particular. In developing this theme, the authors argue that a move away from the current and shortsighted practice of 'performance accounting,' and towards long-range orientation, risk taking, the search for innovative ideas and practices and finally, the championing of them (at the headquarters) is required if current and future candidates for WPMs expect to be taken seriously by headquarters and others (including the host country government). This is due to a combination of organisational and environmental factors. On the organisational side, the performance oriented multidivisional structure of MNEs is more in favour of allocating funds to subsidiaries and strategic business units that have produced good performance 'numbers' in the past and perhaps possess an equally rich potential or produce them again in the future. Usually, these turn out to be the MNE's main divisions. These divisions are also likely to have a rich organisational slack and hence businesses similar to 'miniature replica' operations will be forced to 'piggyback' upon them.

On the environmental side, the reliance on the larger and more innovative divisions reinforces the hegemony of larger divisions and conversely increases the dependence of the smaller divisions on the MNE. The authors argue that such an internal operational context is not conducive to the creation and growth of an autonomous unit such as the WPM. Similarly, the authors state that the absence of international market information and a systematic approach to international markets and marketing in the 'miniature replica' type of subsidiaries makes them incapable of supporting and fostering worldwide operations. Even when a subsidiary assisted by its host government succeeds in securing world-scale production, the sister subsidiaries may not choose to market their manufactured products vigorously, especially when these products begin to infringe upon their own products, rights and jurisdictions. This is not the case for products made by headquarters, large dominant divisions, or those sanctioned by headquarters, as they carry with them an implicit authority which creates a moral — if not a real and tangible — obligation for the sister subsidiaries to market them as vigorously as they would any other product in their portfolio.

When the subsidiary lacks large-scale production and international marketing involvement, the authors reach the conclusion that an entrepreneurially oriented management must replace the conservative — 'play it safe' — and dependent style of current managerial practices to pave the road for new products and efficient production facilities even before engaging in WPM negotiations.

Armed with new products and efficient production, entrepreneurially oriented management is expected to sustain and reinforce its competitive advantages, so that it will not be held hostage by its sister subsidiaries or other agents. Theoretically, this is the ideal orientation which the management of every WPM subsidiary should adopt. As a result, one would expect to find very special attributes and characteristics in the WPM's managerial profile. The next two papers in the third part of the book address these topics.

In an empirically oriented chapter, Bernard Bonin and Bruno Perron aimed to: obtain a comprehensive knowledge of WPMs in the province of Quebec; evaluate the economic impact of their activities; and identify favourable conditions under which MNEs would grant WPMs. In so doing, and after a thorough survey of the literature in order to identify all the pertinent qualities and characteristics of a WPM subsidiary, the authors developed a bilingual questionnaire which was carefully pretested. It was then administered to a carefully selected sample of 126 firms in order to draw pertinent and valid conclusions. The authors' findings confirm the prevalence of some of the better known characteristics, while failing to reject some of the more controversial ones. Within the latter category, for example, there is a question concerning the role of technology and its degree of importance in WPM operations. The authors report that 75 per cent of the respondents rated the parent company's influence in technology as 'strong, very strong and even determining'. Owing to the nature of the research instrument, it was, however, difficult to assess whether a WPM arrangement had resulted in higher or lower R&D than the pre-mandate situation.

In a related chapter, Hamid Etemad and Louise Séguin Dulude addressed themselves to the very question of R&D. In the absence of any WPM related data base, the information on which this chapter is based had to be organised from various sources. Before presenting their empirical findings, the authors state the prevailing view: that R&D and patenting activities are joint products and that the acquisition of a WPM automatically results in increased R&D and patenting activities. In order to develop a perspective on the above, the authors undertook to examine the issue theoretically and empirically. On the theoretical side, the chapter examines the pertinent arguments in favour of centralised and decentralised R&D and patenting operations. Even a favourable interpretation of these arguments does not provide a set of compelling reasons for combining WPM and R&D at one subsidiary.

On the empirical side, an examination of publicly available information on 84 Canadian WPM subsidiaries in the provinces of Quebec and Ontario reveals very interesting results, but is not supportive of the prevailing view. The results imply that 52 per cent of these subsidiaries either lack R&D facilities, or are not involved in patentable activities.

In a theoretically oriented chapter, Bernard M. Wolf examines the trade related aspects of WPMs. Specifically, he addresses two questions:

(1) What is the theoretical basis for the international trade which results from world product mandating, and how does it differ from the underpinnings of more conventional trade theory?

(2) What are the factors contributing to a change in the trade balance when world product mandating is introduced?

To answer the first question, the author reviews the pertinent literature on international trade to identify the conditions under which a WPM arrangement could be enhanced or hampered. The author comes to a clear conclusion. 'WPM and free trade generally go hand in hand'. But nontariff barriers are often used by governments to accomplish their goals and objectives (e.g. securing a WPM) which may not always be compatible with WPM operations, especially when they are based in other countries.

In answering the second question, the author develops a model with three classes of goods (e.g. two final and one intermediate) which characterise a very simple miniature replica operation. The model is rather realistic as it allows for input, intermediate and final goods, of which one of the two final goods initially produced domestically is to become a mandated product and to continue in production, while the other is to be discontinued and replaced by imports. The other final product initially imported would continue to be imported and, finally, all inputs required to produce any good are entered or dropped (as applicable) to accommodate a 'comparative static' analysis of *ex-ante* and *ex-post* effects. The chapter comes to several significant findings, mostly favourable to WPM operations. Specifically, and under certain reasonable assumptions, the model implies that WPM arrangements can positively improve the balance of trade and, in that sense, can be a vehicle for external balance improvements.

PART I

THE EMERGING POLICY AND OPERATIONAL CONTEXT

2 INDUSTRIAL ADJUSTMENTS AND WORLD PRODUCT MANDATES: A ROLE FOR PUBLIC POLICY[1]

Carl E. Beigie and James K. Stewart

After two and a half years of economic recovery, the Canadian economy was still plagued in mid-1985 with double-digit unemployment and the prospect of high rates of joblessness for the rest of the decade. Compounding the economy's difficulties have been the protracted weakness in global resource markets since 1981 and the increasing vulnerability of Canadian manufacturing to lower cost offshore competition. Taken together, these and other problems have focused the attention of policymakers and key segments of public opinion on Canada's need for fundamental structural adjustment in the economy. In particular, concern about the future viability of the inefficient Canadian subsidiaries of foreign owned multinationals has given rise to fears that parent companies will withdraw production from Canada. Hoping to forestall such moves, many commentators and governments have seized upon the notion of world product mandates (WPMs) for these subsidiaries to assist both in maintaining production in Canada and in increasing the Canadian benefits from foreign owned manufacturing.

Many business analysts (including the authors in this volume) have challenged the popular perception of the WPM route as a panacea, as they point to the restricted scope for, and merits of, WPMs from the multinational parent's standpoint. This chapter explores the WPM option from a different perspective, namely its linkage to the policy environment. Its message is twofold. First, the principal focus on direct aid or regulation to encourage WPMs is unbalanced and, in many instances, misdirected; instead, greater emphasis needs to be placed on indirect policies to spur specialised missions, especially WPMs, for existing and future subsidiaries. Second, the nature of the Canadian strategy for encouraging WPMs, as well as its success, will be determined by Canada's strategic policy approach for pursuing the long overdue structural adjustment of the Canadian economy.

Canada's Competitive Challenges and Policy Options²

Despite three years of huge merchandise trade surpluses, the sustainability of key elements of Canada's external improvement is subject to serious doubt. In 1984, a highly favourable Canada-US trade balance accounted for 95 per cent of the total Canadian net export surplus in goods traded. Canadian exports to the United States rose to roughly 76 per cent of total exports, up from 67 per cent just three years earlier. The sharp increase in Canada's continental trade dependence has tied Canadian economic performance even more closely to the US economy's health. In this regard, the dramatic slowdown in US expansion since mid-1984 and the fact that the typical postwar American recovery lasts little more than three years do not augur well for continued increases in the merchandise trade surplus above its 1984 record level.

Looking more closely at the composition of Canada's surge in net goods exports reveals that the shift in Canada-US automotive trade was a key factor, rising from $2.1 billion deficit in 1981 to a $5.9 billion surplus in 1984. Yet the factors that produced this turnaround are diminishing and may have begun to reverse. Automotive sales are very sensitive to changes in cyclical conditions, especially as these affect consumers' purchasing power and confidence. Given weaker US growth prospects and the rebound effect on Canadian imports, the favourable gap in relative automotive demand between Canada and the United States is highly unlikely to continue. Furthermore, fundamental competitive problems persist as Canadian automotive production costs remain significantly higher than in Japan while consumers still perceive European and Japanese car quality as superior to that of North American vehicles (Mac-Donald, 1985, p. 21). Despite the nontariff protection of this industry both in Canada and the United States, Canadian sales remain highly vulnerable to rising imports from offshore, especially from new competitors (e.g. South Korea) that are not bound by explicit or implicit restraint agreements.

From a comparative perspective, Canada's overall growth rate in merchandise sales to the United States from 1981 to 1984 lagged well behind those of Japan and the Newly Industrialised Countries (NICs). Moreover, removing the automotive segment reveals that the percentage rise in Canada's nonautomotive exports was far less than that of West Germany and, especially, the Pacific Rim nations. It is thus hardly surprising that the latter have seen their market share of US nonautomotive imports increase sharply.

Less obvious in the wake of Canada's surging merchandise trade balance is that long-standing deficiencies and more recent weaknesses in Canadian competitiveness have been obscured. Put simply, Canada's traditional approach to economic development, that is, looking outward for wealth from natural resource exports and inward for employment by protecting an inefficient manufacturing sector, is in serious jeopardy.

In the natural resource sphere, advances in new technology are creating a host of substitutes for traditional resource goods, with the future development of additional substitutes assured. On the demand side and on a comparative basis, numerous factors do not optimistically foretell a volume-growth potential of unprocessed and semi-processed natural resource products. Excluding petroleum, commodity based goods have accounted for a declining share of total world trade as global income has grown since World War II (MacCharles, 1984a, p. 18). Technological progress has led to substantial reductions in the amount of raw materials and energy used in the production of many products. The growth in demand has also been restrained in recent years by lower inflation rates relative to those in the 1970s and by the differing nature of business investment in the current cycle. To date, investment in plant structures has experienced far less of a recovery than outlays on machinery and equipment as capital expenditure has favoured productivity enhancement over increasing capacity. Above all, foreign tariff and non-tariff measures continue to limit Canadian resource export opportunities.

The relatively limited real growth prospects for natural resource exports have made it increasingly imperative that the other categories of Canadian goods and services take up the slack as external sources of strength. Yet more recent research has confirmed that many of the conclusions from earlier studies regarding Canada's manufacturing inefficiency still hold. Despite the move to fewer product lines and rationalisation in selected firms and industries, the small domestic market, insufficient scale and specialisation, and the 'miniature replica' nature of many foreign subsidiaries continue to impede Canadian manufacturing competitiveness in general (MacCharles, 1984a, pp. 19–97; Mac-Charles 1984b, pp. 18–19). Inadequate marketing and management exacerbate these production disadvantages (Lazar, 1981, pp. 57–8; Mac-Charles, 1984a, pp. 65–7). Too many Canadian firms have lagged far behind their key foreign competitors in their marketing efforts. In the management sphere, the much slower adoption of improved technologies, production strategies, and employment practices is especially apparent relative to Japan.

Among the costs of these competitive deficiencies is the increasing market penetration of Japanese goods in higher value added manufactured products, especially in technologically intensive goods. In the traditional labour and capital intensive products, producers based in the NICs are rapidly gaining market share in goods whose manufacturing involves standard technologies. The substantial declines in Canadian tariffs under the GATT's Tokyo Round are adding to this exposure of domestic manufacturers to lower cost offshore competition. The expansion of multinational activities across the world is exacerbating these challenges. The integration of NIC based production within the operations of industrialised country multinationals in globalised industries is particularly serious. In rationalising their operations on a worldwide basis, multinationals in these industries shift the production of goods to the most cost-efficient sites across the globe. Where labour costs are the key determinant of plant location, the NICs are the clear-cut choice. Accordingly, subsidiaries based in Canada will face comparative disadvantages in these globalised businesses and will likely be downgraded over time to non-production activities such as local marketing or servicing. Declining Canadian tariff barriers further increase the opportunities for servicing the Canadian market from these offshore locations.

In a host of other products, the lower Canadian tariffs boost the competitiveness of US based versus Canadian based production, thereby affording American multinationals much greater opportunities to export to Canada from US sites. In the case of Japan's multinationals, there has been an increasing willingness to transfer manufacturing abroad to maintain access to key export markets in recent years. These locational decisions, however, are being strongly influenced by market size, economic resources, and policy leverage. The powerful US economic 'pull' in these areas has placed Canada at a substantial disadvantage in this regard. Japanese companies have predominantly chosen American locations for new plants in major industries except where Canadian access to US markets was assured (e.g. the automotive area).

Canada's competitive firms and industries are also at risk in the current environment created from nontariff measures in the United States. Three illustrations are instructive in this regard. There are US pressures to bring Canada into a 'voluntary export restraint' (VER) program that has already been forced on eleven other steel exporting countries. In urban mass transit equipment, there is the ever present threat of subsidy investigations. And in telecommunications, the relationship between Bell Canada and Northern Telecom is being scrutinised by US authorities as a potentially unfair trade advantage. This 'contingency' protection is complementing standing trade barriers (e.g. 'Buy America' provisions) in all three industries that are affecting the exports and investment decisions of Canadian producers.

In sum, the fundamental nature of Canada's competitive challenges is confronting Canadian policymakers with the need for far-reaching and urgent changes. In the past, it has been argued that Canada has four policy options that have strong overlaps but are none the less conceptually distinct:[3]

(1) continuing the current approach;

(2) pursuing closer economic integration with the United States;

(3) improving the Canadian economy's internal performance while diversifying Canada's trade away from the United States; and

(4) pursuing multilateral trade liberalisation through a new GATT round.

In practice, as the authors have seen, the *status quo* has proven to be a woefully inadequate strategy for dealing with either individual sectors or the totality of Canada's needs. With respect to the multilateral option, major hurdles remain to be cleared before a new GATT round begins. As of mid-1985, large differences continue regarding the issue agenda, participants and timing of the new GATT talks. These difficulties virtually ensure that, should agreement be reached on starting a new GATT round, negotiations will be protracted. In the meantime, managed trade agreements are proliferating across the globe while the United States is attempting to pursue bilateral liberalisation where this strategy is feasible. Thus, although the multilateral route remains highly desirable, the risks involved along with the delays inherent in negotiating a new round mean that Canada must focus its immediate attention on the second or third option.

Initiatives under both options have been taken by the Mulroney government as it attempts to achieve the long overdue adjustment of Canadian industry. Prime Minister Mulroney and President Reagan agreed at their March 1985 summit to a joint trade declaration and work plan to enhance Canada-US market access. Following on the heels of its trade and foreign policy discussion papers (Clark, 1985; Kelleher, 1985), the Mulroney government is currently engaged in provincial and private sector consultations regarding its Canadian-American trade approach. A decision is expected by the fall of 1985. On the domestic side, Ottawa has undertaken sweeping changes in the energy and foreign investment spheres and proposed far-reaching alterations in the transportation and financial services areas.

The Scope for WPMs

Despite these initiatives shown by Ottawa, the policy framework needs a host of additional, strategically oriented changes to provide the appropriate policy setting. As important, the response of the private sector to the new competitive environment, although currently uncertain, will be crucial. In particular, the extensive nonresident ownership of Canada's manufacturing sector makes the reaction of foreign owned multinational enterprises critical given that most of these subsidiaries are high cost, inefficient 'miniature replicas'.

In general, the parent companies of foreign owned multinationals face four options with respect to their Canadian subsidiaries.[4]

(1) Production can be withdrawn from Canada as home or NIC based facilities supply the Canadian market, with Canadian operations being restricted to non-production activities such as marketing, distribution, and/or servicing.

(2) The subsidiary's operations can be 'Canadianised' by greater tailoring of the product line to meet unique domestic preferences, thereby 'narrowing the market scope to create a defensible competitive position' (White and Poynter, 1984, p. 65).

(3) Production could be rationalised on a North American or global basis (depending on the industry's characteristics) with Canadian subsidiaries given responsibility for manufacturing specific product lines and/or components for either of the above markets. The parent, however, handles such activities as strategic management, product planning, export marketing, and the vast bulk of research and development (R&D).

(4) Canadian subsidiaries could receive a full WPM which in its pure form involves responsibility for all aspects of R&D, production, and marketing. In practice, WPMs are often limited geographically (e.g. to North America) or functionally (e.g. having some R&D handled outside Canada).[5] To qualify as a WPM, however, significant R&D must be undertaken by the subsidiary; otherwise, the subsidiary has only undergone a production rationalisation or 'Canadianisation' adjustment.

In essence, WPMs provide an organisational vehicle to achieve free trade at the intra-firm level rather than on an economy-wide or sectoral basis. As other studies have outlined, the WPM route for subsidiary adjustment offers real advantages for Canada when such adaptation is efficient (Advisory Committee on Global Product Mandating, 1980).[6] Subsidiary autonomy is enhanced through greater control over product design and development. Management horizons are expanded to encompass international considerations while providing access to the parent's global marketing and distribution channels. To stay competitive, the mandated product and the technology involved in manufacturing must remain efficient in a dynamic sense. Other benefits include the higher value added in production as well as greater subcontracting and productivity spillover effects. The disadvantages of WPMs are basically confined to the adjustment entailed in implementing a product mandate, potentially higher risks from greater exposure to adverse market changes, and limitations on international marketing when other subsidiaries are assigned such tasks.

From the multinational parent's perspective, the merits of the WPM route involve a distinctly different assessment. Although WPMs can generate goodwill on the part of host governments, these charters are almost always earned by subsidiaries on the basis of a 'distinctive advantage'. This advantage can be achieved through such factors as successful innovation, product market access or government incentives. In the absence of sufficient locational benefits in these and/or other areas, analysts have cited numerous considerations that militate against the parent granting its Canadian subsidiary a product mandate charter (Crookell, 1983, p. 26; Crookell and Caliendo, 1980, p. 63; Poynter and Rugman, 1982).[7] The miniature replica characteristics of most subsidiaries create major doubts about these companies' entrepreneurial and product development capacities to undertake a WPM. There are also costs with respect to the parent's capacity to control a subsidiary's R&D and operations with a WPM as well as the need to reallocate existing markets among all subsidiaries to accommodate a WPM charter. Moreover, the number of potential product candidates is relatively limited. The parent is highly unlikely to grant a world charter for a major product line of business in which it has substantial production capabilities. For goods moving into the mature phases of the product life cycle, offshore sites with significantly lower labour costs than Canadian locations will usually have a large comparative advantage. It should also be stressed that the existing US nontariff barriers and the serious threat of additional protectionist measures are significant disadvantages for Canadian based production and thus reinforce the attractiveness of a WPM charter in many businesses.

The Pitfalls of a Direct Approach

Aware of these factors and motivated by both the advantages of WPMs for Canadian subsidiaries and the political concerns regarding foreign ownership, governments in Canada have attempted to help subsidiaries obtain product charters. Public policies to encourage the WPM route have included direct assistance through duty remission schemes and grants for technological development. In certain cases, such aid has been found to have been instrumental in the subsidiaries' receipt of a WPM (Science Council of Canada, 1980, p. 72; Standing Senate Committee on Foreign Affairs, 1982, p. 65). On the regulatory side, FIRA was empowered to seek performance requirements in its efforts to induce WPMs.

Yet there are serious risks in government policies to attract WPMs if the nature and focus of such efforts are not carefully crafted. To begin with, the method of government assistance involves several potential problems when it takes the form of direct aid on a case by case basis. There is a clear risk of excessive subsidisation, given the public sector's difficulty in determining the incentive necessary for a multinational's parent to grant a WPM. Oversubsidisation occurs when a part of or all government inducement ends up as a windfall transfer from the public sector to the corporate purse rather than as an intermediated outlay on desired activities (a WPM), i.e. such aid becomes infra-marginal rather than marginal assistance. This risk is present in public incentives for domestic companies but it is magnified with multinationals. The domestic policy leverage and information available to Canadian governments can be more than offset by the transnational bargaining power and international knowledge possessed by the parent corporations.

Direct assistance for WPMs may also lead to other multinationals withholding product charters as a bargaining tactic to receive government aid which otherwise would not be forthcoming. In addition, such assistance faces the prospect of causing other countries playing host to multinational subsidiaries to respond with their own incentives (Wolf, 1983, p. 102). The consequent competition for WPMs would lessen or could even reverse the gains from a charter should it escalate into a full-scale bidding war.

From a continental perspective, direct measures to encourage WPMs are confronted by the serious risk of countermeasures by the United States. Beginning in the 1970s, and especially in the 1980s, Washington has become increasingly concerned with host-government regulations affecting US multinational enterprises. Washington now perceives the pattern of American international investment as a significant determinant of US trade and economic performance (Drouin and Malmgren, 1981–82, p. 405). In particular, the Reagan administration has actively sought a liberalised international investment regime.

The US government decision in March 1982 to challenge the Foreign Investment Review Agency (FIRA) regarding its performance requirements for foreign investors as inconsistent with the GATT is indicative of the Reagan administration's deep-seated concern in this area. In terms of Canada's ability to achieve WPMs via the regulatory route, the US complaint to GATT revealed that country's major differences regarding the two Canadian policy measures.[8] The United States contended that FIRA's regulations obliging a foreign owned subsidiary to produce specific components or parts of a particular product and its negotiation of export undertakings requiring product mandates to be granted were incompatible with GATT articles III and XVII, respectively.

Despite the fact that the GATT panel did not uphold either contention[9] the Reagan administration has pressed its concerns over these issues in other multilateral fora, most notably before the OECD and in the preliminary talks regarding a new GATT round. Domestically, the Reagan administration has moved to increase dramatically the legislative devices available to take countermeasures against host country regulation of foreign ownership in the 'Trade and Tariff Act' of 1984 (United States Congress, 1984). Under Title 3, for the first time, the President receives specific negotiating authority with respect to US foreign direct investment and foreign export performance requirements. Using the amendments to Section 301 of the 'Trade Reform Act' of 1974, the President may take action against 'unfair' foreign practices on investment. In particular, the Reagan administration can impose duties or other import restrictions in cases involving the products of countries employing performance requirements. The intention in granting this authority is to enable such measures to be used as bargaining levers in seeking the reduction or elimination of such requirements. To assist in its advisory role to the President, the US Special Trade Representative was also given the power to initiate investigations independently under Section 301.

The concern about host country foreign investment policies is symptomatic of the broader phenomena spurring US trade policy militancy. In the face of rising import penetration in traditional labour and capital intensive industries over the past 15 years, affected workers and businesses have suffered fundamental dislocations. Together with the frustration experienced by US corporations in their international operations, these developments fuelled demands for recourse under US law.

Aided by the desire of Congress to increase its role in foreign economic relationships, US trade legislation enacted in the 1970s enabled private interests to seek protection under US law independent of congressional and administrative efforts.

The ballooning US merchandise trade deficits since 1981 have led to a quantum leap in protectionist requests. Although the Reagan administration has been able to contain most of these initiatives, a number of nontariff measures have slipped through (e.g. those affecting specialty steel and surface transportation). For its part, the Reagan administration, while publicly eschewing protectionism, has endorsed 'fair trade' whereby assistance is extended to workers and industries facing 'unfair and predatory trade practices' (Reagan, 1983, p. 7).

With US trade policy activism on the rise, the more widespread use of duty remission schemes to promote exports and other direct incentives by Canada could face the prospects of strong retaliation. The most obvious threat appears to be the potential for the imposition of countervailing duties on US imports from these subsidiaries. These duties are imposed to offset the advantages provided for other countries' export by government subsidies or other forms of assistance. Prior to 1979, under Section 303 of the 1930 'Tariff Act', a countervailing duty could be levied to offset a 'bounty or grant' benefiting foreign customers no matter how early in the production process this subsidy was applied (Lazar, 1981, p. 27). Using this statute, countervailing duties were imposed on two Canadian subsidiaries' (Michelin and Honeywell) exports to the United States because of federal aid, while a challenge to Canada's duty remission scheme for parts imported by domestic auto manufacturers was only preempted by the negotiation of the Canada-US auto pact.[10]

New provisions for countervailing duties came into force with the 1979 'Trade Arrangements Act'. Key among these were elaboration of the test of material injury and a broad definition of what constitutes a subsidy (Lazar, 1981, pp. 30–1). The injury test now only requires that 'harm' be demonstrated that 'is not inconsequential, immaterial or unimportant'. The definition of a subsidy covers a wide variety of incentives that have been used or could be employed directly to encourage WPMs. According to section 701 of the 'Trade Arrangements Act', a subsidy includes:

(1) the provision of capital, loans or loan guarantees on terms inconsistent with commercial considerations;
(2) the provision of goods or services at preferential rates;
(3) the grant of funds or forgiveness of debt to cover operating losses

sustained by a specific industry;
(4) the assumption of any cost or expenses of manufacture, production or distribution.

Despite the broad scope of this definition, the 'Trade and Tariff Act' of 1984 expanded its ambit even further to encompass 'upstream subsidies'. An 'upstream subsidy' involves an 'input product' that provides a 'competitive benefit' such that it 'has a significant effect on the cost of manufacturing' or production. Of special interest for Canada in this regard is that the supply of resource inputs to producers at costs substantially below domestic price levels for other Canadian consumers as a WPM inducement can be countervailed under this new trade legislation.

Another potential legislative impediment can be employed under the amended Section 301 of the 1974 'Trade Reform Act'. Not only can this mechanism be used to counter regulatory constraints on US multinationals, its auspices leave a great deal of room for challenging direct aid for WPMs. Utilising the amended Section 301, any foreign government measures that cause reduced US exports or higher levels of imports into the United States can be subjected to American countermeasures (United States Congress, 1984).

In sum, there are a host of effective constraints upon Canadian regulatory and subsidy measures in the US system of 'contingency' protection. Although the extent to which these impediments might be employed is uncertain, the driving forces behind US trade policy militancy continue to be present, especially when US businesses are actually, or perceived to be, adversely affected. Moreover, the Reagan administration's efforts to achieve an improved code of host country behaviour toward multinationals under the GATT and its focus on investment in the 'Trade and Tariff Act' are telling indicators of American concern in this area.

It also bears emphasis that, from a developmental perspective, governments in Canada need to be concerned with the costs of an excessive focus on the WPM route for upgrading existing subsidiaries. The basis for international cost competitiveness is efficiency, and Canadian authorities seeking to create viable businesses should encourage multinational parents to choose the most appropriate route for their subsidiaries' efficient adaptation. Canada's overriding need is for these subsidiaries to become competitive through 'specialised missions' that substantially narrow the number of product lines manufactured — thereby permitting greater specialisation and, where appropriate, greater scale

— where this form of adjustment is economically viable. Accordingly, while creating an environment conducive to WPMs, policymakers should not pursue a setting wherein other forms of specialised missions — Canadianisation, production rationalisation, or partial WPMs — are made less attractive and thus less likely to occur.

An excessive policy focus on WPMs would also risk obtaining multinational adherence to the 'letter' of the government's desire for WPMs but not the 'spirit', i.e. the granting of WPMs in name only or with a limited life span to satisfy government aims. One recent study of Canadian WPMs found evidence in the computer and computer related industries that a number of subsidiaries use the term WPM for activities that do not qualify as product charters, in an apparent effort to please Ottawa.[11]

Above all, the stress on WPMs for existing subsidiaries raises the issue of whether this principal emphasis is appropriate in terms of the Canadian economy's dynamic needs. A substantial number of these subsidiaries are operating in industries where Canadian based production has no inherent strategic advantage and demand is not expected to grow rapidly. From a dynamic standpoint, creating an environment that makes it attractive for multinationals to establish new subsidiaries in products with higher income elasticities, in niches, and/or in areas where Canada has an existing or comparative strategic advantage (e.g. resource intensive production) is also essential. As well, such an environment could make it worthwhile for parent companies to use the existing infrastructure of subsidiaries to diversify into niches and other product lines where the Canadian operations could be competitive. Therefore, not only is there a need for more indirect support measures to attract WPMs, the focus of such efforts should encompass potential as well as existing subsidiaries' circumstances.

Toward an Appropriate Policy Setting

As the foregoing analysis suggests, an effective strategy to encourage specialised missions, especially through a WPM charter, embraces both specific and framework policies. In so doing, the requirement for integrating indirect and direct policy measures brings us back to the discussion in the first section of this chapter regarding Canada's general approach to structural adjustment. Canada's choice between the second option (closer economic integration with the United States) or the third option (improved domestic policy management and trade diversification) or pursuing some combination of both will be a crucial determinant of

Canadian attractiveness for WPMs.

Foreign owned multinationals will assess a series of locational factors regarding the subsidiary's potential in their decisions about their Canadian operations. Confronted by a turbulent trade environment and faced with a global and North American locational competition, Canada's policymakers need to alter favourably the cost-benefit ratio for subsidiaries in a number of areas. Although many of these are difficult to influence either in the near term (e.g. industrial relations) or at all (e.g. climate), the policy route chosen can significantly affect several key locational factors. By exploring the impact of public policy on these factors, especially in terms of the merits of closer economic integration with the United States versus improved domestic economic management and international trade diversification, the consequences of Canada's policy choice for WPMs can also be assessed.

Among the key locational factors arising from Canada's policy choice for multinational decisions are the following.

Political Risk

This factor can embrace a wide range of elements but for the authors' purposes encompasses general and specific policies aimed primarily at foreign ownership. Since 1982, the climate for nonresident investment has improved markedly, especially with the move to Investment Canada under the Mulroney government. Approval rates for proposed acquisitions have jumped to their highest levels since a regulatory screening mechanism was introduced while the scope for reviewing the establishment of new businesses has been reduced sharply. This emphasis on encouraging improved performance over increasing or preserving Canadian ownership is of distinct benefit to enhancing the multinational parent's perception of Canada. Lessened fears concerning political risk help to alleviate a major problem by reducing concerns about intra-corporate control in granting a WPM.

The absence of major obstacles for multinationals in shifting a subsidiary to non-production activities is a politically unpalatable yet necessary element of an attractive political environment. While some scope for notification and adjustment of aid requirements is present here, excessive restrictions with respect to plant closings can sour the environment for potential upgrading elsewhere or the establishment of new subsidiaries if the parent perceives major constraints upon its future operations. In addition, legislative and/or administrative obstacles can obtain multinational adherence to the 'letter' of government's aims — keeping the plant open — while lacking support for the policy's intent as the subsidiary is starved of much needed multinational resource injections (e.g. cash, technology) in the future.

Discretionary Barriers to Product and Input Flows

This factor encompasses the range of government policies (domestic and foreign) that constitute impediments to product and input movement. Although there are a number of programs that are involved here, the most important is clearly product market access. As this chapter's first section outlined, declining Canadian and American tariff rates together with the growing threat of lower cost offshore competition have made miniature replica subsidiaries highly vulnerable in terms of sales and their locational attraction. The surge in actual and threatened nontariff barriers in the United States is jeopardising the exports of efficient Canadian based subsidiaries as well as the attractiveness of investing in either upgrading existing operations or establishing new businesses. It should also be noted that the Canadian tariff on various imports of machinery and equipment, even after the Tokyo Round cuts, adds to the usually higher costs from the greater transportation requirement for these elements of the production process in Canada.

For specialised missions, especially WPMs, a comprehensive Canada-US trade agreement offers major advantages. Foremost among these — depending on the scope and nature of the accord — is the much improved security of access and, in many cases, improved terms of entry for Canadian exports. On the import side, the lowering or complete elimination of duties imposed on foreign goods would provide a competitive boost through the consequent reduction in the costs of importing components and/or machinery and equipment from abroad. The increased pressures from US imports would also accelerate subsidiaries' adjustment, although this adaptation could occur through the withdrawal of production or the granting of a specialised mission.

It is important to stress, however, that this adjustment is going on already, albeit at a slower pace, without the opportunities present in a comprehensive Canada-US trade deal. The merits of continental trade liberalisation for WPMs were highlighted by the Canadian Standing Senate Committee on Foreign Affairs in its 1982 report (Standing Senate Committee on Foreign Affairs, 1982, pp. 61–6). It found that many WPMs have occurred in the aircraft industry where effective free trade was already present and that the increasing presence of trade impediments hindered existing or potential WPMs elsewhere. The Committee concluded that:

Product mandating assignments and rationalization schemes within transnational firms are easier in a free trade setting, where tariffs could be eliminated and the application of non-tariff barriers mutually agreed to and enforced (1982, p. 65).

One other aspect of the WPM linkage with Canada-US trade liberalisation deserves elaboration. This involves the favourable implications for Canada's exports to offshore markets. The improved efficiency and WPM opportunities in a continental trade pact would significantly enhance Canadian competitiveness as well as expanding management's horizons to North America and beyond. The combination of these benefits would leave Canadian exporters in a much improved position to exploit the growing sales potential in countries outside North America.

The drawbacks of a bilateral accord involve primarily the reduced scope for direct aid for WPMs. Government measures would need to comply with the negotiated code of acceptable policy conduct both during the transitional period of treaty implementation and thereafter. It bears emphasis that this policy room was already substantially limited with respect to any product that would depend heavily on exports to the United States given the likelihood of US countermeasures.

In the absence of a Canadian-American trade deal, governments in Canada would need to offer greater direct incentives to encourage specialised subsidiary missions, particularly through the WPM route. Provided the pitfalls noted earlier are avoided, especially in light of the potential for US protectionist retaliation, such aid would need to be tailored in such a way as to minimise the risk of American countermeasures (e.g. equalising for higher Canadian borrowing costs) or to avoid extending assistance where US contingent protection was highly likely to be invoked.

Taxation

At the direct corporate income tax level, the total Canadian levies by Ottawa and the provinces compare favourably with the combined federal and state corporate income taxes in key US states.[12] Care must be exercised here, however, as tax treatments in each country vary substantially among industries and types of capital outlays. The comparative tax environment is also made less clear by the uncertain status in mid-1985 of the President's tax reform package.

In the indirect area, Canadian based production faces a much heavier burden through a series of levies — sales taxes on equipment and supplies, capital taxes, business and franchise taxes — than their US based competition. The Canadian Senate's study of Canada's indirect tax impact in the late 1970s estimated the cost at approximately one-fifth of the corporate income tax burden (Standing Senate Committee on Foreign Affairs, 1978, pp. 141–2). As well, Canadian gasoline taxes raises fuel costs far above US levels in most provinces.

At the personal level, the more progressive Canadian income tax currently imposes a smaller burden on low income people and a larger cost on high income people than in the United States. If the basic thrust of the President's tax reform proposal gains legislative approval, this bilateral gap at upper income levels will widen substantially. Canadian subsidiaries' capacity to attract upper managerial and other skilled personnel, let alone their ability to retain their own skilled workers, could be seriously impeded if this Canada-US differential increases significantly.

Under either the second or third policy option, governments in Canada cannot ignore the disadvantages faced by Canadian subsidiaries from their higher indirect and personal income tax burdens. Under a Canada-US accord, the scope for targeting tax relief is highly likely to be constrained, making an indirect, across-the-board change the preferable route. Without the limitations of a Canada-US treaty, there appears to be much greater room for specific tax assistance; however, the usual caveat applies with respect to the threat of US countermeasures.

Competition Policy

Potential barriers to the adjustment of Canadian subsidiaries are present in the case of competition policy in both countries. Canadian anti-combines legislation could create legal stumbling blocks to mergers, acquisitions, joint ventures and specialisation agreements because of a focus upon industry concentration and potentially collusive behaviour within Canada. If the future implementation of this law were to fail to take account of the degree of foreign competition, Canadian policy could frustrate the beneficial efficiency improvements from subsidiary rationalisation along the above lines.

The extension of US antitrust laws to American owned subsidiaries is a highly significant area of concern. This extraterritorial application of US antitrust policy becomes a potential threat 'when foreign transactions have a substantial and foreseeable effect on US commerce'.[13] The reach of American legislation is of particular concern given the power to influence the parent's operations. Changes in Canadian law have been made to protect subsidiaries from the impact of US antitrust regulations, but the parent cannot escape Washington's jurisdiction. Moreover, although the Reagan administration has moved antitrust policy toward the pursuit of economic efficiency rather than adherence to legal precedent, this evidence is drawn essentially from domestic cases. Given the current climate of protectionism, the potential threat in this area is uncertain in mid-1985.

A comprehensive trade agreement would, of necessity, have to contain provisions regarding both countries' competition policy practices that take account of the North American and, hopefully, global context of industries. It is likely that special conditions, such as the relaxation of certain competition regulations, would be required during the transitional period to permit the necessary rationalisation and specialisation during this time (Standing Senate Committee on Foreign Affairs, 1982, pp. 98--9). Irrespective of a continental trade pact, the overhaul of Canadian anti-combines legislation to reflect global competitive conditions is long overdue.

Cost and Security of Material and Energy Supplies

Proximity to low cost supplies is important to the competitiveness of many products (e.g. textile inputs for carpets). Canadian policies governing the supply of key input materials will thus influence the potential for WPMs. As an illustration, central Canadian based facilities have equivalent or better energy costs and availability than their neighbouring US competitors because of abundant hydroelectricity endowments and provincial pricing policies. Yet, as noted earlier, the scope for employing low pricing for resource inputs is limited by the provisions against 'upstream subsidies' in the 1984 'Trade and Tariff Act'. The threat of US countermeasures in this area makes it unlikely that the actual constraints upon this mechanism under a Canada-US trade agreement would be much greater than the effective threats inherent in the third option's use of this tactic (they may even be less).

Government Assistance

As noted earlier, the chances of receiving a WPM can be substantially enhanced through various kinds of government aid. Such assistance can be logically divided into direct aid and longer term infrastructural support.

On economic grounds, direct aid can be justified in three areas. One occurs when assistance is given to equalise for the government subsidies and other forms of aid extended to US based production by American states and Washington, provided the Canadian based production can be competitive with these offsetting measures. Another involves current or potentially competitive Canadian subsidiaries where aid can be designed to minimise the risk of triggering the US contingency protection system; or where the bulk of the exports from these subsidiaries is destined for offshore. While care is necessary to avoid oversubsidisation in this area, there is considerable scope for assistance that is effective in increasing R&D, reducing capital costs, and so on.

The third type of direct aid involves assistance to upgrade the knowledge, technology, and other aspects of the management of these subsidiaries. Management, through its shaping of the Canadian operation's competitive position, can exercise considerable influence over the strategic direction of the subsidiary (White and Poynter, 1984, pp. 66–7). Within the confines of the parent's strategy and the comparative strengths of subsidiaries based elsewhere, management needs to develop the competitive strengths of the Canadian subsidiary. This is especially true in light of preliminary research that has found WPMs to almost always be earned by the subsidiary's efforts rather than being granted at the parent's instigation.

Toward this end, there is an informational role for governments in the adoption and diffusion of technology and in encouraging a move to flexible system manufacturing. Despite the better record of technology transfer for foreign owned subsidiaries compared to Canadian owned firms, Canada's poor record in the use of robotics and other forms of advanced manufacturing technology suggests substantial scope for government involvement in spreading knowledge and creating awareness of new technologies among both types of manufacturers.[14] Aiding the efforts of the Canadian Manufacturing Association and the other organisations in promoting the move of firms into market niches, especially in skills intensive goods using flexible system production (e.g. custom-made or precision products),[15] is also warranted. By facilitating the shift into a much narrower and more focused range of product lines, governments help to spur the production specialisation and improved management necessary to carve out a defensible competitive position. Together with improved technology adoption, these policies can help to increase the attractiveness of subsidiaries as potential WPM candidates.

Of longer term concern is the infrastructural support that is crucial to future WPMs through either a major overhaul of existing subsidiaries or the establishment of new Canadian operations with a world product charter. Space constraints and the focus of this chapter do not permit the full elaboration that this subject warrants. However, a brief focus on Canada's R&D environment is worthwhile given the advantages or problems that it creates for subsidiaries' R&D capacities. A policy climate that aids the technological development capabilities of subsidiaries will boost the attractiveness of Canadian sites for WPM charters.

Relative to the major Western industrial powers — Japan, the EEC and the United States — Canada is at a disadvantage in supporting most technologically intensive goods that have large development costs and require high volume production to be economically viable. Canada possesses neither the fiscal resources nor the market size to finance major defence projects like the United States nor the development of massive commercially oriented R&D projects like the Japanese.

Instead, Canada needs to focus its efforts to maximise its comparative advantages through both infrastructural and direct support and through an attractive technological climate. Direct aid must build on areas of existing or potential competitive advantage relating to Canada's natural resources, geographic and climatic setting, or to bolster strengths arising from world class scientific research (basic R&D) in a number of university and government institutions. Infrastructural support should augment these existing strengths and build for future advantages through continued support for both basic R&D and an educational system that to date has provided a good supply of skilled personnel. Beyond government assistance, Canadian policy must provide a competitive environment with the market opportunities and pressures to ensure both static and dynamic efficiency through greater specialisation and, where appropriate, scale. In particular, there is a need for an environment that fosters the application of scientific research through innovation to create marketable products, especially in the so-called 'footloose industries' where small sized firms have advantages, i.e. those with low capital intensity and/or low product development costs (e.g. microelectronics and scientific and professional instruments).

Unfortunately, despite an extremely attractive fiscal environment for private sector R&D and major strengths in basic R&D in a number of university and government institutions and the educational system itself, major flaws characterise Canadian policy in the advanced technology area (Palda, 1984, pp. 90–122; Task Force on Federal Policies and Programs for Technology Development, 1984). Too many programs entail substantial compliance costs for recipients, while too often there is insufficient consideration of user attitudes and needs in designing aid programs. In several high profile cases (e.g. Consolidated Computer Inc.), government assistance went far beyond seed money as the aid became a bailout. Quick fix tax incentives such as the 'Scientific Research Tax Credit' have raised major concerns about the type of R&D encouraged in many cases; the relatively small amount of R&D stimulated per 'lost' revenue dollar; and the potentially large revenue drains on the federal treasury.

In a fundamental sense, public policy toward the advanced technology industry group has too often been misdirected. Much of the government's strategy still focuses on aggregate R&D targets rather than the more appropriate concentration on deficiencies in the policy environment in areas where Canada has achieved or could potentially create a strategic advantage. The emphasis on the supply of technological advance has frequently been at the expense of ignoring the market receptiveness of such products. Above all, government tries to be active in identifying markets when in most cases its record is distinctly inferior to setting a better framework for stimulating advanced technology businesses which can meet the test of the marketplace.

This last reason has led to neglect of less obvious factors that have detracted from the Canadian policy environment. University-business linkages are important sources of innovation and know-how for start-up ventures; yet despite selected Canadian examples of success — especially in the case of Ontario's University of Waterloo — and both federal and provincial efforts to facilitate the corporate-academic interface, Canada has lagged far behind the United States here. In 1982, only 0.2 per cent of Canadian university R&D was financed by business while just 0.1 per cent of corporate funded R&D was performed by universities; the comparable US percentages were 3 per cent and 0.7 per cent, respectively (Grossman, 1984, p. 35). Restraint in provincial funding for higher education has significantly constrained university capabilities to maintain up-to-date facilities and scientific equipment. As well, critics of current government policy point to an inadequate supply of training programs and inappropriate immigration rules that could jeopardise the Canadian supply of qualified scientists and engineers in advanced technologies (Natural Sciences and Engineering Research Council, 1985).

The widespread problems in Canada's technological environment make its upgrading essential for Canadian subsidiaries, both existing and potential, to become attractive candidates for WPMs. As a result, the potential for improved domestic policy to attract WPMs through direct aid and infrastructural support is substantial under either the second or third option. While the type and amount of direct incentives and certain kinds of infrastructrual assistance would be more limited under a comprehensive trade agreement, the impact of such measures in a Canada-US trade pact is likely to be much more beneficial. The greater market opportunities and increased competitive pressures would significantly enhance the incentives and need to achieve technological efficiency. In particular, if a Canadian-American agreement accorded Canadian based producers much better terms of entry to government procurement markets in the United States, the boost to a number of industries where Canada has existing or potential comparative advantages (e.g. telecommunications) could be highly advantageous.

Conclusion

In assessing the attractiveness of foreign owned subsidiaries in Canada for specialised missions, particularly WPMs, it is clear that the nature of Canada's strategic policy choice will have a decisive impact on the locational merits of these Canadian operations. From our perspective, a comprehensive Canada-US trade agreement would be a significant advantage for subsidiaries. The much improved access to American markets, increased competitive pressures, and positive spillovers in other areas improve the chances of a specialised mission considerably.

Yet the foregoing analysis also reveals that there is tremendous scope for improved domestic policy management, especially in terms of indirect measures, to enhance the opportunities for specialised missions, particularly WPMs. While the range of policy measures available is greater under the third option, the policy room for improvement is very large under the second option as well. Indeed, a truly effective Canadian industrial and trade policy should combine a Canada-US trade pact with far-reaching initiatives in competition, R&D and other policy spheres. This applies not just to increasing the comparative merits of Canadian subsidiaries but to enhancing dramatically the general performance of the Canadian economy.

Whether Canada pursues the second or third option, or chooses some combination of both, remains unclear at this juncture as the ultimate policy decision will depend upon many factors, not the least being the political will and foresight of Canadian policymakers. No matter which path is chosen, however, it will be important to frame policy measures in such a way as to maximise the competitiveness of Canadian based operations within the confines of the domestic, North American, and global policy environments.

Notes

1. The authors gratefully acknowledge the benefit of discussions with Peter Clark regarding the GATT and US legislative aspects in this chapter. Helpful comments were also provided by Bernard M. Wolf on an earlier draft.

2. Parts of this chapter draw extensively upon a research project undertaken by the authors for the Science Council of Canada that is still in progress (mid-1985). More specifically, the first section on Canada's competitive challenges and policy options and the fourth section dealing with the appropriate policy setting are taken from the research project.

3. The first three of these options were put forward by Sharp (1972).

4. The framework set out below is a substantially modified version of an earlier set of four options outlined in Crookell (1983, pp. 25–6).

5. See Chapter 12.

6. See Chapter 8.

7. On this point, see Chapter 5.

8. See Chapter 3.

9. The US complaint against FIRA induced undertakings by foreign subsidiaries to purchase products from Canadian sources was upheld by the GATT panel.

10. On the Michelin and Honeywell cases, see Lazar (1981, p. 28). On the automotive case, see Beigie (1970, pp. 38–9).

11. The study by Dhawan and Kryzanowski (1983) also found that most of the subsidiaries surveyed received charters for goods nearing the end of their product life cycle. Although this finding appears to be at odds with the analysts' view cited earlier that parents are unlikely to grant a WPM for a product in the mature phase of its life cycle, at least three possibilities would explain this inconsistency. The US based operations may be moving out of this product line; the parent may be seeking to appease Ottawa at the lowest cost by granting a WPM in products with the least growth potential; and/or Canadian based production may have unique advantages at this stage of the product life cycle for these computer or computer related goods.

12. See for example, Grossman (1983, p. 49).

13. From the US Department of Justice, Antitrust Division, Antitrust Guide for International Operations (1977) cited in Campbell (1981, p. 45).

14. On Canada's poor record in the use of robotics, see the Robot Institute of America and US Department of Labour data cited in Grossman (1984, p. 17). It should be noted that the provinces and Ottawa have created an array of centres to promote the diffusion of technology. Yet corporate representatives have contended that these centres can suffer from duplication of effort, lack of coordination and may often be a response based on political considerations rather than business needs. See Chevreau (1984, p. B13).

15. On the merits of flexible system production, see Reich (1983, pp. 134–8).

References

Advisory Committee on Global Product Mandating (1980) *The Report on Global Product Mandating,* Ontario Ministry of Industry and Tourism, Toronto

Beigie, C.E. (1970) *The Canada-US Automotive Agreement: An Evaluation,* National Planning Association and Private Planning Association of Canada, Washington, DC

Campbell, B.R. (1981) 'Reach of the US Antitrust Laws: What You Don't Know Can Hurt You', *Canadian Business Review,* vol. 8, no. 1, pp. 45–7

Chevreau, J. (1984) 'CMA Attacks Rise in Technology Centres', *The Globe and Mail,* Toronto, 23 March

Clark, J. (1985) *Competitiveness and Security: Directions for Canada's International*

Relations, Supply and Services Canada, Ottawa

Crookell, H. (1983) 'The Future of US Foreign Direct Investment in Canada', *Business Quarterly,* vol. 48, no. 2, pp. 22–8

Crookell, H. and Caliendo, J. (1980) 'International Competitiveness and the Structure of Secondary Industry in Canada', *Business Quarterly,* vol. 45, no. 3, pp. 58–64

Dhawan, K.C. and Kryzanowski, L. (1983) *High Technology Plant Location Decision: US-Based Multinationals in the Canadian Computer Industry,* Concordia University, Montreal

Drouin, M.J. and Malmgren, H.B. (1981–82) 'Canada, the United States, and the World Economy', *Foreign Affairs,* vol. 60, Winter, pp. 393–413

Grossman, L. (1983) *Autumn Pre-Budget Statement 1983,* Ontario Ministry of Treasury and Economics, Toronto

Grossman, L. (1984) *Economic Transformation: Technological Innovation and Diffusion in Ontario,* Ontario Ministry of Treasury and Economics, Toronto

Kelleher, J.F. (1985) 'How to Secure and Enhance Canadian Access to Export Markets', unpublished discussion paper, Ottawa

Lazar, F. (1981) *The New Protectionism: Non-Tariff Barriers and their Effects on Canada,* Canadian Institute for Economic Policy, Ottawa

MacCharles, D.C. (1984a) 'Diagnosing the Competitiveness of Canadian Manufacturers', unpublished paper, University of New Brunswick, Saint John

MacCharles, D.C. (1984b) 'Do Foreign-Controlled Subsidiaries Have a Future?', *Canadian Business Review,* vol. 11, no. 1, pp. 18–24

MacDonald, N. (1985) 'Autos at Peril', *Policy Options,* vol. 6, no. 3, pp. 21–4

Natural Sciences and Engineering Research Council (1985) *Research Talent in the Natural Sciences and Engineering,* Natural Sciences and Engineering Research Council, Ottawa

Palda, K.S. (1984) *Industrial Innovation: Its Place in the Public Policy Agenda,* Fraser Institute, Vancouver

Poynter, T.A. and Rugman, A.M. (1982) 'World Product Mandates: How Will Multinationals Respond?', *Business Quarterly,* vol. 47, no. 3, pp. 54–61

Reagan, R., President (1983) 'Free and Fair Trade: A US Goal', *Economic Impact,* vol. 43, no. 3, pp. 6–8

Reich, R.B. (1983) *The Next American Frontier,* Basic Books, New York

Science Council of Canada (1980) *Multinationals and Industrial Strategy: The Role of World Product Mandates,* Science Council of Canada, Supply and Services Canada, Ottawa

Sharp, M. (1972) 'Canada-US Relations: Options for the Future', *International Perspectives,* Special Issue, Autumn, pp. 1–24

Standing Senate Committee on Foreign Affairs (1978) *Canada-United States Relations: Canada's Trade Relations with the United States,* vol. 2, Supply and Services Canada, Ottawa

Standing Senate Committee on Foreign Affairs (1982) *Canada-United States Relations: Canada's Trade Relations with the United States,* vol. 3, Supply and Services Canada, Ottawa

Task Force on Federal Policies and Programs for Technology Development (1984) *The Report of the Task Force on Federal Policies and Programs for Technology Development,* Supply and Services Canada, Ottawa

United States Congress (1984) *Trade and Tariff Act of 1984, Title 3,* US Government Printing Office, Washington, DC

White, R.E. and Poynter, T.A. (1984) 'Strategies for Foreign-Owned Subsidiaries in Canada', *Business Quarterly,* vol. 49, no. 2, pp. 59–69

Wolf, B.M. (1983) 'World Product Mandates and Freer Canada–United States Trade' in A.M. Rugman (ed.), *Multinationals and Technology Transfer: The Canadian Experience,* Praeger, New York, pp. 91–107

3 DIRECTION OF POLICY ON WORLD PRODUCT MANDATES[1]

A.J. Sarna

Background

Canada has had a long and chequered experience in dealing with the question of world product mandates (WPMs). Prior to the Second World War, many US owned firms were established in Canada's manufacturing sector with exclusive mandates to take advantage of the country's privileged export market access to Britain, the West Indies, South Africa, Australia, New Zealand and India under Imperial tariff preferences (e.g. Ford of Canada). During the postwar period, however, as Canada's external trade became heavily dependent on the US market, concerns developed over export limitations imposed on some Canadian subsidiaries of US corporations from the viewpoint of trade and anti-combines policies (Brecher and Reisman, 1957, p. 157). In the late 1950s and early 1960s, industrial policy concerns as well as trade policy considerations surrounded the behaviour and operations of foreign owned branch plant subsidiaries. In an historic move, Canada boldly opted for a wholesale rationalisation of its inefficient foreign owned automobile industry by concluding a conditional free trade agreement with the US in 1965. The assertion of American extraterritorial jurisdiction over the operations of Canadian subsidiaries which restricted their freedom to export to China and Cuba (nations with which Canada exchanged most favoured nation treatment) led the government to issue a series of voluntary guidelines governing good corporate behaviour. These called on foreign owned firms in Canada, *inter alia,* to:

(1) Seek the maximum development of market opportunities in other countries as well as in Canada;
(2) Develop, as an integral part of the Canadian operation wherever practic.ole, the technological research and design capability necessary to enable the company to pursue appropriate product development programs so as to take full advantage of market opportunities domestically and abroad;
(3) Recognise the desirability of progressively achieving appropriate specialisation of productive operations within the internationally

affiliated group of companies.[2]

Similar recommendations were subsequently made by the Task Force on the Structure of Canadian Industry (1968) which specified the creation of a government agency to secure international charters; by a task force headed by Revenue Minister Herb Gray in 1972 whose report (Government of Canada, 1972) resulted in the passage in 1973–4 of the 'Foreign Investment Review Act' requiring foreign investors to demonstrate 'significant benefit' to the Canadian economy as a condition for having their takeover and new business applications approved. Subsequently, additional guidelines enunciated in 1975 by Alastair Gillespie, the Minister of Industry, Trade and Commerce, urged foreign controlled firms to strive for a full international mandate for innovation and market development, where it would enable the Canadian company to improve its efficiency by specialisation of productive operations (Industry, Trade and Commerce Canada, 1975).

Structural Adjustment and WPMs

The conclusion of the seventh round of GATT trade negotiations in 1979 and the prevalence of recessionary conditions inaugurated an intense concern over the future of Canada's industrial structure, a concern that is likely to exist for the remainder of this century. Briefly, both domestically owned and foreign controlled manufacturing firms were faced with the most severe pressures for structural adjustment since the Great Depression of the 1930s. The unprecedented trade liberalisation carried out under the GATT would result, by 1987, in an average weighted tariff cut of 40 per cent, in addition to immediate free trade in civil aircraft products and limitations on the use of nontariff measures relating to customs valuation, government procurement practices, technical standards and domestic subsidy programs. Despite the positive opportunities afforded by improved terms of market access abroad, the Canadian manufacturing sector appeared more preoccupied with maintaining a strong domestic base as a prerequisite to penetrating foreign markets. Many firms stated they would be unable to compete with low cost imports from Japan and Third World countries which benefited from artificial cost advantages flowing from concessional financing and state supported industrial targeting practices. The option of shutting down manufacturing operations in favour of warehousing and distribution activities became a real one for many firms. The failure of macroeconomic policy to spur and sustain a strong recovery from the recession, high inflation and high interest rates administered an even harder blow to Canada's manufacturing sector resulting in excess capacity, layoffs and the worst unemployment the country has known in the postwar period.

This turbulent economic environment triggered a heated debate, both in Canada and abroad, as to the appropriate industrial strategies that should be adopted and the role of governments in revitalising their economies. Tensions between governments have already developed over what appears to be a universal predisposition for disguised protectionism in the form of national strategies based on subsidising both high technology and traditional industries. Such strategies are being justified by governments as positive adjustment policies in the face of the breakdown of macroeconomic management of the world economy. In Canada's case, world product mandating has been gaining prominence as a centrepiece for a national industrial strategy although other objectives are equally being pursued as prominently, if not more vigorously (i.e. free trade with the US, regional development, manpower retraining, technological innovation, sectoral policies, productivity improvement, framework policies, economic nationalism and reliance on market forces).

Benefits of WPMs and Positive Incentives

In the December 1983 Speech from the Throne, the federal government announced that, as part of an aggressive trade drive, 'active pursuit of world product mandates by Canadian subsidiaries of multinational corporations, and the winning of additional export markets by Canadian companies, will be assisted by competition policy and direct funding' (Speech from the Throne to Open the Second Session, 1984).

The rationale for such assistance was derived from a considerable amount of supportive policy advice received by the government in recent years as well as the visible success of several key policy instruments deployed to obtain WPMs from multinational enterprises.

The most influential policy advice in the 1980s has come from the following quarters:

(1) The Science Council of Canada, which has advanced the proposition that Canada should join the world trend towards technologically intensive production by obtaining specialised mission mandates from foreign firms engaged in Canadian manufacturing. Given the 40 per cent

ownership level in this sector by foreign controlled corporations and an assumption that Canadian owned firms generally lack suitable technological capabilities, the Science Council believes the WPM option would provide a number of important benefits in the form of increased international competitiveness and productivity in the Canadian economy and higher employment through a corresponding reduction in the large trade deficit in fully manufactured goods (Science Council of Canada, 1980, pp. 9–10).

(2) The Standing Senate Committee on Foreign Affairs, which sees WPMs as an alternative to the possible repatriation of the manufacturing operations of American owned firms under a bilateral free trade scenario with the US. In its view, a US parent company would be much less likely to divest itself of a technically oriented engineering group with an efficient facility producing a successful product than to close down a branch plant operation manufacturing similar products for the small Canadian market (Standing Senate Committee on Foreign Affairs, 1982, pp. 61–5).

(3) The Department of External Affairs, whose trade policy strategy envisages WPMs as presenting an opportunity for greater export autonomy, increased scale of operations and hence increased Canadian international competitiveness in technologically intensive secondary manufacturing such as the aerospace, automotive, electronics, electrical equipment and machinery sectors (External Affairs Canada, 1983, pp. 53–4).

(4) The Department of Supply and Services, which has advocated the use of the federal government's $6 billion annual purchasing requirements as an important lever in encouraging multinationals to develop a WPM in Canada (Supply and Services Canada, 1984, p. 22).

(5) The now defunct Foreign Investment Review Agency (FIRA) which sought to maximise the benefits from new foreign direct investment in Canada by obtaining undertakings from applicants to assign to the Canadian business exclusive rights to export either all its products to certain countries, or certain specified products on a worldwide basis, or exclusive corporate responsibility for the research, development and manufacturing of specified product lines (Foreign Investment Review Agency, 1979, pp. 6–7, p. 14). Among the WPMs obtained as a result of these policies were those for pneumatic timing relays, specialty chemicals, sealing compounds, time-division multiplexer products, high-speed multistage tools and dies, metric sized fittings and certain equipment and computer software used in monitoring industrial processes in the chemical and energy sectors (Foreign Investment Review Agency, 1981a, b; 1982a, p. 3; 1982b, c, d).

(6) The Department of Regional Industrial Expansion and its predecessor, the Department of Industry, Trade and Commerce, which have supported the use of duty remission schemes, loan guarantees, industrial assistance programs (e.g. the Defence Industry Productivity Program and the Industrial and Regional Development Program) and corporate development agreements to obtain WPMs. Notable examples are the WPM undertaking of Chrysler Canada to produce the T115 van/wagon (1980); the WPM commitments by Messerschmitt-Bolkow-Blohm and Bell Helicopter Textron to manufacture light twin-engined helicopters and the related WPM undertaking of Pratt & Whitney Canada to develop a new helicopter engine family (1983) (Government of Canada, 1983; Industry, Trade and Commerce Canada, 1980a; Regional Economic Expansion Canada, 1983).

(7) The Government of Ontario, which is considering using a preferential purchasing policy to force foreign companies to grant their Ontario subsidiaries WPMs and has already set up a WPM promotion branch within its Ministry of Industry and Trade. The benefits of such a policy would be to reverse the decline in Ontario's share of world trade (from 2.3 per cent in 1970 to 1.5 per cent in 1984). This decline is estimated to have cost the province $18 billion in foregone exports and more than 200,000 jobs.[3]

Negative Constraints

While there is no question as to the numerous advantages associated with WPMs, it is recognised that some important negative externalities are present. Certainly, sole reliance on the WPM option as the key to a Canadian industrial strategy is not a serious proposition.

The first negative externality is the cost to the public treasury. As previously noted, multinational enterprises may be convinced of the desirability of reallocating or localising particular product development lines in one of their affiliates abroad if suitable investment incentives in the form of up-front grants and government contracts are made available by a host country. Developments in the automotive industry in recent years, which have led to the building of 'world cars', clearly demonstrate how investment wars can erupt between governments competing for such projects.[4] When one considers the government's fundamental commitment to substantially reducing its $34 billion deficit, similar to that of most OECD governments, the psychological and political cost of such wars may be unacceptable. Hence, there would not appear to be much enthusiasm in Canada for a massive spending effort to attract WPMs. Two qualifications need to be made here: if the job creation impact in Canada was significant, it might induce a more forthcoming attitude on the part of government; similarly, if any assistance to the WPM projects required payback commitments and did not entail excessive risk, the financial outlay of the government might be worthwhile.

A second major constraint to embracing the WPM option is the coercive tools that may be deployed. As is well known, the Canadian government was severely criticised by both domestically owned and foreign owned firms for extracting uneconomic export and R&D undertakings from foreign investors seeking entry under the provisions of the now defunct 'Foreign Investment Review Act'. In some cases, such commitments had not been deemed feasible or sufficiently profitable by multinational enterprises but were made to secure a presence in Canada. In others, such commitments were not undertaken, which resulted in disallowance of investment applications. As for established foreign owned firms, the leverage threatened or exerted against them by government procurement practices and the ill-fated proposals to monitor their individual performance[5] to influence such activity as mandating were condemned by the private sector as discriminatory. Widespread dissemination of such negative feedbacks about a host country's policies (e.g. Canada) in the international business community can unduly harm a country's economic development prospects and contribute to a flight of capital, or a rerouting of potential incoming investments.

Bilateral tensions with the US are a third danger arising from the active pursuit of WPMs. The US government has strenuously objected to 'performance requirements' imposed on multinationals by host governments and is leading efforts in the OECD and the GATT to curb or terminate them. Presidential enforcement of the reciprocity provisions contained in recently enacted legislation[6] looms as a countervailing weapon on the horizon unless progress is made internationally on this issue. As well, hostility toward investment incentives has long been a fact in American foreign economic policy. An indication of the depth of US antagonism to 'performance requirements' may be gauged by its 1982 decision to bring a formal complaint before the GATT concerning the negotiation by FIRA with foreign investors for commitments to certain manufacturing and export undertakings. The US included specific references to export undertakings which 'involve assigning to the Canadian business exclusive rights to export either all its products to certain countries or specified products on a world basis' and to undertake the manufacturing in Canada of a product's component which would be imported otherwise (GATT, 1983, pp. 3–4, 11–14, 19–21).

In support of its request to a GATT panel that it recommend that FIRA ceases the elicitation of such undertakings, the US argued that export undertakings violated the provisions of GATT Article XVII: 1(c) which prohibit government actions that prevent private enterprises from conducting their export trade solely in accordance with commercial considerations. Thus, in the US view, export mandates involuntarily granted by foreign investors to the Canadian concerns deny the enterprises and other contracting parties adequate opportunity to compete for participation in such trade. In so far as manufacturing undertakings were concerned, the US contended that the obligations of a foreign investor to produce in Canada specified parts or components of a particular product were inconsistent with the provisions of GATT Article III: 5 because they constituted internal quantitative regulations relating to the mixture, processing or use of products which required that a specified amount or proportion of a product be supplied from domestic sources. Although the US complaints against both types of FIRA related requirements were not upheld by the GATT panel, the US did win against FIRA elicited undertakings to purchase goods from Canadian sources. These issues have also been raised by the US in other international fora such as the OECD with a view to reconciling their validity in terms of the principle of 'national treatment'. It is also likely that, in the event of a new round of GATT trade negotiations, trade related investment requirements will assume prominence.

Policy of the New Conservative Government

The Progressive Conservative Party of Canada, which was elected to office in September 1984, has changed the business climate under which WPMs can be encouraged in Canada. In essence, the new government has largely adopted a market driven approach to economic development with a complementary emphasis on reducing government expenditures much like the developments witnessed earlier under the Reagan administration and the Thatcher government. This has been translated into a greater reliance on horizontal or framework policies, in terms of: (1) rationalised tax measures with a subsequent diminution of direct grant programs, (2) the dismantling of FIRA and the creation of the Investment Canada agency with an 'open door' policy, and (3) the discussions with the United States on a comprehensive approach to the liberalisation of bilateral trade barriers. All three policies are bound to influence the degree in which corporate functions in Canada are broadened to encompass WPMs. Whether the foreign private sector will find these less interventionist measures attractive as incentives to continue to grant WPMs to their Canadian operations, as Canadians clearly expect, remains a matter of intense conjecture.

Notes

1. The material in this chapter appeared originally in *The Canadian Business Review*, vol. 11, no. 4, Winter, 1984, pp. 35–8. Reprinted by permission. The views expressed are those of the author and do not necessarily represent those of the Government of Canada.
2. Trade Minister Robert H. Winter's letter to Canadian subsidiaries of foreign companies tabled in the House of Commons, 31 March 1966, contained a section entitled 'Some Guiding Principles of Good Corporate Behaviour for Subsidiaries in Canada of Foreign Companies'.
3. *The Ottawa Citizen* (1983). Ontario's approach has been influenced by two important reports prepared by executives from leading multinational affiliates in Canada. See Advisory Committee on Global Product Mandating (1980) and Global Product Mandate Promotion Committee (1982).
4. Both the OECD and the GATT have moved to reduce the adverse international effects of investment incentives. See OECD (1979) and GATT (1979).
5. The latter were part of the new national industrial development policy proposed by the government in 1980 under which FIRA would have been considerably strengthened. Details are contained in Industry, Trade and Commerce Canada (1980b).
6. US Trade and Tariff Act of 1984. This law amends Section 301 of the US Trade Act of 1974 to allow the President to retaliate against any foreign actions, including investment policies, which are 'unjustifiable, unreasonable, discriminatory and which burden or restrict US commerce' (United States Congress 1974, 1984).

References

Advisory Committee on Global Product Mandating (1980) *The Report on Global Product Mandating*, Ontario Ministry of Industry and Tourism, Toronto

Brecher, I. and Reisman, S.S. (1957) *Canada-United States Economic Relations*, Royal Commission on Canada's Economic Prospects, Queen's Printer, Ottawa

External Affairs Canada (1983) *A Review of Canadian Trade Policy*, Supply and Services Canada, Ottawa

Foreign Investment Review Agency (1979) *Foreign Investment Review Act: Supplement to the 1978-79 Annual Report*, Supply and Services Canada, Ottawa

Foreign Investment Review Agency (1981a) *Foreign Investment Review Act: Quarterly Report*, Supply and Services Canada, Ottawa, April-June

Foreign Investment Review Agency (1981b) *Releases*, Foreign Investment Review Agency, Ottawa, 6 November

Foreign Investment Review Agency (1982a) *Foreign Investment Review Act: Annual Report 1981-82*, Supply and Services Canada, Ottawa

Foreign Investment Review Agency (1982b) *Foreign Investment Review Act: Quarterly Report*, Supply and Services Canada, Ottawa, January-March

Foreign Investment Review Agency (1982c) *Foreign Investment Review Act: Quarterly*

Report, Supply and Services Canada, Ottawa, April-June
Foreign Investment Review Agency (1982d) *Releases,* Foreign Investment Review Agency, Ottawa, 4 October
Foreign Investment Review Agency (1983) *Releases,* Foreign Investment Review Agency, Ottawa, 6 May
GATT (1979) *Agreement on Interpretation and Application of Articles VI, XVI and XXIII of the General Agreement on Tariffs and Trade,* GATT, Geneva
GATT (1983) *Canada — Administration of the Foreign Investment Review Act: Report of the Panel,* Document L/5504, GATT, Geneva
Global Product Mandate Promotion Committee (1982) *The Report of the Global Product Mandate Committee on Modification to Ontario's Procurement Policy,* Ontario Ministry of Industry and Tourism, Toronto
Government of Canada (1972) *Foreign Direct Investment in Canada,* Information Canada, Ottawa
Government of Canada (1983) *News Release,* Supply and Services Canada, Ottawa
Industry, Trade and Commerce Canada (1975) *New Principles of International Business Conduct,* Industry, Trade and Commerce Canada, Ottawa, 8 July
Industry, Trade and Commerce Canada (1980a) *News Release,* Industry, Trade and Commerce Canada, Ottawa, 10 May
Industry, Trade and Commerce Canada (1980b) 'Economic Nationalism and Industrial Strategies', Notes for an Address by the Honourable Herb Gray, P.C., M.P., Minister of Industry, Trade and Commerce to the Annual Symposium, Ecole des Hautes Etudes Commerciales, Montreal, *News Release,* Industry, Trade and Commerce Canada, Ottawa, 3 June
OECD (1979) *Revised Decision of the Council on International Investment Incentives and Disincentives,* OECD, Paris
Regional Economic Expansion Canada (1983) *News Release,* Regional Economic Expansion, Ottawa
Science Council of Canada (1980) *Multinationals and Industrial Strategy: The Role of World Product Mandates,* Science Council of Canada, Supply and Services Canada, Ottawa
Speech from the Throne to Open the Second Session (1984), 32nd Parliament of Canada, December 7, 1983, *House of Commons Debates, Official Report,* vol. 1, Queen's Printer, Ottawa
Standing Senate Committee on Foreign Affairs (1982) *Canada-United States Relations: Canada's Trade Relations with the United States,* vol. 3, Supply and Services Canada, Ottawa
Supply and Services Canada (1984) *An Annual Procurement Plan and Strategy, 1983-84,* Supply and Services Canada, Ottawa
Task Force on the Structure of Canadian Industry (1968) 'Press Release, No. 2', Ottawa, 15 February
The Ottawa Citizen (1983) 14 December
United States Congress (1974) *Trade Act of 1974,* US Government Printing Office, Washington, DC
United States Congress (1984) *Trade and Tariff Act of 1984,* US Government Printing Office, Washington, DC

4   COMPETING NATIONS FOR GLOBAL PRODUCT MANDATES: SCIENCE POLICIES IN COLLISION[1]

David P. Rutenberg

Introduction

Governments differ in what they want of multinational corporations. It is through the emphasis given to job creation, exports, access to technology and world product mandates (WPMs) that governments' industrial strategies differ. This chapter explains how a rational multinational corporation can match its activities to national objectives, foregoing as little profit as possible, while satisfying each government's demands.[2] In other words, industrial strategies conflict with the multinational's strategies, but the latter can adapt itself to government policy differences, however slight these may be.

This chapter focuses on high technology electronic products for three reasons. First, economies of scale and experience effects are so significant that the international market as a whole can be economically supplied by just one or two plants. Therefore, if there are to be 50 interested governments, then 48 will be disappointed. Second, most governments see electronics as the 'commanding heights of technology' and are determined to do everything in their power so that their nation shall not be eliminated. That is, they shall not be one of the 48 for all products simultaneously. Third, many WPMs involve electrical products.

This chapter builds towards a mathematical model which integrates the different nations' aspirations into the goals of a globally profit maximising corporation (weighted assignment model). Although the model seems to be inappropriately precise, it is simple enough to be run on a personal business computer. It is intended to explore decision implications, but not to make decisions.

As an example, each IBM national manager, as part of his five-year plan, projects his subsidiary's exports and imports. Those national managers forecasting a balance of trade shortfall have a greater claim on some part of the next generation of products to be manufactured in those nations. The purpose of this chapter is to generalise this practice beyond the trade balance focus to all the objectives of different governments. Each government assigns unique weights to these objectives. Some governments focus on their balance of trade while others have different preoccupations.

The centrality of research and development (R&D) to global product mandating suggests that governments' attempts to stimulate R&D are perhaps a good indicator of their enthusiasm and interest in obtaining a WPM. Thus, this chapter examines national research management from a world product mandating viewpoint before proceeding to the formulation of the weighted assignment problem.

National Strategic Differences in Research Support

Industrial strategy used to have many meanings, but the austerity of the 1980s is focusing government attention on high technology. Although the problems of declining sectors and regions are acknowledged, electronics and sometimes biotechnology are seen as the elixirs of industrial growth. During one interview, the Minister of Economic Planning of Czechoslovakia explained that he intends to take his country into electronics, even though he forecast that Czech costs would still be four times those of equivalent Japanese products after allowing for Czech workers to move reasonably far down the experience curve. Among the interviews conducted by the author, only Indonesia and Jordan did not consider electronics as the principal solution. In order better to focus on the following summaries of other nations, the case of Canada will be summarised.

Canada

Canada engages in less than 1 per cent of the world's total R&D activities. Even this minor contribution is spread out over so many economic sectors that Canada does not dominate in any one of them. Thus the models of research domination developed in the USA, UK and France are inappropriate for Canada.

A rational Canadian strategy should be more like Japan's during the 1950s and 1960s: generally learning as much as possible from the other 99 per cent of world research. We are fortunate in this respect since most journals are published in English, and Canadian university science departments closely correspond to the US models. Nevertheless, maintaining systematic access costs money. Canadian government policy provides incentives to encourage corporations to engage in R&D. A study comparing Canadian R&D incentives to those of other industrialised nations (McFetridge and Warda, 1983) concludes that Canada offers a superior number of R&D incentives to those in place in other industrial countries (only Singapore provides more help). When subsidies and contracts are considered, Canada provides one of the most favourable environments for R&D.

However, the ease of access to world R&D is not enough to change the state of R&D in Canada. Canadians are barely attaining the threshold amount of research to stay credible in a number of fields. For example, Canadian military R&D has been long neglected. Canadian contributions to joint US-Canadian research projects have become so insignificant that the US is discouraged from engaging in new ones.

It is customary to say that to maintain access to world industrial and technological developments, Canadians must increase R&D. The point is that Canada must strive to do so effectively. It would not be in Canada's best interest to provide even more liberal treatment of R&D, because technology can be developed in one area and used without compensation in another. Only government pressure to create a WPM tenuously induces the research to be transformed into manufacturing jobs in Canada. Conversely however, world product mandating is one effective way of legitimating access to foreign corporate research and know-how.

Singapore

The city-state of Singapore has developed a wealth of experience in negotiating with multinational corporations. Hewlett-Packard and General Electric now produce technologically sophisticated products in Singapore, but they did not always do so. Visualise Singapore's industrial strategy as a ladder with each rung corresponding to a higher level of technology. The government strategy is to move the Singapore work force up this ladder. The workers learn by working in order to ready themselves for the next level of technological know-how. In order to upgrade the level of technology in Singapore, the government raised the minimum wage, deliberately driving out the textile industry, and reducing jobs for illegal immigrants, thus saving Singapore the capital costs of their apartments and schools. This higher wage bill forced other low technology operations to move out. For example, GE was forced to move a relay manufacturing line from Singapore to Malaysia. As a *quid pro quo* to the government, GE decided it was prudent to create in Singapore an Asian facility for the overhaul of GE jet engines (as used in the Airbus). The former relay assemblers do not overhaul jet engines but some of the GE Singapore workers moved up the technological ladder.

It is the author's impression that Singapore government officials have worked to know the product line details of many corporations, so as to be able to negotiate successfully. They are aware of global product mandating, but are currently interested in manufacturing as Singapore still lacks sufficient qualified engineers and market analysts. This has several implications for Canada. First, a subsidiary in Canada may have a WPM and then find it more profitable to manufacture certain subassemblies in Singapore. Secondly, products that have a static technology are unsuitable for the granting of a mandate to a Canadian subsidiary since it will face direct competition within the corporation from the Singapore subsidiary which is eager to bid on more advanced technology. Expressed another way, it only makes sense to grant a mandate to a Canadian subsidiary if the products in question are experiencing such technical change that they could not be manufactured in Singapore.

Japan

During the past century the Japanese have been watching the development and evolution of foreign technology. They have learned how to learn from foreign experts and have created an excellent human information handling system that spans from market potential assessment to basic research. In the 1970s and 1980s research in Japan has been increasing, applied research being decentralised in corporate laboratories fuelled by intense competition. But basic research is performed in central government laboratories (to reduce duplication) with teams that include corporate researchers.

The government owned inorganic chemistry laboratory in Tskuba Science City is an example of a basic research laboratory whose structure eases the transition from basic to applied research and anticipates the future. This laboratory has 100 scientists who are equally divided into ten basic research teams. Each team works on one inorganic chemical for five years and then disbands. Then some scientists continue to work on the chemical and move to corporate applied laboratories in order to do so. Other researchers start research on a new inorganic chemical. To help select the new chemical worthy of this much effort, the government laboratory convenes a conference of corporate planners who discuss the problems they foresee over the next ten to 15 years that will require basic inorganic research. Every six months, such a conference is held, and a new team launched.

Resource-poor Japan has focused its research on high value added products. Foreign multinationals used to be a welcome source of technology so long as they had unique technological know-how. But now Japanese research has advanced to the point that the Japanese partners in some joint ventures are developing more advanced technological know-how than their foreign partner. In such a case, the joint venture structure and especially its licensing agreement with its foreign parent, is no longer useful to Japan. The Japanese government is less focused on employment and more on the value added so as to support the high Japanese standard of living. Low technology products are being spun off to Singapore, Hong Kong, Korea or Taiwan. Simultaneously the Japanese fear that these 'four dragons' will move too rapidly up the technological ladder. For example, integrated circuit prices dropped precipitously in the 1980s. The US interpretation of this phenomenon is that this reflects US-Japanese rivalry. The Korean interpretation is that the Japanese are deliberately spoiling the market by lowering the price umbrella in order to prevent the Koreans from getting established!

In summary, when a Japanese envisions a new kind of product he sees two constraints. First, does Japan have the technology to develop and manufacture it? Secondly, will the product be so unique that other governments will permit it to be imported? Research eliminates the first constraint and permits decision makers to focus on politically palatable products.

Israel

Israel's high budget for military expenditures has necessitated this country's movement into high value added manufactures where profit margins are high enough to sustain taxes for the military. High technology products, particularly electronics, have been identified by the government as the key sector to achieve such profit margins. Furthermore, the Israeli government believes that computer programming work and electronic assembly can be performed in the isolated Jewish settlements located in the predominantly Arab occupied regions now controlled by Israel.

The government of Israel wants the country to manufacture products with a high added value and very low transportation costs. Foreign multinationals are a welcome source of technology and are encouraged to move parts of their product line to Israel. Some corporations use Israel as a research site. For example, Intel has research laboratories in Israel, California and Japan with superb communication links between them. Global product mandating is seen as a favourable strategy for Israel.

EEC

According to the Commission of the European Communities (1984a, b, c) the first industrial revolution was European, the second one involved Europeans, but the third one is American and Japanese and will leave Europeans behind unless they get involved. Spurred by France and the spectre of overseas competition, the EEC Secretariat and member nations have been redirecting their research efforts towards those few opportunities most appropriate for Europe and within the member nations' financial capabilities. By 1984, the EEC had articulated five strands of research aimed at maintaining European competitiveness:

(1) Industry spanning problems, e.g. catalysis, bonding
(2) Collaborative projects in information technology (ESPRIT) and biotechnology
(3) Introduction of Community Integrated Broadband Communication (RACE)
(4) Assessment procedures for the impact of technology on society (START)
(5) Aid to ailing industries, e.g. research in textiles and steel.

European Community initiatives are intended to eliminate duplication. The European Strategic Program for Research and Development in Information Technology (ESPRIT) is one such project which brings together member states in a collaborative approach to R&D. ESPRIT was initiated when the major European electronics manufacturing companies came together to form a community level lobby. ESPRIT is administered by the European Council; German participation is highly significant.

It is unlikely that the EEC will be overt in discriminating against foreign multinational corporations. Its policies must fall within the bounds of the OECD's definition of 'National Treatment' which declares:

that Member countries should . . . accord to enterprises operating in their territories and owned or controlled directly or indirectly by nationals of another member country treatment under their laws, regulations and administrative practices, consistent with international law and no less favourable than that accorded in like situations to domestic enterprises.' (Committee on International Investment and Multinational Enterprises, 1984, p. 3)

In 1985 it appears that non-European multinationals are being offered token ESPRIT awards, but only on condition that they share some of their other research with European electrical manufacturers.

The management of ESPRIT is faced with a five-year budget constraint of $1.5 billion (Canadian), a trivial amount equivalent to only a few days funding of the EEC agricultural surplus. For this reason, ESPRIT might be interpreted as a structure for a cartel under the guise of a research pool. In fact, European corporations are being urged by their governments to enter into technology agreements with sophisticated US and Japanese competitors.

France

Industrial policy in France stems from a long tradition of centralism. Throughout its economic history, France has favoured the creation and support of domestic manufacturing. Certainly in its funding of research, the government of France makes a sharp distinction between foreign multinationals and either French or European companies. For example, a senior government official explained during an interview that less research was being performed by all French electronics companies combined than by IBM France alone. In his mind, IBM France is not part of French research but part of the competition. Such thinking is not congruent with global product mandating.

The French are extremely wary of depending on the US which they see as capricious in its policy changes. For example, in the French space program (the Ariane rocket) great care has been taken to avoid incorporating any US components; French components are desired, German are preferred, other European components are acceptable. The French government is determined to be independent of the US extraterritorial influence manifested through its control of technology — even through subsidiaries of US multinationals. President Reagan's attempt to prevent US subsidiaries from supplying equipment to a Soviet natural gas pipeline in August 1982 was taken very seriously by the French government. For this reason the French government has quite negative perceptions of global product mandating.

Germany

Research in Germany is divided between theoretical research being carried out in a series of Max Planck government institutes, while applied research is being performed by German corporations. Interfacing between these government and corporate laboratories are a number of hybrid R&D facilities intended to ease the transition from pure to applied research. Paradoxically, because these transitional laboratories have the intellectual respect of neither the Max Planck researchers nor the corporations, their existence has reduced communication and coordination between the two.

Germany is a federation of land (provincial) governments. Only in West Berlin has the government allocated substantial research funds to corporations for product development and enhancement. The first manifestation of this policy was demonstrated in its support for a technology laboratory to the Schering Pharmaceutical Corporation. The attention given to R&D has allowed Berlin to attain world class status in research, supporting more research scientists than the whole of Canada. High technology products have low transportation costs and their manufacture encourages young professionals to remain in Berlin. For this reason the Berlin government is quite enthusiastic towards world product mandating. However, the federal republic's government (located in Bonn) is neutral toward this type of agreement.[3]

The United Kingdom

Japan's ICOT fifth generation computer project jolted the British government from Prime Minister Thatcher's ideological policy of allowing industry to compete on its own. The resulting Alvey Committee of British industrialists and academics identified five key areas where the UK is determined not to be left behind:

(1) Intelligent Knowledge Based Systems (IKBS)
(2) Man Machine Interface (MMI)
(3) VLSI and CAD
(4) Software Engineering
(5) Large Scale Projects (to demonstrate the results of Alvey research in real environments).

Alvey's five-year funding is so low (£350 million; $600 million Canadian) that it serves mainly to nurture an 'old boys' network and to provide a forum for sharing research risk assessments (Institution of Electrical Engineers, 1984).

Unfortunately, Alvey merely maintains British companies in high technology rivalry. Alvey works best when providing social networking to its participants. The British claim a world preeminence in complicated software, yet Alvey is not developing the international legal infrastructure to assure the protection of British software. This is necessary for the collection of royalties from foreign users of the software in order to finance Britain's continuance in this third industrial revolution. Furthermore, there are already such shortages of skilled programmers and engineers as may limit Alvey's vision. Unfortunately, Alvey provides no direct mechanism to educate those students who will be necessary to generate new ideas for the next ten years.

British companies have access to both EEC ESPRIT funds and UK Alvey funds and, by their involvement, they have become members of both sets of liaison committees and review boards. The liaison work itself is extremely time consuming, forcing all but the largest manufacturers to ration executive time. Small British companies are being enticed by opportunities to access the purchasing departments of large corporations, to participate in joint research projects and to offer feedback to government officials. But their research directors lack sufficient laboratory time. Other more self-disciplined British companies are insisting that their research directors establish research programs consistent with their corporate strategy. These companies are funding their research programs internally, and are sourcing Alvey or ESPRIT funds only if they can do so without compromising their corporate strategy. In other words, Alvey/ESPRIT funds are merely backing corporate funds. But no additional research is being performed.

Summary of the National Strategies

As this limited review of national strategies shows, almost all governments want to create jobs, increase exports, bring in technology, etc. In describing how a government makes a decision to give a bigger subsidy to one investment proposal over another, the process is characterised by the cost-benefit criteria, whereby the government assigns a unique set of weights to job creation, exports, technology, etc. The corporate planner interacting with the corporation's government liaison person in each nation has to infer the government's set of weights and corporate expectations. The corporations must set these weights in a manner consistent across nations in order to be viewed as active and competitive within the chosen nations. Each government assigns quite different weights to each of these objectives. These weights will be used in the corporate planner's weighted assignment problem.

Corporate Reconciliation of these Diverse Pressures

The national policy differences of various countries toward technological mandating give some idea of the complex task faced by a corporate headquarters. Usually economies of scale in high technology products are so significant that the entire world can most efficiently be supplied by just one or two plants. If 50 nations aspire to develop the required technological capability, then the assignment of a WPM to one or two nations means disappointment and frustration for the 48 other governments.

Furthermore, the management of a high technology corporation requires that innovation be a pervasive corporate value. If some portions of the corporation are not playing the game, and are merely manu-facturing in a passive mode, the corporation becomes difficult to manage. For example, all major subsidiaries of Hewlett-Packard believe in, and are evaluated on, their ability to develop products. For this reason, what Canadians call world product mandating is a fairly frequent normal way of doing business in certain corporations. But product development is not a clean, logical and predictable process. It depends on inspiration, novel ways of seeing, a rich stream of problems and possible ideas. Thus, the product developments of one subsidiary inevitably evolve into the territory of what another subsidiary believes to be its mandate. The practice of good research management is to encourage a certain degree of duplication, not only as insurance in case the main program fails, but also in the belief that competition can be a spur to creativity. For this reason, a WPM is not a monopoly, but rather it is the right to be the most serious bidder in the ongoing progression of the product's evolution.

Products have to be matched to nations, recognising that the matching may not be permanent. Nations clearly have very different objectives in the kind of products and activities they desire and are willing to subsidise. An inappropriate assignment can irritate many governments.

In 1982 planners of several high technology multinational corporations were interviewed to see how they visualised this assignment problem. All of them were forced to respond to pressures as they arose, and hence could not talk in terms of a globally optimal assignment process. They felt 'nibbled alive' by these government pressures, and distracted from the business and technical decisions they had to make. Each of them wanted some form of conceptual framework in order to understand the trade-offs they were having to make. The following model, admittedly too precise, is a quick-to-solve tool for struggling with these issues.

Weighted Assignment Problem

The problem of assigning mandates to nations can be seen as a game between n governments, all competing for pieces of the corporation. However, such n-person games cannot be solved and so the formulation is sterile. An alternative formulation presented here is as though each government has a set of fixed demands. This model permits a corporate planner to explore the effects of his perceptions of government demands.

In order to build the model the following steps must be taken. First, a matrix must be prepared in which each row represents a nation, and each column represents one of the product lines of the corporation. Economies of scale are usually so significant that only one nation will receive a mandate for a product. Second, two numbers must be entered into each cell of the matrix. The first number (C_{ij}) is an estimate of the after-tax profitability of mandating a specific product to a particular nation. The second number (a_{ij}) is the corporation's assessment of a national government's cost-benefit analysis of the product being mandated to its nation. From the discussion of national differences in supporting research, it is clear that governments have significantly different perceptions of the benefits that might arise from the same investment. Third, an estimate of a national government's demands on the corporation in terms of its cost-benefit criteria (d_i) is placed at the right margin of the matrix. The problem is to assign products to nations in a way that maximises profit, yet satisfies each government's cost-benefit constraints. This weighted assignment problem can be solved by a computer as a generalised network (sometimes called a machine loading problem). Problems involving several hundred products and fifty nations can be solved in a minute. The modelling process is depicted in Figure 4.1.

Figure 4.1: Weighted Assignment Problem

Products

Nations

	1	....	500	
Australia	C_{A1} X_{A1} a_{A1}		C_{A500} X_{A500} a_{A500}	$d_{Australia}$
....				
....				
Zaire	C_{Z1} X_{Z1} a_{Z1}		C_{Z500} X_{Z500} a_{Z500}	d_{Zaire}
	1		1	

Notes:

C_{ij} = after-tax profitability of mandating product *j* to nation *i*

a_{ij} = corporation's assessment of government *i*'s cost-benefit analysis of product *j* being mandated to nation *i*

X_{ij} = assignment variable: $X = 1$, product *j* assigned to nation *i*; otherwise $X = 0$

d_i = government *i*'s demands on the corporation in terms of the government's cost-benefit criteria

where i = Australia . . . Zaire

j = 1 . . . 500

Further Discussion of the Model

Down each column is an estimate of the project's profitability for the corporation. The project could be assigned to the nation where it would be most profitable. However, the corporation is under pressure to consider assigning the project to other nations where it will yield less lifetime profit because of labour costs, strikes, taxes, etc. The corporate analyst must avoid generalising across nations and resist the temptation to penalise all possible projects by the same penalty. The challenge is to find projects that are most appropriate (least inappropriate) for each nation. Included in this is the additional cost to the headquarters of having to manage despite petty government harassment.

Control was found to be the central problem in past studies (Rutenberg, 1981, 1982). Many corporations are split up into product divisions, which are subdivided into strategic business units (SBUs). From this perspective a WPM is simply an SBU that happens to be located in another nation. A corporate executive manages his strategic portfolio by leaving most SBUs to run independently, although systematically funding some and liquidating others. Corporate executives are concerned that if they try to liquidate an SBU which is constituted by a WPM located abroad, the local managers might rally their government to interfere with the liquidation decision or at least restrict the executives' freedom of manoeuvre. For this reason, WPMs can be most safely awarded for products likely to have a long life.

The second control problem occurs at the level of the SBU (WPM) manager when dealing with sales forces in other countries. Each national sales manager has the right not to launch products which he judges unsuitable for his market. If the new product originates from an SBU in the headquarters' country it brings with it the authority of an implicit headquarters' directive. However, products originating from a subsidiary are more likely to be refused by national sales managers, especially the sales manager in the headquarters' country.

Another improvement task is to reanalyse each row of cost-benefit criteria for a nation. Corporate projects can be rated on the criteria of each government objective (260 blue collar jobs, 25 engineer jobs, $0.6 million net per year, exports, etc.). For each government the planner must imagine a set of weights indicating the trade-offs to be made between objectives. The author uses the word 'imagine' advisedly, for it requires that complex societal pressures and coalitions within the government be summarised in a few coefficients. The coefficients constitute the key area of parametric exploration (fortunately easy to do in a weighted assignment problem).

No corporate analyst really knows at what threshold of cost-benefit demands a government will crack down on a corporation and so a computer model permits an exploration of the reassignment effects of such 'what if' modifications.

This section began with an analogy of an *n*-person game (which is incomputable). However, it is possible to compute the consequences to the other nations by parametrically altering a particular nation's demands (right-hand side of Figure 4.1). Because governments monitor other governments' successes with multinational organisations, it is likely that giving too much to one nation will increase the demands of others. This concern cannot be modelled explicitly as it is the substance for dialogue between the corporation's national managers and the planners from headquarters.

The model presented is a static analysis which demands that the corporate analyst envisions projects emerging in the corporation's future with an eye to government pressures and demands and their effect on foreign corporations. Most explicitly this model is not intended to provide 'the solution', but is merely a housekeeping tool to explore some subtle trade-offs as a corporation struggles to assign projects to nations.

Conclusions

This chapter implicitly criticises naïve thinking about the world product mandating. Appendix 4.1 explains that the term 'global product mandate' cannot be as exact as a government contract lawyer desires because it refers to an ongoing process of product improvement which lacks precise boundaries. The criticism so far is that being ethnocentric and preoccupied with their government, Canadians have ignored foreign competition. The brief review of seven other national governments shows their wants and needs. Some, such as Singapore's, are very explicit, while others', such as Berlin's, are quite complicated. Other governments want a piece of the corporation.

Years ago corporations responded to government pressures by building miniature replica plants. Nowadays most electronic equipment can be most cheaply built if one plant supplies the world. As competition gets tougher, corporations find less organisational slack with which to pander to governments' desires to build a plant or fragment their R&D. As governments' pressures are increasing, corporate degrees of freedom are decreasing. Responding to the demands of one government not only foregoes some profit but also reduces the corporation's freedom of action to respond to the demands of other governments. At the focus of such pressure, the corporate planner needs some tool by which to conceptualise this multidimensional bargaining. The tool presented in this chapter is a weighted assignment problem. This tool is easy to use in a 'what if' mode but is inappropriately precise. Even the term 'world product mandate' is beguilingly precise, for it masks difficult control problems, and suggests that the corporation is mandating a fixed product, ignoring the reality of an evolving stream of design improvements. Conceivably, fuzzy set theory or some of the psychometric techniques being developed in marketing research may provide other representations of this problem.

Appendix 4.1: Effective Corporate R&D

It is conventional to say that pure research leads to applied research, product development and missionary sales work. From this discovery-push viewpoint, it logically follows that basic research should be unencumbered. Believers in this convention are generally disappointed by the inadequacy of their salesmen.

Nowadays there is a revisionist demand pull theory based on empirical studies (Walsh, 1984) that shows causality flowing in the opposite direction. The revisionists separate salesmanship from marketing. Marketing means having the vision to understand what product characteristics customers might really desire. The marketers experiment to develop different product ideas for the customers to try. Eric von Hippel (1977) emphasises that some customer segments have already invented one's next product, a point emphasised by Peters and Waterman (1982):

> in the scientific instrument business . . . of eleven 'first of type' major inventions . . . all came from users; of sixty-six 'major improvements', 85 per cent came from users; of eighty-three 'minor improvements', about two-thirds came from users. (p. 194)

The task of product development is to design a manufacturable product and enhance its reliability. The task of research is to understand why the product works in terms of scientific principles, an incredibly difficult task for most products, but an understanding necessary to guide development and to filter out nonsensical ideas.

Product designs evolve. A mandate is not for a product, but it is the right to manage its process of evolution. Most products are made of subassemblies, and it is standard corporate practice to redesign one subassembly at a time, and incorporate it before improving another new subassembly. Selecting the next subassembly to improve involves a cost-benefit discussion, and an interface between marketing and research understanding. This period's authorised subassembly to be improved is selected from a large set of subassemblies, each with problems. In anticipation of subassembly improvements, products can be and are designed in a modular way with an eye to keeping interfaces simple. An example is the electrical black boxes that used to be wired together. As the wiring harnesses became more complicated to manufacture, and excruciatingly difficult to modify, the design evolved to a data bus into which boxes can be plugged and unplugged.

Product management of a WPM involves the realistic assessment of one's competitors in each nation. One aspect of this assessment is the analysis of competitors' products so as to improve one's own subassembly designs. This can be done through dismantling and displaying good subassemblies to one's own workers in order to help make better strategic decisions. Leaf (1978) reports that:

> The Ford Motor Company, for example, regularly takes its competitors' products to bits to find out exactly how they are made and what their cost structure is likely to be. It has even publicly reported the results.

The process follows a five-step sequence:

(1) Purchase the product. The high cost of product teardown, particularly for a carmaker, gives some indication of the value successful competitors place on the knowledge they gain.
(2) Tear the product down — literally. First, every movable component is unscrewed or unbolted; then rivets are undone; finally, individual spot welds are broken.
(3) Reverse-engineer the product. While the competitor's car is being dismantled, detailed drawings of parts are made and parts lists are assembled, together with analyses of the production processes that were evidently involved.
(4) Estimate buildup costs. The cost of parts is estimated in terms of make-or-buy, the variety of parts used in a single product and the extent of common assemblies across model ranges. Among the most important facts to be established in a product teardown, obviously, are the number and variety of components and the number of assembly operations. The costs of the processes are then built up from both

direct labour requirements and overheads (often vital to an understanding of competitor cost structures).

(5) Establish economies of scale. Once the individual cost elements are known, they can be put together with the volume of cars produced by the competitor, and with the total numbers of people he employs, to develop some fairly reliable guides to his economies of scale. Having done this, Ford can calculate model-run lengths and volumes needed to achieve, first, break-even and then profit.

From regularly tearing down the Leyland Mini over the years, Ford's technical and production people had reached two related conclusions: (1) Leyland was not making money on the Mini at its current price; and (2) Ford should therefore not enter that sector of the market as long as current price levels prevailed. Having established these two important points through detailed, factual analyses, Ford was able to make firm strategic decisions.

In summary, the iterative process of R&D gains coherence when interfaced directly with innovative customers. The modular design of a product permits parallel research on many subassemblies, though the resulting improvements are approved for release only when thoroughly tested. Managers of WPMs have to monitor competitors' products, and have the flexibility to incorporate their best ideas by engineering around their patents. Within a domestic corporation the organisational culture may be sufficient to keep researchers close to innovative customers and competitors. In a multinational organisation more systematisation is necessary to minimise the effects of distances and time zones.

The purpose of this Appendix has been to puncture simplistic views on research. Many governments are developing national research policies, but few appear to be congruent with global product mandating.

Notes

1. Support for this research was provided by the Social Science and Humanities Research Council. The research assistance of Julia Dobrzyniewicz has greatly improved this chapter, but the interpretations are solely the author's responsibility.
2. During a 1983–84 sabbatical, the author participated in the National Defence College of Canada and visited 14 countries in order to be present at detailed meetings on their political economy. All the preparation and hundred days of travelling will not be condensed in the terse vignettes of this chapter; however, the purpose is to model a corporate process.
3. More generally, the EEC appears to be mildly opposed to world product mandating though few members are as vehement as France.

References

Commission of the European Communities (1984a) *Draft Council Decision Adopting the 1984 Work Programme for the European Strategic Technologies: ESPRIT*, 13 February 1984, COM (84) 56 final, Brussels

Commission of the European Communities (1984b) *FAST 1984–1987 Objectives and Work Programme*, February 1984, Brussels

Commission of the European Communities (1984c) *Report on R&D Requirements in Telecommunications Technologies as Contribution to the Preparation of the R&D Programme for R&D in Advanced Communications-Technologies in Europe: RACE*, 25 March 1985, COM (85) 145 final, Brussels

Committee on International Investment and Multinational Enterprises (1984) 'National Treatment Publication', 23 May 1984, Paris

Institution of Electrical Engineers (1984) *Alvey Programme Annual Report, 1984*, London

Leaf, R.H. (1978) 'Learning from your Competitors', *The McKinsey Quarterly*, Spring issue, pp. 52–60

McFetridge, D.G. and Warda, J.P. (1983) *Canadian R&D Incentives: Their Adequacy and Impact*, Canadian Tax Paper no. 70, Canadian Tax Foundation, Toronto

Peters, T.J. and Waterman, R.H., Jr. (1982) *In Search of Excellence*, Harper & Row, New York

Rutenberg, D. (1981) 'Global Product Mandating' in K.C. Dhawan, H. Etemad and R.W. Wright (eds.), *International Business: A Canadian Perspective*, Addison-Wesley, Don Mills, Ontario, pp. 588–98

Rutenberg, D. (1982) *Multinational Management*, Little Brown, Boston

Sullivan, S. (1984) 'The Decline of Europe', *Newsweek*, 9 April 1984, pp. 44–9, 53–4, 56

von Hippel, E. (1977) 'Your Customer Has Already Invented Your Next Product', *Sloan Management Review*, vol. 18, no. 2, pp. 63–74

Walsh, V. (1984) 'Invention and Innovation in the Chemical Industry: Demand-pull or Discovery-push', *Research Policy*, vol. 13, no. 4, pp. 211–34

PART II

MANAGING THE SUBSIDIARY IN A CHANGING
ENVIRONMENT AND OPERATIONAL CONTEXT

5 STRATEGIC MANAGEMENT OF SUBSIDIARIES[1]

Joseph R. D'Cruz

This chapter undertakes an examination of the strategic planning and management practices of Canadian subsidiaries of US multinational enterprises (MNEs). Its objective is to present a framework for evaluating their potential response to various World Product Mandate (WPM) policies of the Canadian government. Since similar considerations apply to MNEs' subsidiaries in other developed countries, this framework will prove useful in other contexts. The argument in this chapter proceeds by establishing the role of strategic planning and management in MNEs' subsidiaries, then presenting a framework for understanding business practices of MNEs' subsidiaries and finally examining the WPM issue in the light of this framework.

The data for this study were obtained by a personal interview survey of Canadian subsidiaries of US MNEs (See Note 1). The sample consisted of 50 companies which were on both the *Fortune* 500 list of leading US corporations and the *Financial Post* list of the top 500 companies operating in Canada. In all, 47 companies provided data for this study.

Strategic Planning

The adoption of strategic management practices by MNEs has been well documented. Several recent *Harvard Business Review* articles have shown that MNEs tend to: operate formal strategic planning systems; use analytical techniques such as portfolio matrices; have large planning staffs, etc. Taken together, these studies lead to the conclusion that strategic planning has become a well established way of life in many MNEs. While there are some questions as to whether strategic decisions are really made as outcomes of strategic planning, there can be little doubt that senior managers in many MNEs are required to spend considerable time and effort in formulating, reviewing and working on strategic plans.

The majority of the studies of strategic planning in MNEs have examined issues from the parent's viewpoint. Even when discussing the adjustments made necessary by the demands of host governments, most studies implicitly assume that the corporate protagonists are located at the MNE's head office. The planning system is viewed as a means for exercising headquarters' control over subsidiary operations. This is generally true, particularly when a planning system is first introduced. Even when control is highly decentralised — when each national subsidiary is allowed to operate with a considerable deal of decision-making autonomy — the introduction of a formal strategic planning system will initially result in a tendency to centralise the decision process.

Planning in Mature Subsidiaries

When the planning system matures, centralised decision-making is not an inevitable outcome. National subsidiaries of MNEs are frequently large-scale, multi-business enterprises in themselves. When a substantial measure of decision-making autonomy rests with local managers, a well established system of strategic planning at the subsidiary level may develop. Understanding how such systems operate provides new and valuable insights into strategic management of MNEs.

This chapter reports on a study of strategic planning among Canadian subsidiaries of US multinationals. Just as the United States is the home country for some of the largest, most sophisticated MNEs, Canada is the host for some of the most mature national subsidiaries of these organisations. Geographic proximity, and similarity of economic and social conditions made Canada the first choice for a non-US location for a great many US companies that established operations outside their home base. Many Canadian operations of US companies date back before the turn of the century. Some of them have served as jumping-off points for further international expansion. Others have grown and diversified, sometimes even into product markets that go beyond the scope of the parent's operations in the US.

Today, Canadian subsidiaries of US multinationals are significant corporations in their own right. In many cases they dominate the industries in which they operate. More importantly for this study, they have mature, well established management systems, including planning systems. By studying how these systems cope with the special problems that Canadian subsidiaries face in strategic decision-making, one is able to anticipate response patterns that are likely to emerge in other countries when subsidiaries reach a similar level of maturity.

Four Phases of Planning

Canadian subsidiaries vary considerably in terms of the maturity and sophistication of their planning systems. It is useful to distinguish four phases of maturity, much in the same way as Gluck, Kaufman and Walleck (1980) have described the phases of evolution towards strategic management. Corresponding to these four phases of maturity of the planning systems, four types of subsidiaries exist. Table 5.1 shows the proportion of firms in the study in each category. What explains this diversity? Some insights into this issue can be gained by examining the profile of each type of subsidiary.

Table 5.1: Maturity of Planning Systems

Planning System	Type of Subsidiary			
	Type I	Type II	Type III	Type IV
Annual business plans	No	Yes	Yes	Yes
Strategic plans	No	No	Informal	Formal
Per cent in sample	9	32	27	32

Type I: Truncated Businesses

These subsidiaries do not have a formal system for developing business plans in Canada. They frequently do have formal systems for planning in one or more functional areas. For example, they may have systems for sales forecasting and planning, inventory and production management or personnel management, but there is no formal system bringing these plans together in order to develop an overall plan for business operations in Canada. In other words, there is no formal planning for profit or return on investment. Such overall business planning is usually done by the parent in the United States. The Canadian operations are 'truncated businesses' which usually do not perform the full range of functions that would be necessary for the subsidiary to operate as an independent.

Type II: Miniature Replicas

These subsidiaries have formal systems for annual planning, but have neither formal nor informal strategic planning systems. Their planning systems are heavily budget oriented, and consist largely of extending figures of previous years into the future, and modifying these figures to take account of changes in the market or directives from the parent. Such subsidiaries do perform the full range of functions that would be found in an independent business, though typically their capacity for innovation and development is minimal. Their Canadian activities are small-scale replicas of parts or all of the parent's operations and strategic changes in Canada tend to follow those made in the parent organisation.

Type III: Mature Non-strategic Subsidiaries

These subsidiaries have mature, sophisticated systems of annual business planning, and perform strategic planning on an informal or *ad hoc* basis. Their annual budgeting systems are usually well established. Annual operating plans, once approved, are treated as commitments by the managers involved. They are expected to deliver the results specified in the plans, and are evaluated and rewarded on this basis. In addition, these subsidiaries also do a considerable amount of informal strategic planning. Changes in strategy for one or more businesses do take place from time to time, apart from following strategic changes initiated in corresponding units of the parent company. The latter changes usually occur because the chief executive officer (CEO) of the Canadian operations has initiated courses of action based on his judgement and inclination. Formal strategic planning for such subsidiaries is often part of a parent company's process in which members of the Canadian subsidiary participate. Thus, Canadian managers may be deeply involved in formal strategic planning, but have very limited autonomy in strategic decision-making.

Type IV: Strategically Managed Subsidiaries

These subsidiaries have formal systems for strategic planning in Canada. A formal strategic plan is prepared by the Canadian subsidiary, and key strategic decisions are made in Canada, with the participation and interaction of the parent's strategic planning process. Needless to say, these organisations also have formal systems for annual business planning. Such subsidiaries are quasi-autonomous area-mandated corporations that are usually in lines of business similar to those operated by the parent. Further, they are usually multi-business corporations, with business units that compete in different product markets and industries. The strategic planning process at the Canadian corporate level includes a strategic portfolio management system. Many of these business units may themselves contain the full range of functions necessary to operate an independent business in that industry. The degree of interdependence of these business units with corresponding business units in the parent organisation can vary considerably.

Opportunity for World Product Mandating

WPMs cannot exist without a substantial degree of strategic autonomy in the subsidiary. Typically, such autonomy is not to be had as a gift from the parent; it must be earned, usually over a long period of time by management that is successful. It is only in Type IV companies that the author finds a substantial measure of strategic autonomy at the Canadian corporate level. These companies conduct corporate portfolio analysis for the Canadian businesses and they have varying degrees of authority regarding resource allocations to these businesses. Company *X* is a good example. It is a Canadian subsidiary that is 92 per cent owned by the US parent. Canadian operations have been in existence for more than half a century and its management has been granted considerable decision-making autonomy. The board of directors of the Canadian subsidiary plays an active role in the strategic decision-making process.

Canadian operations have been divided into business units along similar lines to those of the parent's organisation, although with some significant differences. Some businesses in Canada are too small to be operated as separate units and therefore have been combined with other units, unlike the situation in the US where they operate as quasi-autonomous businesses. Thus, Canadian operations are divided into ten operating businesses grouped into three divisions whereas US operations have over 50 business units in seven sector groupings. The Canadian subsidiary reports to the parent through an international division. While there is frequent communication between Canadian business units and their counterparts in the parent organisation, there are no formal lines of authority linking them.

Company *X* can therefore be said to have a well developed strategic management system in operation. The basis of this system rests on the autonomy exercised by Canadian management in making strategic decisions. This autonomy is not unconstrained. There are both formal and informal constraints within which the Canadian subsidiary operates. The most important of these relates to the mandates of the various operating divisions. Most divisions are mandated for operations within the Canadian market only. A few are mandated to service world markets for some product lines or North American markets for others.

In addition, senior Canadian management shares an understanding with their US colleagues about the nature of the corporation and the kinds of industries in which corporations will choose to compete. Company *X*, like its parent, sees itself as a diversified manufacturing corporation operating within a clearly defined set of industries. It does not believe in unrelated diversification. It strives for excellence in a limited number of areas. And, like its parent, it is concerned about maintaining world-scale cost competitiveness in manufacturing. To that end, it constantly devotes its efforts to developing cost advantages from economies of scale and from cumulative production experience.

The Subsidiary Mission Grid

Multinational enterprises are large complex organisations. Similarly, Type IV subsidiaries of multinationals are also large and complex. To cope with the management problems of complexity, their firms usually adopt an organisational device known as the strategic business unit (SBU), which can be thought of as an organisational subunit which possesses the resources and capabilities of operating as an independent business (Abell and Hammond, 1979). Each SBU can be thought of as competing within a somewhat narrowly defined product/market environment which is somewhat loosely referred to as an industry.

When considering policies that concern MNEs, the need to take into account the complexity of the companies involved can hardly be overstated. With a few notable exceptions, each corporation is engaged in a great variety of businesses — some mature, with stable competitive structures, others fast moving and constantly evolving; some global in scope with a few competitors who are present in almost every national market, others of a more local nature with important Canadian competitors who are not major factors in many international markets. Given such a diversity in the strategic characteristics of the environments in which a corporation's business units compete, it is to be expected that management and planning approaches will exhibit considerable diversity. It is not unusual for an MNE to follow different strategies and different strategic planning processes for different business units. This makes it difficult to develop simple generalisations about strategic planning processes in such corporations. Different processes apply to different business units. Indeed in some business units, strategic planning may be truncated because that business is part of a parent company's business unit which does its strategic planning on a global basis. In other business units in the same Canadian subsidiary, extensive strategic planning may occur under conditions of quasi-economy from the corresponding parent-level business unit.

An additional factor that determines the extent and nature of strategic planning is the organisational policies of the parent. On the one hand, the parent may prefer highly centralised decision-making processes, with limited autonomy for subsidiaries. In such organisations, strategic planning is performed mainly at the head office in the home country. Other corporations have adopted a decentralised management style, with a high level of decision-making autonomy granted to subsidiary management. A principal finding of this study is that the level of decision-making autonomy can vary considerably within a single corporation, as well as from corporation to corporation. Thus, it was found that in a number of instances within a single corporation, some business units were allowed to operate with a high level of autonomy, whereas other business units were required to follow decisions made on a centralised basis.

This leads to the conclusion that decision-making autonomy should be examined at the business unit level, rather than at the corporate level. This is quite consistent with the proposition that the business, rather than the corporation, is the appropriate unit of analysis for many issues in strategic planning as well as for public policy analysis (Abell, 1980).

This conclusion is most effectively illustrated by Figure 5.1 which is drawn from the planning system of a subsidiary which has been in operation in Canada since before the turn of this century. Many of its businesses were well established in the marketplace. While the Canadian subsidiary is majority owned by the US parent, a significant minority of shares are Canadian owned. The subsidiary has an active board of directors, and its senior management is well known in Canadian business circles.

Figure 5.1: Subsidiary Mission Grid

		Low	High
World		GLOBALLY RATIONALISED	WORLD PRODUCT MANDATE
North America		SATELLITE	BRANCH PLANT
Canadian only		IMPORTS	LOCAL SERVICE

EXTENT OF MARKET INVOLVEMENT

DECISION-MAKING AUTONOMY

The first step in the analysis process is to position each business unit on the grid. The horizontal axis depicts the degree of autonomy that the subsidiary's business unit has in strategic decision-making. This axis is divided into two zones — to the left are business units where decision-making authority rests mainly with the home office business unit. The subsidiary does not determine product and pricing policies, or make decisions about technology, production processes and marketing approaches. At the other end of the spectrum are business units where major decisions of this nature are made locally, with some coordination from the home office. The vertical axis is used to depict the scope of market involvement of the subsidiary, and is divided into three levels. At the lowest level are subsidiaries that are concerned only with the Canadian market. At the opposite end of the scale are business units in industries that have become global in scope, with only a few competitors, all of whom have rationalised production and marketing on a global basis.

When a multinational starts a new line of business in Canada, the simplest way to get going is to import products from a plant in its home country. The new business may be conducted either directly or through agents, but in any case is totally dependent on its parent for products and technology. It often chooses only a minimal involvement in the Canadian market, concentrating its attention on one or two provinces. Such businesses occupy the lower left-hand corner of the grid. Historically, many businesses in this category were set up to distribute new products which had not been previously available in Canada.

Satellite Business

If the new product gains market acceptance, competition often develops as sales expand. It becomes important to be able to offer competitive prices, and pressure begins to develop for a reduction of costs. One way to accomplish this without substantial capital investment is to import subassemblies and put together the final product in Canada. Often tariffs on components and subassemblies are lower than those on finished products, and some savings may be made in transportation costs. This is called a satellite business. Although it may be called a 'local manufacturing unit' for purposes of demonstrating to government officials and the public that the corporation is committed to host country economic objectives, a satellite operation is still heavily dependent on the parent. Its decision-making autonomy remains severely curtailed, with technology, prices and product features all following the patterns set at the home office.

Local Service Business

Alternatively, an imports business may face non-price competition, and may have to respond by providing services along with the product. It may find it necessary to open a network of local sales and service outlets, or it may become involved in training customer personnel and/or providing service support to wholesalers and retailers. The development of local service capabilities is often accompanied by an increase in local decision-making autonomy. While remaining dependent on the parent for the product and technology, a local service business unit can establish and manage its own market linkages. To the extent that its ability to compete in the Canadian marketplace depends on these local service linkages the business will be granted a certain measure of autonomy.

Branch Plant

When both price and non-price pressures combine, the corporation may choose to convert the business to a 'branch plant' mode. In the past, this decision was heavily influenced by tariff considerations. The Canadian government, anxious to promote the development of local manufacturing, had erected tariff barriers to protect manufacturing activity from price competition from imports. Initially, most branch plants used technology 'imported' from the parent and adapted to a smaller scale of operation suited to the size of the Canadian market. Over time, branch plants often took on additional product lines, with the result that each branch plant produced a wider range of products, each in small volume, than corresponding plants in the home country. Over time, the branch plant could become more independent of the parent. It could develop some of its own technology and it often sought to establish local supply sources for much of its required input, often from branch plants of other MNEs.

As long as the branch plant is adequately protected by tariff barriers, it can remain viable and is likely to be allowed to exercise considerable decision-making autonomy. Understanding the key competitive factors for success in such a business often requires detailed knowledge of local conditions in Canada. Once the subsidiary establishes a track record of profitable operations, its expertise in Canadian conditions tends to reinforce and extend the parent's willingness to allow Canadian managers to exercise decision-making autonomy. The branch plant business unit develops into a small-scale replica of the parent business. Its scope of operations is generally limited to the Canadian market with occasional opportunistic exports to third countries. These are 'at the pleasure of the parent' and will be allowed to continue only as long as they are not troublesome to the home plant or do not lead to the development of a satellite or branch plant operation in the importing country.

Recent developments have threatened the viability of branch plant operations. A principal factor in their decline has been the lowering of tariff barriers that has resulted from the various rounds of the GATT negotiations. This has eliminated much of the protection these businesses required to compensate for their uncompetitive cost structure.

Additionally, some industries have undergone technological changes that have made obsolete the existing modes of operation. Often competitors with new technologies are able to offer product alternatives and features at prices which cannot be matched by existing producers. Often the scale required for efficient operations using the new technology cannot be supported by the Canadian market.

World Product Mandate

Strategic choice is severely limited for Canadian branch plants faced with this kind of lower priced competition. The obvious answer, and one that has certainly caught the attention and imagination of Canadian public policymakers is to seek a WPM for the Canadian subsidiary. Supposedly, a business with a mandate to sell its products anywhere in the world can contemplate setting up a world-scale production facility and operate at a competitive unit cost level. Further, it can devote the appropriate amount of resources to research and development (R&D) to continue to maintain the leading edge in technology. Such businesses appear in the top right-hand corner of the grid.

A business unit with a WPM tends to operate with a high degree of independence. It has considerable control over the fundamental technological thrusts that will sustain development, it makes decisions on the timing and direction of product development and it is substantially involved in making investment decisions on production facilities, marketing and distribution. The business unit has the primary responsibility to serve as 'product champion' in corporate decision-making processes, particularly those involving resource allocation. With such independence comes a far greater degree of responsibility; the business unit is assigned a larger measure of financial responsibility for its operations. If profits falter, it has no parent level business unit to absorb business losses in the cause of growth. The subsidiary may find that the parent expects it to raise debt independently of the parent. Despite such difficulties, managing a WPM business unit can be one of the most challenging and rewarding jobs in a subsidiary. When it succeeds, not only is it an attractive business from a profits and growth viewpoint but it also comes to be viewed as evidence of good corporate citizenship in Canada.

Why are WPMs Scarce? In the first place, it is not easy to obtain a WPM. The subsidiary has to earn the right to the mandate, by proving to the parent that it can operate that particular business better than any other part of the corporation. In many cases, other parts of the organisation will lose decision-making autonomy when the Canadian subsidiary is granted a world mandate. This is not particularly difficult for new businesses or industries in which other parts of the multinational perceive themselves as not having a major stake. Thus, Canadian subsidiaries will find it rather easy to acquire world mandates for relatively obscure products or industries where the entire global market is small.

On the other hand, acquiring a world mandate for a major line of business in which the parent has a substantial stake is difficult and often impossible. If the business is in a maturing industry, the parent is likely to have substantial production facilities which have been designed to serve a US market that is at least ten times as large as the Canadian. It is unlikely even to consider closing down its US facilities in order to transfer production to Canada. In fact, according to the international product life cycle theory, if a multinational does transfer production outside the US for a mature product line, it is likely to consider locations with significantly lower labour costs. This would exclude Canada, where labour costs are perceived to be higher than those in the US. Finally, organisational realities will tend to make such a transfer difficult. Typically, general managers of major domestic business units are among the most senior executives in the corporation. They are often candidates for top corporate management positions, and would as such outrank the CEO of the Canadian subsidiary. It is therefore unrealistic to expect the parent to be willing to transfer control of these operations to Canadian managers of lower status.

For totally different reasons, it is equally difficult for Canadian subsidiaries to acquire WPMs for relatively new businesses in technologies at the leading edge. In the first instance, it may be difficult for the Canadian subsidiary to assemble the talent, laboratories and pilot facilities which are needed to develop the new technology. Indeed, it may be difficult to build a convincing case that the infrastructure needed for some emerging technologies exists in Canada, since that often develops out of a juxtaposition of military, industrial and academic institutions that is not common even in the US. Second, even if it can be demonstrated that the Canadian subsidiary is capable of putting together the human and other resources for the business, the parent may still prefer to locate development activities in the US. During the early stages of establishing a new technology, the need is especially urgent for swift and effective communication within the corporation. Senior management often finds it preferable to keep close personal contact with the nascent business, to lend support to its champion(s) during the period before they have acquired sufficient internal stature on the basis of the track record of the business, and to participate in the critical decisions about the specifications of the product likely to be most successful (Vernon, 1971). For these reasons, multinationals prefer to locate new high technology businesses close to their corporate headquarters, and indeed sometimes in the same physical complex.

Global Rationalisation

It is obvious that all of these conditions will be met in only a limited number of cases. Therefore, conversion to WPM status is not a solution which will be widely applied. Yet Canadian subsidiaries cannot continue operating 'branch plants' that have become unprofitable. One answer to this dilemma is the conversion to a 'globally rationalised' business. These are businesses that operate as integrated global entities, with the management team of the parent's business unit assuming worldwide responsibilities for strategic management and control. The Canadian subsidiary is structured to supply a limited portion of the product line for the entire world market, and imports the remainder of its requirements from plants in other parts of the world. Each production facility is world-scale and concentrates on becoming the low cost producer of those parts of the line for which it is responsible. A recent *Harvard Business Review* article by Theodore Levitt (1983) describes the economic imperatives behind the emergence of global industries.

Rationalisation is primarily a production concept. The attention of Canadian managers of a rationalised business is focused on doing the production job right and on lowering costs wherever possible. Development of the supporting product and process technology is usually centralised in the business unit of the parent, as are most of the managerial decision-making functions. There is limited room for decision-making autonomy in the subsidiary. The mission of the subsidiary's business unit is to carry out its assigned production functions as and when called upon to do so. Under such a system, it is counterproductive to attempt to vary the product to suit each local market. Product variety is often seen as detracting from cost control and scale economies.

Global rationalisation does bring with it some advantages. Since each production facility becomes a low cost producer for its part of the line, the corporation as a whole is able to compete effectively with other low cost producers. For some manufactured products, a worldwide low cost production position is essential for survival. This is particularly true of product lines where transportation costs are low relative to selling price and where market requirements have become relatively standardised. In such product lines, Canadian business units which do not participate in a globally rationalised production network may find they will have to shut down Canadian manufacturing altogether when a branch plant ceases to remain competitive. It may then be reduced to importing the product or may have to give up the business entirely. For this business unit, the only way to continue manufacturing in Canada would be to seek a role in a globally rationalised manufacturing structure.

Many of the managers interviewed in this study were deeply concerned about the future of their branch plant businesses. They recognised that such businesses are finding it increasingly difficult to survive. The WPM option is not practical for the majority of branch plants. Therefore, it is likely that most will be converted to importation businesses and a few will be integrated into globally rationalised structures. In both cases, decision-making autonomy will be reduced, which explains some of the reluctance of Canadian branch plant managers to embrace these options. Yet international developments over which they have no influence may force their hands.

Implications for Public Policy Regarding WPMs

There appears to be considerable enthusiasm for this concept among Canadian policymakers at both the federal and provincial levels. Multinationals are being urged to seek and develop world mandates in order to ensure that their manufacturing activity in Canada will become world class in its competitive capacity. Provincial governments have made formal statements of their support for such policies, and they continue to advocate them in informal contacts with multinationals. World mandates are mentioned frequently in federal policy statements concerning manufacturing and multinationals.

It is not clear that across-the-board advocacy of WPMs is in the Canadian national interest. First, it is neither feasible nor desirable to seek world mandates for industries that are global or North American in scope. Many high technology industries fall into this category. Unless companies in such industries are organised on a global basis with centralised planning and control of such key functions as R&D, production and marketing, they will not be able to match their competitors in innovative capacity, cost reduction and market acceptance. An across-the-board public policy posture in favour of subsidiaries with WPMs creates an unfavourable climate for companies that are proceeding towards global rationalisation. The Canadian activities of the latter companies may well make valuable contributions towards Canadian

national interests despite the fact that planning and control of these operations is a centralised process at the parent's home office. The mandate
does not have to rest with the Canadian subsidiary for it to be assigned
world-class functions in R&D or production. Indeed, such a business
unit may well be a net exporter even though it produces only a narrow
part of its product range in Canada and imports the rest. The central
public policy issue should be whether the production activity in Canada
is carried out on a scale and at a cost level that is equal to or better than
that of its major competitors.

Similarly, many business units have come to be integrated across the
Canada-US border. Production and development functions are
rationalised on a North American basis, with planning and control
centralised in an office located logically in the larger US market.
Admonishing Canadian subsidiaries of such businesses to seek WPMs
amounts to telling them to give up the scale and cost advantages of North
American rationalisation. The automobile industry is a clear example
where such a policy posture would be inappropriate. Canadian engine
and assembly plants of the Big Three automakers are able to achieve
scale economies as integrated parts of a North American system that they
would not be able to accomplish on their own. The future of the
automobile industry in North America depends critically on its ability
to achieve world-class quality and cost competitiveness. Under such
conditions, it does not appear wise to urge Canadian subsidiaries of US
automakers to seek WPMs.

WPMs may not be wise even in those industries where it is possible
to develop a Canadian production unit to serve the world market. It is
highly unlikely that a foreign multinational will assign such a mandate
to its Canadian subsidiary for a product line of substantial importance
to the corporation merely because this would please Canadian
governments. Indeed, the more important the line of business is to the
corporation, the more likely it is that the world mandates, if they are
assigned at all, will be assigned to a business unit in the home country.
Canadian WPMs will in all likelihood be assigned in those areas which
the parent has identified as being unimportant to the corporation. Thus,
the Canadian subsidiary may find itself with such mandates in industries
which are declining, in areas where the parent has limited competences
or in cases where parent level access to world markets is blocked by
political factors.

The conclusion from this discussion is that a public policy posture
that is neutral towards WPMs may be more appropriate than a policy
which strongly advocates them. When such mandates are appropriate

they should be allowed to evolve naturally. For example, a Canadian business unit devoted to exploiting natural resources which are not economically available to a business unit in the parent's home country will find itself with a clear case for acquiring such a mandate. Similarly, world mandates may devolve to the Canadian business unit that has developed a superior product or production process. World mandates are not granted as gifts from corporate parents to subsidiaries: they have to be earned by the subsidiaries on the basis of superior competence and resources. Across-the-board advocacy of WPMs by public policymakers exposes the country to important risks: other forms of global integration may be inadequately recognised; attempts may be made to seek such mandates in inappropriate circumstances; and, those mandates that are granted may be confined to trivial areas or those with limited prospects. What is needed is a rifle-shot approach with careful targeting rather than a shotgun approach that hits numerous unintended targets in its efforts to score on productive marks. Adroit nudges from Canadian policymakers in cases where a Canadian subsidiary has a natural advantage can be extremely helpful when inertia is holding a parent back. Sensitive urging by well informed policymakers in appropriate cases can be most helpful and will undoubtedly be welcomed by managers in Canadian subsidiaries. Inappropriate advocacy, on the other hand, will elicit resistance and may actually prove counterproductive.

Note

1. The research on which this chapter is based was funded by the Institute for Research on Public Policy. Further details may be obtained from the publication entitled *Strategic Planning in Canadian Subsidiaries of US Multinationals.*

References

Abell, D.F. (1980) *Defining the Business: The Starting Point of Strategic Planning*, Prentice-Hall, Englewood Cliffs, New Jersey

Abell, D.F. and Hammond, J.S. (1979) *Strategic Market Planning: Problems and Analytical Approaches*, Prentice-Hall, Englewood Cliffs, New Jersey

Gluck, F.W., Kaufman, S.P. and Walleck, A.S. (1980) 'Strategic Management for Competitive Advantage', *Harvard Business Review*, vol. 58. no. 2, pp. 154–61

Levitt, T. (1983) 'The Globalization of Markets', *Harvard Business Review*, vol. 61, no. 32, pp. 92–102

Vernon, R. (1971) *Sovereignty at Bay: The Multinational Spread of US Enterprises*, Basic Books, New York

6 THE STRATEGIC MANAGEMENT OF MULTINATIONALS AND WORLD PRODUCT MANDATING[1]

Alan M. Rugman and Sheila Douglas

Introduction

Public policy proposals in the area of world product mandating appear to be based on the premiss that large-scale multinational enterprises (MNEs) are monolithic entities. They are not; often they are coalitions of strategic business units, linked together by the centralised strategic planning of the corporation. Nearly all large corporations in Canada, including the majority of the parent firms of foreign owned subsidiaries, use strategic planning. Yet, government officials and most politicians do not appear to understand the concept of the business unit nor the complexity of parent-subsidiary relationships and the manner in which structure and strategy are integrated within the internal markets of MNEs. We review in this chapter the nature of corporate strategic planning, the role of strategic business units and the implications that these have for Canadian public policy toward multinational corporations in general and world product mandating in particular.

This chapter first outlines the stated objectives of Canadian policy regarding world product mandates and reviews the problems of such a policy. Next the world product mandate (WPM) is defined and then the parent-subsidiary relationship within the MNE is reviewed. The discussion then turns to how the organisational structure and strategic planning of the MNE and its subsidiaries affect the success of the WPM option for Canada. Finally, the relationship of WPMs with the degree of global competition currently facing MNEs is examined.

Canada's Proposed WPM Policy and its Problems

The proposal to confine research and development (R&D) subsidies to subsidiaries of MNEs with a WPM is part of a Canadian industrial strategy set out in a study by the Science Council of Canada (1980). The latter's primary concern has been Canada's deteriorating balance of trade in manufactured goods. The reason for this policy position has been attributed to Canada's reliance on imported manufactured goods which embody a high technology component. This policy position was also supported by the Hatch Report (1979). These studies suggest that Canada must both increase exports and decrease imports of technology in the form of manufactured goods, especially with its major trading partner, the United States, which accounts for over 70 per cent of its trade. Decreasing imports necessitates the development of viable technologies within Canada for use by Canadian industry. Increasing exports requires that the traditional branch plant structure of Canadian industry be altered so that US subsidiaries, originally set up in Canada to supply the Canadian market without facing Canada's high tariff barriers, become more outwardly oriented in their production and marketing strategies. The latter development must be given more emphasis as tariff reductions of the last round of GATT proceed, progressively removing the initial economic justification for the establishment of branch plants of MNEs in Canada (although nontariff barriers between the United States and Canada remain an important obstacle in exporting and explain much of the two-way foreign direct investment that still exists between the countries).

The underlying basis of the Science Council of Canada position, which is strongly nationalist and indeed mercantilist in its consistent advocacy of an independent Canadian technological capability, has been criticised or the grounds of conventional economic theory by Safarian (1979) and the Economic Council of Canada (1981).

The Science Council of Canada (1980) proposed that the federal government should encourage Canadian subsidiaries of MNEs to seek WPMs from their parents outside Canada. It is argued that such a policy would result in increased output and reduced unit costs for the subsidiary, as well as increased employment and improved management capabilities in Canada. The increased volume of components should justify sourcing from Canadian suppliers. Exports from Canada would increase, and possibly the truncated nature of Canadian industry would evolve into expanded innovative operations.

Rugman (1983) has shown that such a WPM strategy is likely to fail due to the centralised nature of control in the MNE, especially of the R&D function, but also of the strategic planning decisions typical of most large MNEs. Generally, ongoing R&D expenditures are the source of technological knowledge, embodied in new product lines, which constitute the firm specific advantage (FSA) of the MNE. The recovery of private expenditures on this public good requires the protection of the FSA from excessively rapid dissipation. In turn, this requires that the

MNE establish property rights over its knowledge advantage by the use of its internal markets for the exploitation and use of the new product lines. The granting of a WPM would require the parent MNE to surrender some degree of control over its R&D, especially over the strategic decisions about which new product lines are to be pursued. As it will be shown later, more autonomy in the marketing function would also be necessary. Both of these situations lead to an increase of uncertainty for the parent MNE, equivalent to an increase in transaction costs, which raises the costs of operating internal markets (Rugman, 1981). In short, a WPM strategy increases the internal organisational costs of the MNE by its complication of the parent-subsidiary relationship. Poynter and Rugman (1982) have shown that such costs need to be offset by government subsidies, or significantly higher expected returns, to make WPMs viable from the viewpoint of the MNE which must grant them.

Only if it is assumed that the R&D capabilities which Canada wishes to develop are not necessarily 'pure', but include 'downstream innovations' in design and engineering, can a sensible argument be made that the FSA of the MNE is not threatened. This may occur, for example, when aspects of the R&D function can be decentralised with overall strategic decision-making remaining centralised (a policy followed by IBM and some other large MNEs, but not by most of those operating in Canada). Then the risks facing the MNE are not as great. But it is difficult to generalise across MNEs. Internal costs may be overcome when the technology being transferred through a mandated product is at a mature phase of its product life cycle. Yet, for a transfer of 'downstream' R&D responsibility to satisfy Canadian policy objectives of increasing technological exports, newer product lines are clearly required. These are unlikely to be awarded by the MNE to the Canadian subsidiary unless there is also some way of changing the nature of the subsidiary's strategic orientation and/or capabilities. This is the essential, but often neglected, aspect of WPM policy. It is ironic that while these managerial problems of the proposed WPM policy have not drawn the universal acceptance of economists with a nationalist streak, they have been understood and incorporated into the work of political scientists such as Atkinson (1985).

The Definition of a WPM

A WPM should be defined as the full development, production and marketing of a new product line in a subsidiary of an MNE. Others writing on WPMs are frequently not so precise in their definitions. This leads to needless confusion. There are three aspects of the definition of a WPM which give rise to disputes in the literature.

First, there is a disagreement about the degree of R&D undertaken by the subsidiary within Canada which is necessary to constitute a 'pure' WPM. It has been argued that pure R&D capability is not essential for autonomy in technology (Bourgault and Crookell, 1979). More importantly, 'downstream innovation' appears to be the preferred objective of Canadian policy, since it embodies a high value added component (Hatch Report, 1979). Therefore, it can be concluded that some degree of design and engineering research done in Canada would suffice to qualify a subsidiary for a WPM incentive.

Second, there is confusion as to whether the product or product line for which the subsidiary gains responsibility must be 'new'. Case studies of successful WPMs in Canada (Rugman and Bennett, 1982; Science Council of Canada, 1980) indicate that a WPM granted to a Canadian subsidiary often comprised an existing product, using existing technology, which was transferred to Canada from within the MNE. For example, Black and Decker Canada received permission to produce the orbital sander in high volume in 1969, but the manufacturing of this product elsewhere in the world did not cease until 1973. Since then, B&D Canada has introduced new product lines such as the Workmate, the Workwheel and the Workhorse worldwide. Similarly, a WPM for producing aircraft temperature control systems was transferred to Garrett Manufacturing Ltd of Toronto from its California division in 1961. GML Canada now has five new lines of business, developed through its in-house R&D. Westinghouse Canada received a WPM for producing small industrial gas turbines at the time when its parent was concentrating on larger turbines for different applications. Westinghouse Canada now has a strategy aimed at developing new products worldwide in which its parent has no involvement. Litton Systems Ltd of Toronto received its WPM for commercial inertial navigation systems when its parent was involved in military work, but the subsidiary currently undertakes other custom electronic systems work. It appears that, in all cases, the subsidiary gained responsibility for a product which was already being produced within the organisation, although in the latter two cases (Westinghouse and Litton Systems), the product manufactured by the subsidiary had different applications from the one produced by the parent. Perhaps this supports the argument of Rutenberg (1981) that the second, or mature, phase of a product's life cycle is most amenable to a WPM strategy being adopted by a parent MNE. The danger is that a WPM may be granted for a product with no growth potential, so that in effect the Canadian government would be subsidising 'sunset' industries.

Third, the definition of a WPM often ignores the critical role of the marketing function of the subsidiary. Clearly, a 'world' product mandate suggests that the subsidiary should have global markets. Yet, as pointed out by Wolf (1983), the mandate is often geographically limited. Such an arrangement would constitute only a 'partial' product mandate (Poynter and Rugman, 1982; Proulx, 1982). There is some concern that any limitation of the subsidiary's mandate will result in mere 'product rationalisation' (Crookell and Caliendo, 1980). In that case, increased economies of scale would improve efficiency, but would not necessarily have a beneficial impact upon Canadian managerial or innovative capabilities. For a WPM to be successful, it is necessary for the subsidiary to acquire control of the marketing function, especially for the products subsequently developed by the subsidiary through its in-house R&D. In all of the cases reviewed above, the scope of the marketing mandate was worldwide. In order to satisfy Canadian policy requirements of increasing exports of technologically based products through WPMs, the marketing scope of the subsidiary must then go beyond the domestic market.

In summary, only when a WPM is defined as the responsibility of an MNE's subsidiary for developing, producing and marketing a product or product line worldwide does the full complexity of the WPM become apparent. Some R&D capability must be transferred, although it need not be of a 'pure' type. Similarly, the product does not have to be 'new', but responsibility for seeking future associated products and market niches must be transferred. Finally, the marketing functions of the subsidiary must become worldwide in scope in order that the WPM strategy be economically viable.

Strategic Planning and the MNE

The MNE's form of strategy is long-term planning, basically qualitative and pragmatic, which integrates and directs the functional areas into an overall company goal. There is an emphasis on the assessment of external, environmental conditions, as well as internal factors. This is the critical characteristic which distinguishes strategic planning from operational planning or budgeting. There are two levels of strategy in a diversified company: corporate and business level strategies.

Corporate strategy uses the strategic business unit (as defined below) as its basic unit of analysis. Such strategy is concerned with the optimal integration of the business units. The tools of analysis used in corporate strategic planning include environmental and political scanning as well as portfolio analysis. Portfolio planning requires a corporation to define its business units and classify them in a portfolio grid according to their competitive position and the attractiveness of a particular product market. Then, each unit is assigned a strategic mission, and resources are allocated accordingly. The resources allocated include the FSAs of the MNE. Such FSAs arise in areas of proprietary knowledge, technology or marketing skills. Business unit performance is evaluated, not as an independent profit centre, but in terms of correspondence with overall corporate strategy (Rugman, 1985). The corporate strategy eventually chosen will depend not only upon environmental factors, but also upon corporate objectives that have been established and the personal values of top management. The options will require differing strategic responses by the business unit.

A strategic business unit (SBU) consists of a set of products that share manufacturing, marketing and technical bases and common customers and competitors (Davidson, 1982). SBUs do not necessarily correspond with operating units, but usually consist of aggregations of existing operating units or segments of single units (Haspeslagh, 1982). Business strategy encompasses the tasks of positioning a particular business unit within its competitive environment, and integrating the various sub-strategies of the business. The SBU will be responsible for setting out sub-strategies which exploit most efficiently the FSA allocated to it at the corporate level. An SBU can itself be considered to be a portfolio, not of businesses, but of product/market segments. In positioning the business, consideration must be given to the stage of the industry in its production life cycle, the business's specific strengths (e.g. FSAs) and weaknesses, and the outside environment. Business level strategy requires the SBU to identify its product/market niche and its FSA within that niche.

The issue of world product mandating will have implications on the two strategic levels. At the corporate level, it appears that a subsidiary must be viewed as an SBU with growth potential. The case studies of successful WPMs mentioned previously appear to be examples of corporations choosing an extended growth strategy for their subsidiaries. The decision to award a WPM involves a change in the present thrust of corporate strategy and a new commitment when allocating the MNE's internal resources. In particular, the MNE must be willing to give up some measure of control over its FSA. Yet, as discussed earlier, most MNEs have a centralised R&D function aimed at the protection of technological FSAs.

At the business level, the subsidiary must constitute an SBU with responsibility for integrating its various sub-strategies. A WPM, in any form, will require major changes in at least one of three sub-strategies (in the areas of technology, manufacturing and marketing), which in turn will require changes in the complementary sub-strategies. To achieve the successful evolution toward the acquisition of a WPM, the managers of the subsidiary must be capable of implementing and monitoring the required change. Yet, an SBU with a dependent technology would be so constrained in its choice of manufacturing and marketing strategies that a WPM could not be implemented. Since a particular technology is often an important FSA of the MNE, it is logical to expect that an SBU's technology strategy will be a dependent type (dependent, that is, on the MNE's corporate headquarters' strategy). Similarly, an SBU with an undifferentiated marketing strategy is limited to a particular combination of manufacturing and technology strategies. Since many of Canada's subsidiaries were originally installed to serve the entire Canadian market as miniature replicas of their US parents, one would expect an undifferentiated approach to marketing. To some extent, the marketing pattern of subsidiaries has been modified over time, especially as the relative influence of Canadian managers working in the subsidiaries has increased due to better management training programs in Canada. In general, however, the marketing function of subsidiaries is focused primarily upon the host nation market of Canada. To the extent that the Canadian market may have different characteristics from the home market of the MNE some decentralisation of the marketing function is encouraged. However, few MNEs in Canada are truly polycentric in their outlook, and most of them engage in centralised strategic management even when there is limited decentralisation of marketing decisions.

It is apparent that an SBU requires some strategic control over its portfolio of product/market segments in order to undertake a WPM successfully. Yet, it is clear that when a subsidiary does not consist of at least one complete SBU then it has no strategic planning capability whatsoever. In such cases a WPM is inappropriate. The introduction of a WPM requires changes in technology, marketing and manufacturing sub-strategies. These internal managerial changes necessitate a long-term strategic capability on the part of business managers, a capability which most branch plant subsidiaries do not have. Some recent empirical work confirms that Canadian subsidiaries do not possess the managerial autonomy required to launch successful WPMs.

Evidence on the Strategic Planning of Canadian Subsidiaries of US Multinationals

D'Cruz (1983a, b) has identified several phases of maturity within the strategic planning processes of MNEs, ranging from no formal business planning to formal strategic and annual planning. He interviewed the subsidiary managers of the 47 largest US multinationals in Canada in order to determine into which phase each of them fell. These firms account for the major slice of manufacturing foreign direct investment in Canada, of which 80 per cent comes from the United States. His research shows that only one-third of the Canadian subsidiaries surveyed carry out any type of formal strategic planning. This would appear to indicate that the majority of subsidiaries located in Canada lack the managerial capacity to plan strategically in any sense. Generally, subsidiaries which can be categorised as having no strategic planning played a limited role in resource allocation decisions. Portfolio analysis was seldom if ever used. It appears that managers of approximately half of all informal strategic planning subsidiaries identified by D'Cruz participated in portfolio analysis, but actual resource allocation decisions were still made by the parent. Only a few subsidiaries made extensive use of portfolio analysis and were responsible for allocating resources among their business units. In total, 60 per cent of the firms interviewed by D'Cruz did not use portfolio analysis at all. Similarly, 26 per cent performed no analysis of the economic environment, and 51 per cent performed no analysis of the political environment. Only 10 per cent of the subsidiaries had a Canadian board of directors playing an active role in the strategic process. Participation by the board of directors in the strategic planning of the subsidiary was significant only for a few companies.

The results indicate that, at present, relatively few US subsidiaries in Canada have strategic planning processes in place which are compatible with world product mandating. Although D'Cruz (1983a) states that over half of the firms interviewed used the SBU as their basic unit of planning, the key process of portfolio analysis is not widely used. His work raises questions as to whether the typical Canadian subsidiary is viewed by the MNE as an SBU with important strategic planning responsibilities. Even if the subsidiary is considered by its parent to consist of one or more SBUs, it is probable that the present technology, manufacturing and/or marketing strategies within the SBU put severe limitations on the subsidiary's choice and autonomy. One obvious conclusion to be drawn is that world product mandating is not a strategy which fits in well with

corporate and business strategic processes which are now practiced by
MNEs in Canada. To be successful, a WPM policy will require not only
a change in corporate attitudes, but also in business capabilities. It is
also important to note that any change in technological strategy for the
business unit requires corresponding changes in the manufacturing and
marketing strategies on the part of the entire network of the MNE, not
just the Canadian subsidiary.

WPMs and Global Competition

Another reason why WPMs may fail to be granted by MNEs is that in
today's globally competitive marketplace, many MNEs need to achieve
either economies of scale or economies of scope on a worldwide basis.
Porter (1980) and Levitt (1983) have argued that the globalisation of
markets leads to competition on price and that scale economies are
necessary for a US based MNE to be competitive with Japanese and
European rivals. Rugman, Lecraw and Booth (1985) came up with a
slightly different argument, to the effect that MNEs need to be concerned
with not only scale economies, but also scope economies, the latter
including the ability to adapt product lines to meet the special
requirements of consumers in different segments of the national markets.

Both of these models of global competition have an important
implication for Canadian public policy toward MNEs, and the WPM
policy in particular. The reason for this is that most MNEs today need
to plan and organise to meet global rivalry. They do this by the use of
highly centralised strategic planning. Environmental variables are scanned
to identify changes and the effects that such changes will have on internal production and marketing policies. Modern management techniques
are used to run internal markets effectively. In such MNEs decentralising key decision-making, for example, about the launch of a new product
line, is far too risky. Giving such autonomy to subsidiaries serves to
compromise the ability of top management to respond quickly and efficiently to changes in environmental and internal factors, which have
repercussions on the entire network of the MNE, not just on one
subsidiary.

Probably the key constraint of the use of WPMs from the MNE's
viewpoint is the risk of losing control of the marketing function. A
subsidiary with a WPM needs to develop an autonomous marketing
capacity. This can threaten the overall structural design of the MNE,

in which marketing decisions are related to the use of all the product lines of the MNE, not just a new product line from a small subsidiary. Only if the MNE has a really satisfactory matrix organisation (which is rarely observed) may it have the capacity to decentralise R&D, production and marketing of a new product line to a subsidiary. Yet, for most MNEs there will be a danger of the loss of world market share to keen global rivals if an autonomous subsidiary develops a WPM. There are risks to the MNE's innovative and cost saving capacities and worldwide market acceptance. The WPM serves to reduce the ability of most MNEs to engage in global production and marketing.

Given these constraints of strategic planning and global competition, what types of WPMs will work in Canada? The WPMs will be restricted to mainly vertically integrated MNEs which operate in Canada to take advantage of its natural resources. WPMs based on the processing and marketing of Canadian resources in the areas of minerals, forestry, agriculture, food processing and other related sectors will have the best chance of succeeding. In contrast, WPMs based on horizontally integrated MNEs, where an attempt is made to generate more technology in branch plants, are not likely to succeed. Instead, scarce public funds for R&D should be directed (if any discrimination is really necessary) toward improving Canada's technological competence in its resource based sectors. It is in these sectors that there exists a group of Canadian owned MNEs which is competitive on a global scale and in which foreign ownership is not such a problem. Rugman and McIlveen (1984, 1985) have identified and analysed the 20 largest Canadian owned MNEs. They find that these mature and resource based MNEs have strong strategic planning skills and successful FSAs at the marketing end of the business, rather than at the R&D based production end.

Conclusions

Some Canadian policymakers would like to encourage increased activity, especially R&D, in the subsidiaries of Canadian MNEs. Such a sectoral change would help to increase the value added component of goods manufactured in Canada, and lead to increased exports of technologically intensive goods. Yet, the majority of MNEs will not readily grant WPMs to their subsidiaries in Canada since a WPM serves to increase the costs of internal management of the parent-subsidiary relationship.

The introduction of a WPM policy will have dramatic effects upon the existing corporate strategy of the MNE. First, the R&D function, in most MNEs, is centralised in order that their technologically associated FSAs be adequately protected and efficiently exploited. Second, in most MNEs operating in Canada, formal strategic planning is done at the corporate (parent) level, not at the subsidiary level. The result is that the Canadian government will find that parent MNEs are unwilling to undertake the risk of losing control over R&D and business strategies at the subsidiary level. A WPM strategy simply will not be attractive to the parent MNE, especially in a world of global competition.

The fact that a number of WPMs have been successfully implemented in Canada indicates that some types of MNEs are amenable to such a policy. However, in three of the four cases discussed here, the Canadian government had to play an important role in subsidiary-government negotiations with the parent company by articulating its policy objectives and providing funding for the program. Therefore, it seems that the government must be actively involved in each WPM. Is this degree of government intervention in the private sector desirable?

It has been argued in this chapter that parent-subsidiary relationships are complex and that proposed WPM policy has ignored these complexities. Clearly, future government policy concerning WPMs should take the complexity of the management of MNEs into account. It is likely that a case by case analysis is required, in order to identify the business or product lines which are most compatible with a WPM strategy. The costs of such involvement in the economy are probably high enough to make WPM policy unworkable.

Note

1. The material in this chapter will also be published by *Canadian Public Policy — Analyse de Politiques*. Reprinted by permission.

References

Atkinson, M.M. (1985) 'If You Can't Beat Them: World Product Mandating and Canadian Industrial Policy' in D. Cameron and F. Houle (eds.), *Canada and the New International Division of Labour*, University of Ottawa Press, Ottawa, pp. 125–44
Bourgault, P. and Crookell, H. (1979) 'Commercial Innovations in Secondary Industry', *Business Quarterly*, vol. 44, no. 3, pp. 56–64
Crookell, H. and Caliendo, J. (1980) 'International Competitiveness and the Structure of Secondary Industry in Canada', *Business Quarterly*, vol. 45, no. 3, pp. 58–64
Davidson, W.E. (1982) *Global Strategic Management*, John Wiley and Sons, Toronto
D'Cruz, J.R. (1983a) *Strategic Planning in Canadian Subsidiaries of US Multinationals: Current Practice and Public Policy Implications*, Working Paper no. 5, Faculty of

Management Studies, University of Toronto, Toronto

D'Cruz, J.R. (1983b) *Strategic Planning in Multinational Subsidiaries*, Working Paper no. 6, Faculty of Management Studies, University of Toronto, Toronto

Economic Council of Canada (1981) *The Bottom Line: Technology, Trade and Income Growth*, Supply and Services Canada, Ottawa

Haspeslagh, P. (1982) 'Portfolio Planning: Use and Limits', *Harvard Business Review*, vol. 60, no. 1, pp. 58–73

Hatch Report (1979) *Strengthening Canada Abroad*, Industry, Trade and Commerce Canada, Export Promotion Review Committee, Ottawa

Levitt, T. (1983) 'The Globalization of Markets', *Harvard Business Review*, vol. 61, no. 3, pp. 92–102

Porter, M.G. (1980) *Competitive Analysis*, Free Press, New York

Poynter, T.A. and Rugman, A.M. (1982) 'World Product Mandates: How Will Multinationals Respond?', *Business Quarterly*, vol. 47, no. 3, pp. 54–61

Proulx, P.-P. (1982) 'Integration and Mandates', *Policy Options*, vol. 3, no. 2, pp. 28–32

Rugman, A.M. (1981) *Inside the Multinationals: The Economics of Internal Markets*, Columbia University Press, New York

Rugman, A.M. (1983) 'Multinational Enterprises and World Product Mandates' in A.M. Rugman (ed.), *Multinationals and Technology Transfer: The Canadian Experience*, Praeger, New York, pp. 73–80

Rugman, A.M. (1985) 'Multinationals and Global Competitive Strategy', *International Studies on Management and Organization*, vol. 15, no. 2

Rugman, A.M. and Bennett, J. (1982) 'Technology Transfer and World Product Mandating in Canada', *The Columbia Journal of World Business*, vol. 17, no. 4, pp. 58–62

Rugman, A.M., Lecraw, D. and Booth, L. (1985) *International Business: Firm and Environment*, McGraw-Hill, New York

Rugman, A.M. and McIlveen, J. (1984) 'The Strategic Management of Canada's Multinationals: Who Needs High Tech?', *Business Quarterly*, vol. 49, no. 3, pp. 64–70

Rugman, A.M. and McIlveen, J. (1985) *Megafirms: Strategies for Canada's Multinationals*, Methuen, Toronto

Rutenberg, D. (1981) 'Global Product Mandating', in K.C. Dhawan, H. Etemad and R.W. Wright (eds.), *International Business: A Canadian Perspective*, Addison-Wesley, Don Mills, Ontario, pp. 588–98

Safarian, A.E. (1979) 'Foreign Ownership and Industrial Behaviour', *Canadian Public Policy — Analyse de Politiques*, vol. 5, no. 3, pp. 318–35

Science Council of Canada (1980) *Multinationals and Industrial Strategy: The Role of World Product Mandates*, Science Council of Canada, Supply and Services Canada, Ottawa

Wolf, B.M. (1983) 'World Product Mandates and Freer Canada-United States Trade' in A.M. Rugman (ed.), *Multinationals and Technology Transfer: The Canadian Experience*, Praeger, New York, pp. 91–107

7 SPECIALISATION AND INTERNATIONAL COMPETITIVENESS[1]

Harold Crookell

That Canada, in just five short years, should have moved all the way from the insularity of its National Energy Program to the aggressive pursuit of sectoral free trade with the United States manifests a profound shift in public mood. Surveys report a sharp decline of confidence on the part of Canadian business in the ability of the federal government to intervene and regulate intelligently in the private sector.[2] It is as though the public has given government its chance at the helm, and government has failed the test. The preponderant view now is that the market can do the job better, that government should impede the efficiency of the market less and that nationalistic protectionism has to go. This has been a difficult message for a government steeped in the habits of paternalistic intervention to pick up. But change is in the electoral winds and the message is likely to get through regardless of who prevails in the political arena.

Outside Forces at Work

It isn't just the United States' outspoken ambassador, or the United States' surprisingly accommodating position on our sectoral free trade initiative that brings outside influence on Canada's policies. There are real outside forces at work too; real in the sense that they are independent of political rhetoric. They include the reduction of Canadian import tariffs by up to 40 per cent under the Tokyo Round of the GATT; the growing homogenisation of global tastes leading to more world products; and the movement of technology leadership away from the United States. Each of these forces is fraught with notable exceptions which add spice and characteristic untidiness to the world. But still the trends are visible and corporate strategies in multinationals have begun to reflect them (Levitt, 1983) in ways strangely familiar to Canadian economists. A number of multinational subsidiaries in Canada are starting to do what Canadian economists have long recommended (Eastman and Stykolt, 1967). The outcome, however, may contain some surprises. What the firms are starting to do is specialise their Canadian production so that their costs are internationally competitive and export heavily into world markets. Some products that used to be made in Canada are then imported, largely from the parent company. Economists have long recommended this kind of structural arrangement because the miniature replica alternative of making many products in small volume, for the Canadian market only, is inherently inefficient (Economic Council of Canada, 1975) and permanently dependent on tariff protection for its efficacy. It results in unfocused research and development (R&D) and poor export performance because of high production costs.

But the multinationals are not moving toward specialisation because economic theory has finally penetrated. They are moving because they have seen the outside forces at work. Subsidiaries in Canada feel vulnerable to attack under low tariffs from competitors in the Far East and Europe, and their parents cannot as often bail them out with superior technology. The evolution of world products, accelerated by satellite television and enhanced global communication systems, has lent greater power to global rather than national strategies. Specialisation has emerged as the answer to these changing market forces. No more branch plants or tariff factories. World-scale, internationally competitive, efficiency-seeking production facilities are the way of the future.

Underlying the argument for specialisation are two assumptions that may not work out. The first is that recession induced protectionism is a temporary aberration in a world of otherwise diminishing trade barriers. One hopes this will be so but the recession is proving stubborn and recovery very uneven between nations. A great deal of political will is still required to prevent a debilitating round of nationalistic protectionism. The second assumption is that some solution will be found to the Third World debt problem that will not throttle trade and economic growth in nations with such enormous potential. Many Third World countries are resorting to countertrade and other forms of trade distortion for the simple reason they have no assurance of foreign exchange availability. New institutions (Daly, 1983) are going to be needed to solve this problem, because the austerity imposed on some nations by representatives of their creditors often lacks political sensitivity. Some firms are taking the view that strategies of specialisation apply to the developed world only, while for the Third World nationalistic strategies still prevail. Other firms are taking the view that specialisation is eminently suitable to the Third World's present dilemma, because subsidiaries which export from host countries are more likely to help resolve the foreign exchange problem, and are less likely for a host of reasons to be expropriated. However, in some Third World countries, foreign exchange is so scarce

— or mismanaged — that even export oriented foreign exchange earners cannot get import licences to keep their operations going.[3]

The Sectoral Free Trade Initiative

If it were not for these two troublesome assumptions, the pace of specialisation might be a lot faster than it is, but Canada's sectoral free trade initiative with the US might not have gotten underway so fast. It was the fear of US protectionist measures that gave the initiative its urgency. Access to the US market is absolutely imperative in any scenario of specialisation in Canada. The free trade initiative, even though bilateral and sectoral, could well be the basis for exempting Canada from defensive US trade measures aimed at other countries. Since foreign subsidiaries in Canada have been among the first to respond positively to the sectoral free trade initiative, it seems reasonable to assume that they have specialisation strategies on their mind. It matters a great deal to Canada, and to the managers of those foreign subsidiaries in Canada, just what form of specialisation arises from the ashes of the miniature replica branch plants. There are choices. And the choices might be influenced to a point.

Types of Specialisation

The balance of this chapter draws heavily from a research study recently completed for the Federal Department of Finance by Paul Bishop and this chapter's author.[4] Its focus was on forms of specialisation, their implications and effects. The research differentiated between rationalisation-integration as one form of specialisation and world product mandates (WPMs) as another. Both approaches to specialisation resulted in improved productivity and export performance, and both required extensive worker retraining. The differences between them were more subtle and not so readily apparent to industry outsiders. It may be that one has to be biased to see the differences as important. Certainly, the economist's expectations from specialisation could be fulfilled by either approach. From the standpoint of subsidiary executives, however, the differences were clear and vital. WPMs led to more R&D, greater subsidiary autonomy and more export marketing responsibility for the more dynamic subsidiaries. To understand how these effects occur requires a closer look at the two forms of specialisation.

Rationalisation-integration

Rationalisation-integration occurs when a subsidiary produces a component or product under assignment from the parent for the multinational firm as a whole. Product design and specification are handled by the parent division which is close to the relevant market. Since the product assigned is familiar to the parent no export marketing effort is needed by the subsidiary. Exports arise automatically as soon as production in the subsidiary gets underway.

Why would the parent agree to make such an assignment to its subsidiary? Well, partly because the subsidiary is giving up production of some other products in order to specialise and the parent supports this move and benefits from the economic activity flowing from it. But also because subsidiaries are asking for specialisation. Under lower tariffs they simply cannot compete in the full range of products they have become accustomed to producing under protection. The parent is, however, reluctant to assign a growth product to its subsidiary unless the subsidiary has earned a right to it through innovation. More often, the product assigned is a dying product or one which has never reached the volume projected for it. Canadians are good at small volume production. Sometimes, like Canadian General Electric's blade and vane plant in Bromont (Quebec), it is a component for a high technology product (e.g. aero-engines) but is produced in Canada for other strategic reasons (e.g. a defence sharing offset).

A subsidiary that operates entirely as a rationalised operation ends up with less autonomy than the old branch plant. What it produces is largely for export to the parent. What it markets is largely imported. Both production and marketing report along parallel lines to the parent. There is little point in trying to integrate them strategically in the subsidiary. Some R&D is still done in the subsidiary but the money is spent largely on process technology for cost reduction rather than product innovation or technology absorption from the parent, and the amount is not impressive.

The move from multiproduct output for the Canadian market to focused production for the multinational firm necessarily involves closer integration with the parent, major capital expenditures on special purpose equipment and some retraining of the work force. But it is a sure thing strategy without major market risks for the subsidiary, as long as the parent can be depended on to keep the flow of product assignments coming as existing ones weather the storms of the product life cycle. Depending on the parent has been a familiar and profitable strategy for many subsidiaries in the past. Under rationalisation-integration the dependence deepens with serious risk of debilitating effect on subsidiary management if it is not handled well (Bishop and Crookell, 1983).

World Product Mandates

For decades Canadians have wanted their foreign owned sector to export and do more R&D. Rationalisation will generate the exports, but to get both exports and R&D, especially product innovation, requires a WPM. In this scenario, the subsidiary in Canada becomes more like a division of the multinational firm, a fully-fledged partner so to speak. It obtains an area of specialisation either by virtue of its own research and innovation or by agreement with its parent. With that specialisation, it obtains the responsibility for product renewal and export marketing. The parent cannot provide a lot of direct help because as a rule the entire corporate expertise in the product resides in the subsidiary. So the subsidiary has a lot of autonomy, a substantial challenge and a lot more influence over its destiny. No wonder the concept is popular in Canada. It has all the right ingredients. It sounds like a kind of cost free Canadianisation of foreign owned subsidiaries (Poynter and White, 1983).

There are flaws, however. Admittedly one has to look hard. But they are there. For one thing, converting from a branch plant to a mandated subsidiary means a substantial change of corporate culture in the subsidiary. Subsidiary management has to move from copier to innovator, from the safety of protection to the risks of competition, from importer to exporter. And the subsidiary president has to enter the parent culture as an equal to major divisional line managers. The change is traumatic. Many will not be able to make it. Some heads will have to roll.

Furthermore, exports from WPMs will arise more slowly and will cost more than exports under rationalisation. Under rationalisation, the parent has assigned a known product to be produced in Canada instead of the US. The parent already knows how to market the product. All rationalisation does is change the locus of production. Multinational marketing activities barely skip a beat. When WPMs are involved, however, the corporate multinational marketing group may not know the product or how to sell it. If the product is a subsidiary innovation, the subsidiary will have to segment and define its market, select appropriate channels of distribution, develop supportive advertising and generally motivate and reassure the multinational sales force on product quality, after-sales service and selling techniques. Parent company divisions are used to this process. To them, the marketing requirements of innovation are familiar. To the subsidiary in Canada they are not. There is a lot of learning and a lot of cost involved.

From a management perspective, the problems with WPMs are really challenges to the subsidiary. But they are very major challenges, not to be underestimated. WPMs would force subsidiaries to face risk head on — both technical and market risks. The resulting transformation would make them more like Canadian owned firms, and would reduce the tendency to treat them differently in public policy. Table 7.1 presents an abbreviated comparison of the implications of the two forms of specialisation.

Table 7.1: Forms of Specialisation

	World Product Mandate	Rationalisation-Integration
Initiative Arises in	Subsidiary	Subsidiary
Selection of product(s) for specialisation results from	R&D in the subsidiary	Negotiation between subsidiary and parent (demonstrable cost savings)
Impact of Specialisation on:		
(a) Subsidiary Autonomy	Increased (innovation is power)	Reduced (parallel lines of reporting)
(b) Subsidiary R&D	Increased (skewed toward innovation)	No change (skewed toward process)
(c) Subsidiary Employment	Increased through product innovation (usually skilled labour intensive)	Reduced through greater productivity (unless balance of trade improves)
(d) Subsidiary Exports	Increased but slowly as new product gains acceptance	Increased quickly but longer term not so attractive
(e) Subsidiary Export Costs	High cost of informing and motivating parent marketing system	Modest — product already familiar to parent
Transition costs required to achieve specialisation	High in R&D, export marketing and management development/worker retraining	High in capital costs for transformation of factory worker retraining

Making the Choice

Multinationals face a choice when it comes to specialisation in their subsidiaries. Rationalisation-integration is by far the easier route to choose. Like most easier routes in life, it gets you a pale imitation of what you really wanted but were not willing to pay the price for. But it is less costly and less traumatic than the alternative.

The way large divisionalised subsidiaries have approached the choice is both pragmatic and informative. They have chosen different strategies for different divisions. Under the same corporate umbrella, the two forms of specialisation coexist along with some divisions that are not specialised at all and others that simply import their needs. In general, large subsidiaries have made these choices because of constraints on managerial time and R&D resources. They have chosen mandates where they have felt they had sufficient in-house expertise and have opted for other structures in other divisions to make the transition more manageable.

Sometimes product-market imperatives have dictated the choice. Where the technology is massively expensive, as with aero-engines, an import strategy with some component production makes sense. Where the subsidiary has a protected market niche difficult to displace by imports, the miniature replica approach continues to serve well. The choice between rationalisation and mandate seems to be influenced by the age of the product and culture of the parent. Most organisations face the task over time of reconciling innovation and efficiency (Lawrence and Dyer, 1983, p. 8). When innovation dominates (often when the product line is relatively new) the overall corporate culture tends to reinforce product mandates that arise from subsidiary research initiative. When the majority of products are older and efficiency concerns dominate, control becomes more centralised and specialisation more likely to be by assignment in the rationalisation-integration mode. Add to this the general dynamism of the marketplace and corporate structure becomes a changing adaptive mechanism rather than a permanent institution. Such is the untidiness of the real world. To make matters worse, it is probably much harder in human terms to change a subsidiary structure from rationalisation to mandate than it is to go the other way. Given the scope and general complexity of the problem of corporate structure and its tendency to change over time, it is tempting to take the public policy position of encouraging international competitiveness by tariff reduction and letting the firms sort out how to specialise in the competitive marketplace. One could, however, go further and take measures to make Canada a more attractive place for product innovation. In the past, federal policies have been cautious in this area, because, under the branch plant structure, there was too great a possibility of research being done in Canada and the economic activity arising from it taking place elsewhere. Under a more specialised, less protected economy this abuse is less likely to occur. The public payoff to innovation incentives should increase.

Specialisation and the Canadian Owned Firm

So far we have looked at specialisation from the standpoint of multi-national firms and have outlined the structural choices open to them, given a less protected environment. But underlying the logic of the specialisation argument is an assumption that is valid, by and large, for multinationals but not for Canadian owned firms without foreign affiliates. The assumption is that restructuring to obtain the gains of production specialisation will not affect the company's market share position. This is true for multinationals because what they do not produce in Canada they can import reliably from the parent and can still present a full line to their dealers and distributors. If a Canadian owned firm specialises its production to get its costs down, it faces formidable marketing challenges both at home and abroad. Somehow, at one and the same time, it has to develop markets abroad for its Canadian output and find reliable import sources to round out its line for the domestic market. The risk-free rationalisation route is simply not open to the Canadian owned firm on the surface. There is no one to participate in this rationalisation. Excessive specialisation in production can also lead to the lack of perceived differentiation by consumers between various brands carried by the same manufacturer, and to the subsequent loss of market share. Whichever way one looks at it, a world of freer trade favours multinational or global enterprises. The indigenous firm, raised and nurtured in a protected market has a harder time responding to the call for specialisation and international competitiveness, especially if it competes in a relatively mature industry. Over time, of course, newer firms in 'sunrise' industries freed from the habits of insularity will embark on international strategies as a matter of course. But the transition will be difficult and the time allowed to make it will be shortened by the improved competitiveness of specialised multinationals. The short-term outlook for Canadian owned firms in a freer trade scenario is distinctly hostile.

Implications and Conclusions

The economic thrust of Canadian industry is moving from nationalistic protectionism to international competitiveness through specialisation. Behind the move is a rejection of government intervention and a public preference for market based discipline. There are outside forces too and they are the more influential. The trend toward trade liberalisation and more global products is making it harder to survive profitably with insular corporate strategies based on tariff protection. Thus multinational firms in Canada are starting to specialise and can be influenced to do this in more innovative ways through the right kind of climate. WPMs are worth encouraging as long as we keep in mind that any form of specialisation is better than resorting to imports.

Productivity, entrepreneurship, labour negotiations and government policy all need to be reexamined in an international light. Productivity improvement under specialisation means extensive worker retraining, and, in the case of product mandates, it means management development and product innovation both of which are important elements in the calculation of productivity. Entrepreneurs of the future need more often to think of product specialisation and market diversity rather than product diversity and market specialisation; that is, fewer products for international markets rather than many products for the domestic market. Labour negotiations need to give more weight to international wage and productivity comparisons, especially among OECD nations, and less to the concept of sharing the domestic profit pie. And policy needs to help firms in Canada to be internationally competitive by making government services and their related costs and base levels internationally competitive.

For public policy in Canada, specialisation will bring some problems with its benefits. There is no such thing as a problem-free economic structure. With specialisation, Canada's complaints that foreign owned firms do not export and do not do R&D will quickly fade away, only to be replaced by other complaints. With time the complaints will start to surface about transfer prices and loss of autonomy. And the new complaints will be voiced more loudly and persistently than the old ones because fear and suspicion are endemic when it comes to transfer pricing. We will also discover that a heavily specialised economy is more difficult to stimulate by conventional fiscal means because stimulation of domestic demand through tax cuts would result in more imports; that is, in job creation largely abroad. There will also be concern about the plight of Canadian owned firms, especially those in mature industries with strategies based on market protection. The option of specialisation is less readily available to Canadian owned firms without foreign affiliates, but the outside competitive pressures are still there. The plight of Canadian owned firms under a scenario of international competitiveness through specialisation clearly warrants further examination. Because, whatever the difficulties and whatever the dangers, Canada's thrust toward international competitiveness is necessary. In the long run it is difficult to overestimate the potential economic damage to Canada if foreign competition catches Canadian firms with their barriers down but still steeped in the habits of a protected economy.

Notes

1. The material in this chapter appeared originally in *Business Quarterly*, vol. 49, no. 3, 1984, pp. 26–31. Reprinted with permission.
2. A survey of Canadian business leaders was completed on 16 December 1982 by Kenwin Communications Inc. of Toronto. A sample of the results of this survey is provided below. The columns may not add up to 100 per cent due to computer rounding.
Should the Canadian government take an active role in the marketplace?

Those who feel there should be . . .	%
Less government regulation	83
Same amount of government regulation	12
More government regulation	4
No opinion	1

Those who feel there should be . . .	%
Less financial assistance	53
Same amount of financial assistance	22
More financial assistance	21
No opinion	5

3. The need for new institutions was underscored in a speech by Grant Reuber, Vice-Chairman, Bank of Montreal to the Canadian Economic Association on 28 May 1984.
4. Data obtained from managers attending the International Management course at the University of Western Ontario, May 1984.

References

Bishop, P.M. and Crookell, H. (1983) 'Specialization and Foreign Investment in Canada', unpublished paper prepared for the Department of Finance, Ottawa, October

Daly, D.J. (1983) 'Canadian Productivity Performance: Some Guides for Business Decisions', *Business Quarterly*, vol. 48, no. 1, pp. 55–60

Eastman, H.C. and Stykolt, S. (1967) *The Tariff and Competition in Canada*, Macmillan, Toronto

Economic Council of Canada (1975) *Looking Outward*, Information Canada, Ottawa

Lawrence, P.R. and Dyer, D. (1983) *Renewing American Industry*, The Free Press, New York

Levitt, T. (1983) 'The Globalization of Markets', *Harvard Business Review*, vol. 61, no. 3, pp. 92–102

Poynter, T.A. and White, R.E. (1983) 'The Strategic Management of Foreign Subsidiaries: Implications for the Multinational Enterprise', working paper, School of Business Administration, University of Western Ontario, June

8 INDUSTRIAL POLICY ORIENTATION, CHOICE OF TECHNOLOGY, WORLD PRODUCT MANDATES AND INTERNATIONAL TRADING COMPANIES

Hamid Etemad

Introduction

The discussion of different components of industrial strategy as they affect the industrial structure and commercial policy has assumed importance in the contemporary literature. Although the interdependence of all the different components is recognised, the effects of these components on each other are not fully discussed. For example, in discussing trading houses or state trading companies, their effects on the industrial and technological structure of the country or industry are not integrated for the most part. Nevertheless, the relative success of Japanese and Korean (among others) trading companies has generated a great deal of interest (Dhawan and Sheeri, 1982; Fournier, 1972; Japan External Trade Organization, 1980; Kozo, 1976; Lancaster, 1980; McMillan, 1981; Morikawa, 1970; Roehl, 1982b; Tsurumi and Tsurumi, 1980; Yoshihara, 1981; Young, 1979). These discussions, for the most part, are rather isolated, as they do not address the other related components (e.g. a country's or industry's orientation, industrial structure, technological requirements, or governmental choice of commercial, technological or industrial policy) at the same time.

On the industrial strategy side, an equally impressive interest has developed and has dealt with the formulation, characteristics and other aspects of industrial strategy in isolation (Ebrele and Moller, 1982; Guisinger and Miller, 1982; Holland, McLennan and Frank, 1982; Jones, 1982; Magaziner, 1982). The main objective of this chapter, therefore, is to show that these topics are related and the choice of one affects the choice, feasibility and effectiveness of others. Specifically, this chapter presents three general topics and discusses their interrelations as follows:

(1) The characteristics of inward and outward orientation and their comparison;
(2) Selection of technology and the constraining effect of orientation on valuation of the choice as compared to another; and finally,

(3) The comparison of world product mandates and trading companies as vehicles for penetrating into international markets once orientation and technology are determined.

Inward Oriented Development Strategy

The primary focus of an inward oriented (IO) development strategy is on the internal and national (domestic) markets (Balassa, 1980a, p. 13).[1] Whether the inward outlook of a nation is in response to externally imposed constraints, or is a genuine manifestation of the nation's economic and cultural nationalism, the end results remain the same: narrow and internal outlook.[2]

Externally imposed constraints are numerous and are symptoms of a variety of problems ranging from balance of payments deficits to inability to compete in the international marketplace. The latter can contribute single-handedly to many other severe problems, including a chronic deficit in the balance of payments merchandise account, deteriorating technological base, raising of tariffs, and forcing of local production on foreign companies that would not operate otherwise (Balassa, 1980b; Caves, 1975; Helleiner, 1977; Pincus, 1975).

Most IO policies are restrictive and cause a long-run misallocation of resources. Theories of 'second best' have provided the main theoretical justification for the implementation or reinforcement of IO strategies, despite their shortcomings in allocation efficiencies. The policy instruments recommended in these theories include a variety of tariffs, encompassing optimal tariffs, quotas, and other forms of nontariff barriers, plus various local content requirements. Total bans on importation of certain items, and policies of import substitution as opposed to export stimulation, are among the distinct consequences of inward orientation. Implementation of 'second best' theories has resulted in consequences similar to those of IO. In terms of their resource allocating efficiency, in a Pareto optimal sense, inward orientation and 'second best' theories also yield the same result. In a dynamic setting, therefore, whether the 'second best' theories cause, provide justification, or only facilitate inward orientation, is of no significant interest, in so far as the end result is the same. In a theoretical and static setting, however, the distinction between IO and 'second best' seems to have facilitated analysis.

Inward oriented strategy is reactive in nature, and it usually responds to short to medium-run problems. In the reactive or short-run mode,

IO strategies and their resultant policy recommendations remain sub-optimal, as most resources are constrained in the short term. Hence, IO policies can at best achieve local maxima (or minima), based on constrained optimisation of short-run objectives through short-run alternatives, as opposed to global maximisation (or minimisation) of longer-run goals over a less binding set of long-run alternatives.

In an internally oriented nation, the government is open to domestic producers' objections to international competition and usually responds to calls for protection. These assume a variety of different guises: unfair competition, dumping, cheap labour, low quality, etc. The final result, however, is greater isolation of internal markets from international markets through the imposition of more tariff and nontariff barriers. Protectionist policies share the following features:

(1) Their implementation requires bureaucratic and governmental administration. This leads to more intervention and more disruption of normal market processes.

(2) They fail to reward efficient producers and to punish the inefficient and slothful.

(3) They tax the final consumers indirectly by not encouraging competition and stimulating efficiency (i.e. by the amount of tariff).

(4) Although they may stabilise current employment or save it from falling in the protected industry, they hinder the increase of long-run employment.

(5) They apply an upward pressure on prices. Such pervasive policies may institutionalise price level inflationary pressures. The price level inflation can harm exporting industries. This in turn may further reinforce the original protectionist policy or inward orientation.

(6) The small size of the domestic market combined with protection may exclude effective external competition and internal competition in some cases. Lack of effective competition may give rise to industrial concentration (i.e., oligopolistic structure).

(7) They may discriminate unduly against export industries, as these industries may be dependent for components on the protected industries.

The argument is rather clear. Protectionism perpetuates the inefficient use of constrained resources in the uncompetitive industries, instead of accelerating a shift to more advantageous industries that can compete on open international markets and do not need protection.

In summary, because of government intervention in normal market processes, the taxing of the consuming public, the misallocation of resources, and the inefficiencies in production that are associated with IO, the aggregate social welfare of the nation does not reach its potential. The nation may also suffer from underdevelopment in comparison to the other nations that do not fully subscribe to IO policies, or that exercise them sparingly only when absolutely necessary.

Outward Oriented Development Strategy

The primary focus of outward oriented (OO) strategy is on open international markets (Balassa, 1980a, p. 18; 1978a, b). These offer competition and variety of value to all market participants. Importing nations receive the best value for imported goods and can also conserve on their constrained resources by buying from international markets. Exporting nations are forced to compete in these international markets if they are to enjoy the benefits of a large volume of sales. Competition forces the sellers (exporting nations) to draw upon their comparative competitive advantage in order to maintain their position in the marketplace.

The delivery of quality and value at a reasonable price to the right market and to the final customer is the ultimate objective of marketers. Any comparative efficiency in the chain of transactions can enhance overall comparative advantage and competitiveness. Marketing principles are often critical in international marketing. Therefore, the shift of focus from domestic markets to open international markets forces a country to institute far-reaching changes that go well beyond mere shifts in policy from import substitution to export stimulation, etc. The change in orientation is bound to affect the country's outlook, competition and market regulating policies, price levels, state of technology, and long-range employment, and as a result it will enhance aggregate social welfare.

Outward or open market orientation does not require any regulatory intervention. In the longer run the international market mechanism rewards the efficient supplier (combination of producer, distributor and marketing agent) and shies away from the inefficient and indolent. Resource allocation schemes are bound to favour comparatively advantageous industries and activities (e.g. marketing activities) and to work against uncompetitive or comparatively disadvantageous industries.

To remain vigorous, a country or industry must also adopt a proactive strategy formulation approach. Those who only react to market forces are bound to remain behind those who affect markets proactively. The proactive nature of open market competition has several interesting and related features:

(1) It allows the proactive country to be selective about current and future areas of specialisation. The selectivity allows a combination of current and future comparative advantages within the emerging market trends in order to guarantee medium to long-run competitiveness and to stay ahead of other reactive market participants.

(2) Proactive suppliers can use time to their advantage in order to search for and identify latent and emerging marketing trends (Keegan, 1980, p. 211). They can then develop industrial and technological capabilities that respond to or match these market trends in order to satisfy such latent and incipient markets. Therefore, proactive nations can stay in the forefront of product life cycles for a long time (e.g. Japanese automakers in the US markets).

(3) Proactively oriented countries or industries can develop new capabilities and open up new markets (exports) in an orderly and planned fashion and preoccupy inward oriented countries with finding ways to catch up with them. Such preoccupation may unduly tax these countries from dealing with both latent and emerging demands to stop or slow down further erosion of their position in the international marketplace. Early response patterns are characterised by incentives for imports substitution and barriers or restrictions on imports, which through their own distortions further bias the plight of reactive sectors.

In the process of identifying latent markets and capitalising on emerging market trends, proactive countries have ample time to formulate an optimal industrial development strategy that will respond to developing trends as efficiently as possible. To promote a smooth transitional process, authorities may identify strategic industries (e.g. 'vision of the next decade' issued by Japan's MITI) as targets for their resource reallocation process. They may also provide incentives and programs for the retraining of their human resources, and they may help to retool their overall manufacturing facilities optimally (Roehl, 1982a, b; Van Tho, 1982).[3] Structural unemployment is thus minimised or at least controlled, resources are efficiently allocated, and finally, there will be no need for extensive governmental or administrative intervention to rescue jobs or dying industries.

Inward vs Outward Oriented Industrial Development Strategies

Inward and outward strategies must be viewed as the two pure extremes of a set of mixed strategies along a continuum. In view of the increasing level of international interdependencies between nations, strict inward outlook is not economically practical. Nevertheless nations still use policies which imply a high degree of inward orientation (e.g. textiles and footwear in Canada). Adopting an outward outlook is not difficult but is time consuming. Its proper implementation requires access to, and active participation in, international markets (Balassa, 1980a). Marketing research tools and techniques for uncovering market needs, wants and trends are an important ingredient. Deep marketing knowledge in order to understand and interpret marketing research information (from international markets) is also paramount. Traditionally, economic development planners and bureaucratic cadres have lacked marketing tools and techniques, and undermined the role of marketing in economic and industrial development. A much smaller role even than that of marketing is attributed to international marketing (Etemad, 1982, pp. 18–20; Sethi and Etemad, 1983, pp. 2–6). In an outward oriented strategy, however, international marketing does play a vital role, without which the enhancing benefits of international markets are not feasible.

The critical difference between IO and OO strategies is in their reactive and proactive features, respectively. The proactive feature of OO strategies seems to be a strong reinforcing factor that allows proactive countries/industries to stay ahead. In that sense it forces reactive type responses on others, and leads them to weaker competitive positions in the future. To remain ahead of worldwide industry members, a leader must start off by defining new products, technologies and marketing in new markets. This requires a very early start on marketing research in order to identify new trends or uncover markets needs and wants. Market testing of prototypes, full production and marketing must follow within the lead time before others can copy or produce their own versions. The length of this lead time is shown on an extended product life cycle in Figure 8.1.

In fact reactive producers start the process of product development, production, testing, etc. when a proactive producer is expanding as rapidly as possible in order to preempt all others in as many markets as possible. During this period, proactive producers enjoy a virtual monopoly and can increase sales and accumulate profits rapidly.

While others are busy trying to find ways to emulate the process and catch up in order to stop the erosion of their international market position, a proactive country (or industry) can redefine and identify yet another strategic portfolio (i.e. a new generation of products or a new product class) for concentrating effort and further development. Although there is no absolute guarantee that the process would be successful every

Figure 8.1: Critical Time Periods on an Extended Product Life Cycle Curve

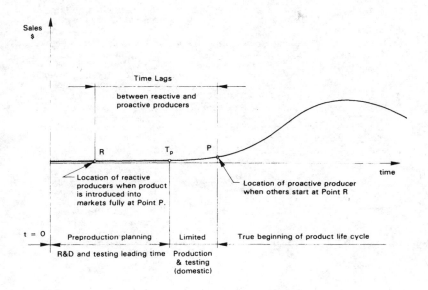

time, the lead time allows the country to experiment sufficiently with identification and development of successful strategic industries (or products). In contrast, in addition to overcoming other adversities, reactive countries must race against time. Other differences are summarised in Table 8.1.

Selection of Technology: The Choice between Developing and/or Transferring

The choice of industrial development strategy (i.e. IO to OO) affects the process of selection, development and transfer of technology necessary for further industrial and economic growth and development. For example, the choice of inwardly oriented strategy prohibits a country from identifying an emerging market trend or incipient markets.[4] This in turn excludes them from developing and producing goods (or services) to satisfy those markets. An outwardly oriented strategy, however, can very well accommodate the necessary lead time involved in developing

Table 8.1: Comparison of Inward and Outward Strategies

	Inward Orientation	Outward Orientation
1. Point of Reference (or focus)	Domestic markets and industries	International and domestic markets and industries
2. Guiding Indicators	Domestic consumption and imports Debit side of balance of payments Infant industries and import substitution	International consumption and growth rate Export potentials, stimulation and growth International market position of competitors
3. Time Perspective for Policy Effectiveness	Immediate and current problems Short to medium-run concerns	Current and future potentials Medium to long-run concerns
4. Main Objectives	To preserve internal political and economic equilibrium To save and/or create employment To respond to externally imposed constraints To decrease dependence on imports Stimulate growth in infant industries	To preserve internal and external equilibrium To reach a leading position in strategic industries To insulate their economy from drastic worldwide/ domestic fluctuations To create industrial/ employment flexibilities To minimise structural inflexibilities
5. Underlying Motives or Forces Stimulating the Process	Domestic political pressures: (e.g. from organised labour and/or business) Nationalism Infant industry concerns Self-sufficiency and security issues Balance of payment problems Lack of international marketing orientation Relative isolation from international trade and investment	Desire to participate in international trade and investment To increase integration into international trade and investment system To benefit from international trade investment and competition To further support industrial and technological advancement To increase effective market size beyond domestic markets
6. Nature of Response/ Action	Reactive to imminent problems Stabilising or minimising damages	Proactive Strategic and future orientation Creating and preserving dynamic comparative advantage
7. Type of Problems/Issues Triggering Action	Mostly domestic problems Unemployment (layoffs) Balance of payments deficit Lobbying pressures	Strategic choices Sign of possible erosion in dynamic comparative advantage Erosion in worldwide market share

Table 8.1 *contd.*

	Inward Orientation	Outward Orientation
8. Policy Tools or Choice of Policies Employed	Direct regulations and restriction by: Tax on consumption imports Tariffs, quotas, NTBs Local content rules Review and regulatory agencies for FDI activities	Indirect and minimal intervention by subsidies and grants for: Exports R&D International marketing intelligence Incentive for developing future comparative advantage Incentives for shifting from sunset (comparatively disadvantageous) to future strategic industries
9. Effect of Policies on Industrial and Economic Structure	Pushing protected industries toward domestic monopolies Lower long-run employment Misallocation of resources in favour of import competing industries Decrease interdependencies	Increasing international competition Opening up of the country Increasing interdependence Enhancing comparative advantage and hence increasing country's share of world trade Phasing out of inefficient industries
10. Necessary Requisites for Achieving Objectives	Full power to enforce regulations (e.g. sovereignty and jurisdiction)	Combination of: Marketing intelligence and information Creation of innovative capabilities Establishing access to and presence in international market Creation and presentation of quality and value in the international marketplace

leading industries for capturing substantial global market shares in the emerging markets. Longer-run versus shorter-run orientation of strategy also interacts with choice and development of technology. Short-run orientation cannot usually accommodate long and extensive lead time. Criteria for selection and development of an industry with internal orientation are expected to specify a shorter time span, a lower break-even point, and a quicker payback period than those of their counterpart in OO type strategies. Of equal importance are criteria for absorbing and hence taking risk. Outwardly oriented strategies, with their longer-run perspective have a more diversified portfolio and can accommodate more risky projects. In this sense they can absorb higher risks. They are, of course, expected to enjoy higher than average returns on their successful projects. In contrast, the expected shorter payback period (of IO) excludes IO strategies from considering projects with longer fruition periods and, by definition, more risky involvements.

Criteria for evaluation of projects also influence the outcome. Inwardly oriented type strategies are expected to value projects at current or close to current prices based on current domestic production and imports; while OO strategies are bound to consider the impact of export demands combined with current and future international prices.

In a general equilibrium model of international trade, a small country with full access to international markets and with no monopolistic power to set prices, takes prices as given. Although policy choices of such a country are assumed not to have any effect on international prices, they do influence prices and quantities in the country itself. Adoption of IO strategy and its consequent policies, as opposed to OO strategy, therefore, may result in the following shifts and disparities:

(1) The relative prices of exports will be lower than international market prices.
(2) The relative prices of imports will be higher than international market prices (by at least the value of tariffs).
(3) Relatively higher prices of import-competing goods shift resources toward import-competing production and away from export production.
(4) The production level of exports will be lower, and conversely, the production level of import-competing goods will be higher than otherwise.

Adoption of IO strategy and its resulting shifts and disparities is bound to affect the basis on which new products, processes or technologies are to be evaluated. In contrast to an evaluation based on international prices under the OO regime, an IO based system of evaluation will reflect the above distortions. Although the research and development cost of a new product, process or project is a function of technological opportunities, their full-scale deployments are very much dependent upon the valuation system. Commercial orientation of a country can influence the choice and subsequent development of such new projects, especially when the project is sensitive to current and future prices, quantities, revenues and/or profits.

In comparing the two orientations as a basis for evaluation and full-scale development, one would expect export oriented invention (or innovation) to be adopted faster and more extensively under an OO regime and to be deferred or not to reach its potential under an IO regime. Conversely, import oriented inventions (or innovation) are expected to be adopted and fully deployed (by import competing industries) faster and more extensively under an IO regime, and deferred or discounted under an OO regime. Therefore, each orientation will have its own biases and, as a result, leads to the adoption and development of certain new products or processes at the cost of others. Under an IO regime, technological innovation (in products or process) is expected to help import competing industries to become more competitive and at a faster rate than the exports; and conversely, export oriented industries are expected to flourish faster and more persuasively under an IO regime. In short, the rate and extent of adoption, and the pattern of technological diffusion in a country are affected by its industrial orientation. Although the above are general trends, the sector of activity, the stages of product life cycle and state of competitiveness of the sector are expected to give rise to specific differences.

A shift in industrial orientation can begin to change the structure and orientation of industries. For example, mature industries with standardised products which are generally subject to strongly increasing pressures from their international competitors are always forced to become more cost competitive. These industries are naturally more open to adopt new process oriented innovation to help them cut costs than equally potent product oriented innovations. Should such an openness be left to itself, the industry is bound to follow its natural reactive path of evolution. Adoption of an OO strategy, however, may bring policies that can check, stop or even reverse such trends. The impact of such policies may just be enough to swing the pendulum and reverse the process, however slowly. The stimulating force of these policies, combined with the prospects of a potential future lead time even in a limited number of products (see Figure 8.1) may be attractive enough to these industries to force a reexamination of their past standard practices. These industries are likely to begin to examine new products and product oriented technologies alongside process oriented technologies. They may even begin to change their evaluation criteria away from reinforcing the safety of protection (under IO) to preparing to take the risk of international market competition. This process can slowly sway these problematic industries towards more diversification within or outside their own industries. It may also help to change their orientation toward proactiveness and away from their accustomed reactive stance. Should such an evolutionary trend start to set in, its demonstration effect will help to diffuse it, and before long, a new outlook is bound to develop. Without such an outlook and predisposition to proactiveness, acceptance of current and future international market prices and quantities as a basis of project evaluation cannot easily come about, and thus the disparities and their associated distortion are expected to continue. Continuation of even a mild IO policy will tax the more proactive or export oriented sectors, while their absence can at least provide for an interplay of natural market forces.

In summary, the policy for developing new technologies, especially when international markets can play a stronger role than domestic markets (e.g. higher international prices or larger international demand), must be devised in concert with that of commercial and trade policy. Conversely, the orientation in industrial development strategy of a nation can affect the choice, the final selection, and the future of technological development in that nation.

The Role of World Product Mandates in Industrial and Technological Strategy

World product mandates (WPMs) can play a significant role in implementation of industrial and technological strategy. WPM is a mandate that a local subsidiary earns or receives from its parent company to produce a particular product or product line for international markets or even, if necessary, for the entire world. The transition from a typical subsidiary operation — which is normally a miniature or truncated operation — to a fully developed WPM is a time consuming process. But, during the transition, the mandate holder develops, acquires, and/or transfers the technologies and products which are necessary for WPM. Furthermore, it adopts and implements an outlook toward presence and competition on open international markets as opposed to limited scale operations under protection of inwardly oriented host country policies. As a result of the mandated operations, a subsidiary decreases its dependence on domestic markets while it increases its international sales and dependence on international markets. Of equal importance is the fact that the mandated product and the technology or processes by which it is produced must become and remain efficient in a dynamic comparative advantage sense (Bruno, 1970) to compete on international markets on a sustained basis.

The change in outlook, production efficiencies, technology, and other activities involved in the mandated subsidiary is bound to influence and revitalise the firm and perhaps the industry.[5]

WPM is one possible vehicle for gradual transition from inwardly oriented policies of closed and protected markets to outward orientation, overhaul of outmoded industries, and subsequent industrial and technological development. As an instrument of transition, WPM offers the following advantages:

(1) It provides an immediate presence and access to international markets through the parent company's sister subsidiary system, while reducing the subsidiary's exposure to the uncertainty of such markets.
(2) It will not require extensive international marketing expertise or knowledge that is necessary for success in the international marketplace, as local sister subsidiaries provide such expertise in foreign markets.
(3) Its resource requirements are relatively low as compared to other options (e.g. international trading companies, joint ventures, etc.).
(4) Its return in terms of employment benefits, tax revenues, value added contribution, foreign exchange contributions, secondary and tertiary effects (e.g. subcontracting, spillover, etc.) are significant.
(5) It can reach a high degree (up to 100 per cent) of internal autonomy with respect to the mandated product.
(6) It can benefit relatively quickly from economies of scale and learning.
(7) It lends itself to planning for internal control and regularity on the one hand; and on the other hand, to smooth transition from one product generation to the other.

In terms of disadvantages, however, the world product mandated subsidiary loses its external autonomy and control over its international marketing, when other sister subsidiaries perform such tasks. As a result, only minimal residual marketing expertise is accrued to the subsidiary or to the host country, unless the subsidiary starts simultaneous exporting independently. In contrast, a substantial amount of expertise in other areas — e.g. production, finance, logistics, international communication, information processing and R&D — is amassed and exercised when a WPM operation reaches a reasonable degree of success. Therefore, the disadvantages of the low degree of external control and minimal marketing spillover must be balanced against the benefits of WPM, before a country can decide in favour of WPM as a vehicle for linking itself to international markets for gradual implementation of an outwardly oriented industrial and technological strategy (Etemad, 1982, 1983).

The Role of Trading Companies in OO Strategies

Other vehicles for establishing linkage to international markets and for transforming industrial technological strategy from IO to OO range from private and small-scale Export Management companies (Terpstra, 1983) to much larger and, at times, publicly owned and organised international trading companies (ITC). ITCs (e.g. Brazilian, Japanese and Korean trading companies) are national organisations that are active domestically as well as internationally (McMillan, 1981; Tsurumi and Tsurumi, 1980). They can provide the linkage, access, and international marketing expertise to small and medium sized domestic manufacturers, to large sized subcontractors with little or no international marketing contacts or experience, and to most internally oriented companies which would otherwise remain outside international markets. Because of their large-scale operations, ITCs have been able to provide their services (e.g. commercially valuable information, access to international markets, marketing knowledge and expertise) to companies lacking such requirements, at a very reasonable cost, thereby opening international opportunities to domestic producers.

Once an ITC is fully developed and is operating internationally, it compares very favourably with WPM as a provider of access to international markets only for those companies that possess competitive and internationally adapted products. For small and domestically oriented companies that lack advanced technology or products, an ITC is not a viable option, for it cannot provide them with access to the results of more advanced technology, R&D and/or products. In contrast, ITCs do not suffer from the alleged disadvantages of foreign direct investment (in terms of transfer of profits from the host to home countries), nor do they expose their suppliers to externally imposed decisions or constraints. Selective features of ITCs and WPMs are compared in Table 8.2.

In short, both the WPMs and ITCs are powerful vehicles for establishing an active linkage to international markets. They both can help inwardly oriented countries to change their orientation to outward and open market operations. WPM provides access to international markets through the sister subsidiary network of its parent which is already present and active in the marketplace. An ITC, however, must establish its presence in international markets and build up its international marketing expertise before it can become active and effective. A subsidiary holding a WPM can enjoy internal autonomy and control at the cost of very little or no external control. An ITC is capable of offering internal and external control to its subcontractor or supplier but it cannot provide them with new R&D. In contrast, a WPM allows the mandated subsidiary to tap the parent's pool of technology expertise and support staff, but it has to remit a portion of its profit to its parents. An ITC, in contrast, ploughs all its profits back into its country of origin. In summary, ITCs and WPMs accomplish similar tasks, but the utility of the actual mix of their respective features (in terms of their costs and benefits) for different countries, industries, or even firms may assume drastically different values.

Concluding Notes

A permanent linkage to, and strong participation in, international markets is a necessary ingredient for the success of an outwardly oriented industrial development strategy. Without such a linkage and presence vital functions are not performed. Among these functions are:

(1) Identifying latent markets and emerging trends toward incipient markets
(2) Conveying of the above information to domestic industries or producers
(3) Active marketing of goods and services in international markets
(4) Immediate attention to, and analysis of, problems as they develop
(5) Information feedback to producers and suppliers on market acceptance, performance, and success or failure of goods and services (including those of the competition)
(6) Feedback on global competitors and their strategies.

It will take a long time before the above functions can be disowned or delegated to others, as a slight disparity in quality, content and timing of the above functions may be responsible for global success or lack of it.

Total commitment to international markets is another essential ingredient of success for outward oriented strategies and overall industrial and economic development. In the absence of complete commitment, temporary fluctuations and short-lived setbacks may put the soundness

Table 8.2: Comparison of WPM and ITC

	World Product Mandates (WPMs)	International Trading Company (ITC)
1. Required Span of Time to Develop	Immediate to short term for: developing access to international markets and active marketing, as sister subsidiaries are already present and active in those markets. transferring required technology/product from parent (if necessary). pooling of R&D and expertise of parent, for developing new technology or product.	Medium to long term for developing access to, and active marketing in international markets, as the ITC establishes its presence and starts to train its international marketing personnel.
2. Level and Composition of Resources Required	Requires low number of marketing oriented personnel but high number of other support staffs, which may remain national, but must handle international requirements.	Requires a high level internationally oriented cadre, preferably locals in their own domestic countries. This cadre must be found, trained and kept on staff in their indigenous countries. A central office cadre must also be developed to work as liaison between international offices and domestic producers.
3. Level and Composition of Knowledge and Experience	May begin with exclusively domestic knowledge and experience in all areas and functions, because sister subsidiaries provide local knowledge and experience. Development of an internationally oriented cadre to better utilise the international information and knowledge which help to smooth operations.	ITC staff must have international knowledge and experience to handle internationally derived information. Centrally located staff must have domestic and international knowledge and experience to unite the international cadre (located overseas and domestic producers mostly domestically oriented).

Table 8.2 *contd.*

	World Product Mandates (WPMs)	International Trading Company (ITC)
4. Magnitude and Composition of Risks and Returns	Magnitude of risk of lower than domestic risk due to geographical and market diversification. When sales are finalised, risks are shifted to the buyers (sister subsidiaries of the parent). When mandate holder retains title, risk remains unabsorbed. Risk is spread among many nations in general. Overall subsidiary risk is higher due to specialisation and international market competition.	Magnitude of risk is lower than domestic risk and depends on the extent of ITC's active presence at points of international sales. All risk is absorbed by ITC and its suppliers. In transactions between suppliers and ITC, ITC must absorb risks. When products are on consignment, producers absorb risks. Therefore ITC's country of origin absorbs all risk.
5. Magnitude of Returns	Profits are distributed between a sister subsidiary, the mandate holder, and the parent company. The magnitude of final returns to WPM country/subsidiary is considerably lower compared to direct or independent sales on international markets.	All profits are accrued to the ITC's country of origin. Profits are not distributed between nations; instead they are distributed between ITC and its suppliers.
6. Degree of Control	WPM enjoys full internal control, but minimal external control, since the locus of ultimate control is at point of sale. Controls depend on coordination of efforts between the WPM holder and the sister subsidiary network. Hence control is diffused.	Locus of control will remain in the country of origin, as both the producer's and ITC's locus of control is in that country. The degree of actual control in international markets depends on the ITC's capabilities and flexibilities in international markets.

	World Product Mandates (WPMs)	International Trading Company (ITC)
7. Required Size for Desired Returns (or Lowering Costs)	WPM holder's ultimate success depends on size and total number of subsidiaries in the network to reach economies of scale and learning.	Size can play an influential role to lower charges; the presence and intensity of marketing activities in international markets can compensate for a lack of size.
8. Degree of Receptivity to Planning and Coordination	As receptivity to planning is mirror image of the degree of control, a WPM does not offer much opportunity for planning for external activities to the WPM holder. Internal activities are open to full planning. Internal operations and plans may suffer from changes in external and internal activities which are highly coordinated.	Linkage between ITC and domestic producers is open to planning and coordination. ITC's required external flexibilities should be viewed as a constraining factor. ITC can plan every function internally and externally when domestic producers act as if they are subcontractors for ITC.
9. Locus of Authority, and Responsibility (A/R) of Functions	A/R rests with sister subsidiaries and the parent. WPM is autonomous internally, hence internal A/R rests with the mandate holder. A/R depends on the relative bargaining power of the WPM holder and the parent.	External and internal A/R rests in the country of origin. Domestic producers have A/R over internal production and financing. ITC has A/R over marketing, logistics and financing in the international market and it has A/R over everything when domestic producers act as subcontractors.
10. Benefits, Taxes, Employment and Dividends	Large-scale employment, spillover and industrial benefits accrue to the mandate holder's country. Because of increased production, value added, and sales, profits and higher tax revenues should result.	Everything being equal, employment spillover and industrial benefits should be equal to or higher than those of WPM. Tax revenues are expected to increase, as all profits and dividends are transferred to the country of origin.

of the policies in question. When OO policies are questioned, strong pressures from a group or coalition of disenchanted groups, including inefficient producers, their suppliers and their displaced labour force, can strongly influence the situation. They may even force the country, or the industry, to change course toward a more internally oriented strategy than was previously in practice. Disruptions in the servicing of international markets, either due to the actual or perceived weakening of commitments and internal dissent (e.g. sympathy strikes, delays, etc.), can damage an otherwise successful presence therein, as international buyers start to shift to more stable and trouble-free suppliers. It is obvious how such pressures, coupled with disruptions (even temporary ones), can influence a successful outward orientation and force it to change course.

In contrast to the above case, outward orientation and active presence in international markets reinforce each other, and can accomplish certain industrial and economic development goals that cannot be otherwise achieved. For example, when OO strategy and active presence in international markets complement each other, the country (industry) can start to enjoy numerous benefits. A list of these follows.

(1) The benefits of economies of scale and learning: larger plants, higher employment, higher revenues, and lower cost per unit
(2) The benefits of early lead times (as regards the newness of technology or products)
(3) The benefits associated with monopoly, or quasi-monopoly positions, or simply being the first in the marketplace
(4) The benefits due to the proactive nature of their activities, including the selection and implementation of strategic choices in advance of others
(5) The benefits which correspond with being a market leader as opposed to a market follower.

Active linkage and presence in international markets can be accomplished in various ways, and each has its own benefits and disadvantages. Multinational enterprise (MNE), as an institutional model, presents a very interesting and powerful choice. MNEs have been active in international markets for a long time and enjoy a relatively strong success record. Despite this apparent strength and success, they do not appear to be viable options for many countries or companies. The MNE is a complex institution which requires a substantial amount of resources (including human resources). In addition, their developmental process is complicated, involved and very time consuming. However, they are capable of providing their parent company with a high degree of control and relatively high returns.

A WPM is an option which takes advantage of an already existing MNE to establish an explicit and active linkage to international markets through the MNE's subsidiary network. Although a WPM holder may start to enjoy the advantages of international markets rather quickly, and avoid the painstakingly slow process of internationalisation, the implicit costs will be present nevertheless. The sister subsidiary network or the parent company will be the actual controller of external activities. Its decisions will include the degree of market penetration, the extent of marketing activities and the amount of informational feedback. In short, the locus of control of external activities remains outside the mandated subsidiary and its host country (Etemad, 1983; Rugman, 1983; Rutenberg, 1981; Science Council of Canada, 1981; Witten, 1981; Wolf, 1983).

ITC is another interesting option for establishing linkage to international markets. It shares some of the features (in terms of benefits and disadvantages) of the above two options. As an institution, it can be as complex as an MNE. It may not take as long to establish a network comparable to that of an MNE in international markets, but it does require comparable resources. In short, an ITC is an in-between (i.e. WPM and MNE) choice, which allows the country of origin to exercise a greater degree of control than on a WPM.

A WPM subsidiary usually has access to new technology and new products that have been developed by its parent, if both decide that transference is a better choice than developing new technology or new products. ITCs do not offer this choice. That is, products and technologies (new and old) used by an ITC's suppliers, or subcontractors must be acquired or developed independently and an ITC cannot provide help with those processes as it is an international trading and marketing organisation at best. Figure 8.2 depicts the complexity that characterises the relationship between an ITC and its suppliers or subcontractors on one side and customers on the other side.

One very apparent shortcoming of the ITC in comparison with a WPM is the clear absence of technology and product related flow between the ITC and its suppliers. This shortcoming may have serious implications for the implementation of outward oriented strategies that depend on new products and new technologies, and that are incapable of developing them internally. This could be a short-run problem however. In the long run it is possible that the investment of all additional returns in R&D and

Figure 8.2: ITC Linkage between Domestic Firms and International Markets

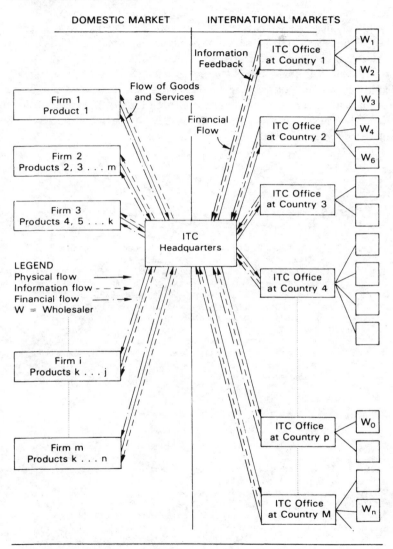

Note: ITC establishes linkage between domestic firms and international markets. ITC provides domestic firm with access to international markets. Domestic firms supply ITC with their goods and services. ITC provides the firms with financial and information feedback.

related activities will surpass the MNE's capabilities in that area, although the risk and short-run problems remain. The additional returns accrue to the parent company under the WPM option.

In conclusion, as a part of a well formulated strategy, governmental authorities can sponsor a series of policy steps to respond to the needs of all their corporate citizens — small and medium sized, local or foreign owned and controlled alike. These policies must facilitate the creation of a WPM option to revitalise foreign owned and controlled subsidiary firms, and should also put in the foundation for establishment of ITC, through which indigenous firms of all types can participate actively in international markets.

Notes

1. Throughout this chapter, it is assumed that countries are market oriented.
2. For a detailed discussion of narrow and internal orientations see Economic Council of Canada, 1976, pp. 1–37 and Institute of Contemporary Studies, 1979.
3. Roehl (1982a) argues that although the Japanese Ministry of International Trade and Industry (MITI) may act as 'control tower' (in an airport) and suggest policies and directives for an industry, industry members may not follow it if they think it may conflict with their own company objectives. The behaviour of small car companies in the 1970s is cited as an example. However, the smooth transition in textiles is attributed to modification of trade policies in response to changing comparative advantage and resulted in the restructuring of the industry before it reached crisis.
4. For a detailed definition and examples of incipient markets, see Keegan, 1980, p. 211.
5. The more efficient operations of a mandated subsidiary gradually establish higher standards in industry. To survive and compete in an industry with a mandated subsidiary, other industry members must either become as efficient and competitive or accept a secondary role (e.g. specialise in subassemblies).

References

Balassa, B. (1978a) 'Export Incentives and Export Performance in Developing Countries: A Comparative Analysis', *Weltwirstschaftliches Archiv*, vol. 114, no. 1, pp. 24–61

Balassa, B. (1978b) 'Exports and Economic Growth: Further Evidence', *Journal of Development Economics*, vol. 5, no. 2. pp. 181–9

Balassa, B. (1980a) *The Process of Industrial Development and Alternative Development Strategies*, World Bank/Staff Working Papers No. 438, World Bank, October

Balassa, B. (1980b) 'Prospects for Trade in Manufactured Goods between Industrial and Developing Countries', *Journal of Policy Modelling*, vol. 2, no. 3, pp. 437–55

Bruno, M. (1970) 'Development Policy and Dynamic Comparative Advantage' in R. Vernon (ed.), *The Technology Factor in International Trade*, Columbia University Press, New York, pp. 27–64

Caves, R.E. (1975) *Diversification, Foreign Investment, and Scale in North American Manufacturing Industries*, Economic Council of Canada, Information Canada, Ottawa

Dhawan, K.C. and Sheeri, J. (1982) 'The Evaluation of National Trading Corporation

134   *Industrial Policy Orientation*

Alternatives for Canada', *Proceedings of the Annual Conference of the Administrative Science Association of Canada, International Business Division (ASAC)*, vol. 3, Part 8, pp. 65–73

Ebrele, W.D. and Moller, J.V. (1982) 'Industrial Objectives: The Right Course for the United States', *Journal of Contemporary Business*, vol. 11, no. 1, pp. 17–28

Economic Council of Canada (1976) *Looking Outward, A New Trade Strategy for Canada*, Information Canada, Ottawa

Etemad, H. (1982) 'World Product Mandates in Perspective', *Proceedings of the Annual Conference of the Administrative Science Association of Canada, International Business Division (ASAC)*, vol. 3, Part 8, pp. 107–19

Etemad, H. (1983) 'World Product Mandates' in A. Rugman (ed.), *Multinationals and Transfer of Technology*, Praeger, New York, pp. 108–25

Fournier, R.B. (1972) *Trading House/Export Middleman*, Industry, Trade and Commerce Canada, Ottawa

Guisinger, S.E. and Miller, R. (1982) 'Industrial Policy in Developing Countries: Strategic Issues for Managers', *Journal of Contemporary Business*, vol. 11, no. 1, pp. 139–50

Helleiner, G.K. (1977) 'The Political Economy of Canada's Tariff Structure: An Alternative Mode', *The Canadian Journal of Economics*, vol. 10, no. 2, pp. 318–26

Holland, R.C., McLennan, K.M. and Frank, I. (1982) 'Defining an Industrial Strategy', *Journal of Contemporary Business*, vol. 11, no. 1, pp. 5–15

Institute of Contemporary Studies (1979) *Tariffs, Quotas, and Trade: The Politics of Protectionism*, sections 6, 8, 9, and 10, Institute for Contemporary Studies, San Francisco

Japan External Trade Organization (1980) *The Role of Trading Companies in International Commerce*, JETRO, Tokyo

Jones, T.M. (1982) 'Industrial Policy: Political "Hot Potato" of the 1980s', *Journal of Contemporary Business*, vol. 11, no. 1, pp. 1–3

Keegan, W.J. (1980) *Multinational Marketing Management*, (2nd, ed.), Prentice-Hall, Englewood Cliffs, New Jersey

Kozo, Y. (1976) 'General Trading Companies in Japan — Their Origin and Growth' in H. Patrick (ed.), *Japanese Industrialization and its Social Consequences*, University of California Press, Berkeley

Lancaster, J. (1980) 'Sectoral Paper on Trading Houses in Canada', unpublished paper, Industry, Trade and Commerce Canada, Ottawa

Magaziner, I.C. (1982) 'The Rationale for a U.S. Industrial Policy', *Journal of Contemporary Business*, vol. 11. no. 1, pp. 29–44

McMillan, C.J. (1981) 'The Pros and Cons of a National Export Trading House' in K.C. Dhawan, H. Etemad and R.W. Wright (eds.), *International Business, A Canadian Perspective*, Addison-Wesley, Don Mills, Ontario, pp. 242–59

Morikawa, H. (1970) 'The Organizational Structures of Mitsubishi and Mitsui Zaibatsu — 1868–1922: A Comparative Study', *Business History Review*, vol. 44, no. 1, pp. 62–83

Pincus, J.J. (1975) 'Pressure Groups and Pattern of Tariffs', *Journal of Political Economy*, vol. 83, no. 4, pp. 757–78

Roehl, T.W. (1982a) 'Industrial Policy and Trade: Three Myths of Japan', *Journal of Contemporary Business*, vol. 11, no. 1, pp. 129–38

Roehl, T.W. (1982b) 'The General Trading Companies: A Transaction Cost Analysis of their Function in the Japanese Economy' in M.G. Harvey and R.F. Lusch (eds.), *Marketing Channels: Domestic and International Perspective*, American Marketing Association, Dallas, Texas

Rugman, A.M. (1983) 'Multinational Enterprise and World Product Mandates' in A.M. Rugman (ed.), *Multinationals and Technology Transfer, The Canadian Experience*, Praeger, New York, pp. 91–107

Rutenberg, D. (1981) 'Global Product Mandating', in K.C. Dhawan, H. Etemad and R.W. Wright (eds.), *International Business, A Canadian Perspective*, Addison-Wesley, Don

Mills, Ontario, pp. 588–98

Science Council of Canada (1981) 'Multinationals and Industrial Strategy: The Role of World Product Mandates', in K.C. Dhawan, H. Etemad and R.W. Wright (eds.), *International Business, A Canadian Perspective*, Addison-Wesley, Don Mills, Ontario, pp. 582–7

Sethi, S.P. and Etemad, H. (1983) 'Marketing: The Missing Link in Economic Development' in G. Hampton and A. Van Gent (eds.), *Marketing Aspects of International Business*, Kluwer-Nijhoff, Boston, Mass., pp. 95–113

Terpstra, V. (1983) *International Marketing*, The Dryden Press, New York

Tsurumi, Y. and Tsurumi, R.R. (1980) *Sogoshosha, Engine of Export Based Growth*, The Institute for Research on Public Policy, Montreal, Quebec

Van Tho, T. (1982) 'Industrial Policy and the Textile Industry, the Japanese Experience', *Journal of Contemporary Business*, vol. 11, no. 1, pp. 113–28

Witten, M. (1981) 'Branch Plants Bear New Fruit' in K.C. Dhawan, H. Etemad and R.W. Wright (eds.), *International Business, A Canadian Perspective*, Addison-Wesley, Don Mills, Ontario, pp. 600–10

Wolf, B.M. (1983) 'World Product Mandates and Freer Canada-United States Trade' in A.M. Rugman (ed.), *Multinationals and Technology Transfer, the Canadian Experience*, Praeger, New York, 1983, pp. 73–90

Yoshihara, H. (1981) 'Research on Japan's General Trading Firm', *Japanese Economic Studies*, vol. 9, no. 3, pp. 61–86

Young, A. (1979) *The Sogo Shosha: Japan's Multinational Trading Companies*, Westview Press, Boulder, Colorado

9 WORLD PRODUCT MANDATES: THE NEED FOR DIRECTED SEARCH STRATEGIES

Norman W. McGuinness and H. Allan Conway

The acquisition and exercise of more technological capability within Canada continues to be a worthy objective. As one approach to reaching this objective, some Canadian governments have been strongly urging foreign based parent companies to grant world product mandates (WPMs) to Canadian subsidiaries for the development of specific products. The intended benefits of WPMs for both Canada and the subsidiary have already been described (Advisory Committee on Global Product Mandating, 1980; Science Council of Canada, 1980). Governments seem to believe that a combination of research and development (R&D) incentives along with pressure exerted on corporate offices will induce foreign parents to assign more WPMs to Canadian subsidiaries. This chapter argues that this approach will probably prove unsuccessful in generating substantial increases in the number of WPMs in Canada unless the subsidiaries themselves become much more adept at the entrepreneurial development of new opportunities.

A policy to encourage WPMs must be compatible with how large multinational organisations operate. Multinationals are not composed of one big central brain with a lot of small appendages that operate only as directed. Rather, they are internally competitive markets wherein the business unit with a strategically sound idea and the will to see it through gets the rewards and resources for further expansion. It might be added that it also incurs the risk of suffering the penalties of failure. The corporate office (the central brain) decides in broad terms what types of businesses and new enterprises will be encouraged and supported, on what basis financial resources will be allocated to the various businesses and how the business unit and individual success will be measured and rewarded. In other words top management at the corporate level sets up the context under which the various business units within the corporation (sometimes over 100) will compete for resources and recognition. The actual development of new products and application of new technologies, however, are usually initiated by the business units themselves. Therefore, corporate decisions affecting product responsibilities may not be appropriate, as the locus of real action may be elsewhere.

In this kind of a system the critical elements in achieving more technological development in Canada are the willingness and ability of the Canadian subsidiary to engage in more innovative and search oriented behaviour. The best product mandates will be earned, not allocated. In fact, within the multidivisional context that characterises most multinationals, the need for innovative behaviour and the locus of the prime responsibility for its initiation at the business unit level are currently highly fashionable managerial concepts (Conway, 1983). More dedication to decentralisation and away from strict concepts of administrative efficiency (the parent rigidly measuring the subsidiary's financial performance) creates opportunities for Canadian subsidiaries to acquire their own product mandates. The challenge, then, is for the Canadian managers within these corporations to become more development, rather than short-term profit, oriented. They must alter the strategic directions of their subsidiaries so that much more effort is devoted to searching for and nurturing new product opportunities. Although the authors argue that this is what corporate management will also want, Canadian managers must create opportunities to prove their capabilities in product and market development. It is the authors' contention that a constant search for new opportunities (often new solutions to recognised problems) must constantly take place throughout the Canadian subsidiary if the effort is to be successful in the long term. Thus, understanding search activity as an ongoing process is critical to the success of Canadian subsidiaries. The encouragement of an intensive search process is the vehicle whereby these subsidiaries will earn WPMs within the multinational context.

In the remainder of this chapter these themes will be expanded. The authors will then review the pattern of search behaviour exhibited in some of the most widely reported examples of WPMs. In addition, the authors will add recent information on the entrepreneurial search going on in a company widely cited in early examples of WPMs.

The Multinational's Organisational Structure

Developing the state of mind inside a subsidiary that leads to a search for product mandates calls for changes along a number of dimensions. Such a search for new products places more emphasis on the longer than the shorter term, calls forth an entrepreneurial rather than a 'play it safe' approach and depends heavily on voluntary and informal activities. To encourage this search process the subsidiary's management must be willing to support proposals that carry the organisation into product market areas in which the parent has little strength. Searching, then, entails new risks, additional costs and new strategic directions. Since a subsidiary is a component of a multinational system, these changes ought to be considered in the light of that overall context. The following discussion will attempt to relate some of the broader aspects with which management must grapple to world product mandating.

Most multinationals have a multidivisional (M-form) organisation. The M-form organisation, however, is in reality more complex than how the two prominent scholars on the subject, Oliver Williamson (1970) and Alfred Chandler (1962), have described it. Williamson, for instance, described an organisation made up of a corporate office and many independent divisions. In this structure Williamson conceptualised the corporate office as a kind of central brain with responsibility for all high level planning and strategic functions. It was crucial, in Williamson's view, for the M-form organisation to avoid mixing these functions with the operational responsibilities of the divisions. This is not unlike Sloan's (1963) organisational concerns in creating the ongoing structure of General Motors. Since the corporate office houses only have staff and general overseer functions, it would imply that the top-down road to a product mandate for a division would arise from the strategy making resource allocation responsibilities of the corporate office.

Multinational companies, however, are broken down into divisions not only by product, but also by country. Not uncommonly the whole Canadian subsidiary reports as a single unit for all its products and related marketing and assembly activities. Various parent divisions, though, would have primary product development responsibility for one or more of the subsidiary's products. First, when the parent is American, the US divisions are larger, more specialised and close to the Canadian division. In such a case, it is convenient in an efficiency oriented world for the Canadian firm to 'piggyback' on the American capabilities. In doing so, economies of scale are offered to the corporation as a whole. Second, it reasserts the hegemony of the large American divisions within the company. Even more importantly, perhaps, it provides for very little risk taking on the part of the Canadian subsidiary. In a world where corporate promotion, pay and security are linked to this month's profit plan with only some vague notion of long-term development, a natural response for Canadian management has been to 'let George do it'. In each situation it must be questioned whether Canadian managers even want to take on responsibility for a WPM. Can Canadian managers, schooled to be dependent on the parent organisation, learn the new entrepreneurial game that WPMs entail?

Not only are the multinationals' organisations more complex than the simple M-form described by Williamson, but the strategy making process is not nearly as concentrated in headquarters. In fact, early research by Berg (1965) concluded that the resource allocation process in a multidivisional firm was multilevelled rather than top-down. Later Bower (1970) showed that strategy making was not only multilevelled but that the ideas and initiative for new products actually came from lower level business units. Divisional and group management then provided the impetus to get the ideas implemented. Headquarters, in Bower's model, had no direct role in the strategic process. Rather, Bower's conclusions suggest that the headquarters' role is to set the parameters through which strategic search and decision-making will occur. Based upon these 'rules' (Bower's term was 'corporate context'), managers throughout the organisation compete for resources and for personal and unit recognition. The single, centralised, corporate brain of Williamson, then, does not exist. Instead there are a lot of small, active ones at the bottom of the multinational hierarchy. One of them should be at the Canadian subsidiary.

In this view of strategic processes, where ideas come from the bottom rather than the top of the structure, product mandates should not be allocated to Canadian subsidiaries through top-down decisions. The subsidiary must generate the WPM possibilities itself. If, however, the subsidiary has traditionally been a geographically limited selling and manufacturing unit set up to secure the Canadian market and valued on measures such as monthly profit versus budget or return on investment, which most are, then it will be driven by efficiency considerations only. The long-run effectiveness of the division will be determined by the applicability of new products developed by the US operations for their home markets. Canadian development will tend to be limited to customising those products to maximise returns in the Canadian market.

But the overall corporate outlook within multinationals seems to be shifting in directions that will demand more innovative effort by all parts of the organisation, including foreign subsidiaries. Recent research (Conway, 1983; Peters and Waterman, 1982) indicates that organisations may be trying to foster the ingenuity present in smaller business units. Conway (1983) traces themes in M-form companies, which are remarkably consistent across companies, and describes how the grand strategies of diversification in the 1960s gave way to an emphasis on corporate control in the early 1970s. That fashion was in turn replaced by a focus on strategic planning during the late 1970s which is now being converted to a new devotion to increasing innovative output in the early

1980s. The latest theme tries to be concerned with evaluating the quality of decision processes and their ability to ensure the organisation's long-term competitive strength. If a subsidiary is fortunate enough to have a parent that is promoting this approach, then the climate may be ideal for the subsidiary to embark on a hunt for WPMs. Conversely, if the parent continues to only press for 'good numbers' in the short term, then it may be very difficult for the subsidiary to develop the search activities required to find WPMs.

All this creates the dilemma of determining how such a bottom-up new product development system affects the status of the Canadian subsidiary. The following elements are worthy of consideration.

Overall Corporate Context

The chief executive's style of management and the signals he sends throughout the whole multinational organisation are critical dimensions in determining the type of strategic behaviour pursued by the company. If, as touched upon previously, top management seeks to improve operations by cost cutting, streamlining and rationalising, then the measurement of current results becomes the critical element of the overall context. In such a case, there will be opportunity for innovation in only the most profitable divisions. Canadian divisions with extremely good numbers will have slack resources (in the current sense) while those without good numbers may be forced to operate with even less resources than they really need. Such a system is not necessarily bad if you can make the heroic assumption that the past and present states are true forecasts of the future. It forces the businesses with a poor performance into disinvestment patterns and gives the resources for expansion to the better ones. The successful divisions of the present, however, are more likely to use any investment resources to improve present operations than to search for new products. Risky developments are not the 'solution set' in this kind of corporate context. Long-term strategic development is still needed but will not be initiated by the division or subsidiary under such a system. Often, in fact, such a firm will eventually be forced to buy growth through acquisition.

If, however, the corporate context is concerned mainly with evaluating management's ability to understand its business environment, its competitors, etc. and to plan effectively, all but the most poorly performing divisions can, and indeed will have to become more innovative. For a Canadian subsidiary the main challenge in these circumstances may be to find the right kind of managerial talent. Subsidiary managers who have spent many years learning how to survive in the 'good numbers or else' school of management can find the new situation very uncomfortable and may be highly inappropriate leaders for a strategy that emphasises more product development. In truth the enemy may no longer be the foreign parent but Canadian management.

Resource Allocation

If multinationals are thought of as groups of businesses that compete internally for resources to expand and innovate, it makes sense to expect that those businesses within the company that have a distinctive competence in an attractive market will have an edge in winning resources. This poses the question of how the Canadian subsidiary will stack up against the others. If it has nothing to recommend why should the parent risk capital for product development work there? This issue strikes at the heart of the product/market strategies of the subsidiary. To acquire WPMs it appears that the subsidiary must venture into new areas which calls for some redefinition of its traditional role. For effective search to take place, people in the organisation need a clear understanding of what it is they ought to be looking for. Subsidiary management, if it is serious about developing WPMs, must do more than simply exhort the organisation to be more innovative. It must also be prepared to specify the kinds of strengths, technologies, and markets it hopes to build around. Once specified, these criteria form the framework against which new product ideas are evaluated. Without them search, if it happens at all, may be focused in inappropriate areas. Or, very worthwhile new product ideas might well be rejected because of being judged by the criteria of the past rather than those of the future. Either way rejection results for reasons which are not well understood and that can have a considerable dampening effect on what little enthusiasm may exist in the subsidiary for taking entrepreneurial risks.

New Product Search

What then is the nature of the search processes which subsidiaries may need to develop? The following discussion is intended to highlight the main features of the search processes in order to show how management may encourage and manage them.

Search, as it applies to product innovation, refers to all those purposeful activities that precede, and result in, concepts for new products. Crawford (1983) refers to this phase of innovation as 'concept generation'. Other writers use designations such as 'exploration' (Feldman and Page, 1984), or 'opportunity identification' (Urban and Hauser, 1980) or 'idea generation' (Wind, 1982, p. 229). 'Search' is the term used here because it conveys the idea of a hunting process that may be collective, having some direction, that takes place over time. It can, of course, involve quite a bit of the individual's creativity that is implied in designations such as 'idea generation'. But much more is involved than just creative thinking.

The output of the search process is a concept for a new product. Crawford's (1983, pp. 201–62) definition of what constitutes a new product concept is the most rigorous and comprehensive and is, therefore, worth following. The elements that make up a product concept offer many insights into the nature of the search process itself, although Crawford is quick to point out that search, or concept generation, is a very poorly understood set of activities. One of the strengths of Crawford's definition is its recognition that a product concept is more than an idea. Instead, a product concept is a carefully drafted vision of what the new product will ultimately be. This vision always includes three elements: a clear idea of the benefits to be offered and the needs to be met in a particular market; the technology that will provide the benefits; and the physical form the product will take. Only after a concept is carefully defined can effective development proceed. Downstream activities may greatly modify the original concept but Crawford (1983, p. 224) is quite emphatic in stating that the concept usually cannot be properly evaluated or technically developed until it is at least verbalised in a complete form.

Obviously many ideas may contribute to the development of a fully blown new product concept. The original notion may have started with the recognition of a market need, or a new material offered by a supplier, or a suggestion from a customer. From there it is elaborated, perhaps by one inventive person, but more likely by various interested people having different kinds of expertise. The process tends to be iterative and circular rather than linear as notions are progressively and more carefully defined. In the end, as Crawford notes, it may be impossible to say where the ultimate product idea, or concept, arose. A recent study by DeBrentani (1983) seems to bear this out as managers were unable to recall in about half of the new products studied whether the source of the idea was inside or outside the company. Search, therefore, takes time and effort. It is also purposeful and should be distinguished from what Aguilar (1967) termed 'undirected viewing' of what is going on with no particular purpose in mind. Information gathered from scanning may trigger search, but it is not considered here to be part of the search process.

Although search may involve activities such as market research and technical exploration that are quite structured, there are also many aspects that are highly informal. This would seem to be especially true of the very preliminary stages of search where embryonic notions tend to be nebulous and tentative. Formal modes of communication are unlikely to be used for conveying such information as has been found by Allen (1977). Not only did two-thirds of the information used by R&D laboratories in this study come from outside the organisation but a great deal of it was transmitted through person-to-person networks. Another study of smaller manufacturing firms (Allen, Hyman and Pinckney, 1983) found an even greater reliance on outside sources. Less than 20 per cent originated internally, and nearly all the outside ideas were obtained through direct personal contact.

In addition to being heavily dependent on informal networks, ideas are also very fragile — they are easily ignored, or squelched. In one R&D laboratory it was found that many ideas were never submitted for any kind of review (Baker and Freeland, 1972). To the loss of that organisation the unsubmitted ideas were found to contain an above average proportion of good ones. In 60 per cent of the cases the reason given for non-submission was 'time pressures' due to other work. Negative reactions from various sources, or no response at all, which could be interpreted as a negative response, together made up the remaining 40 per cent of the unsubmitted cases.

Product concepts, therefore, evolve by way of both formal and informal processes that blend fragmentary information from many sources into the final conception. It seems reasonable to think of the search process as going through stages as depicted in Figure 9.1. In this diagram search is presented as essentially a problem solving process — with the difference that search must first find its own set of product related problems and opportunities to solve. While a solitary inventor may go through the whole process alone and emerge with the finished concept, it seems more likely that in an organisation a number of people will be involved. In the idea generation literature there is no shortage of references to problem identification although it is often cited in relation to the creative process within individual minds (Crawford, 1983, p. 105; McGuire, 1972). Tangible evidence of search as a problem solving process is offered by Baker, Seigman and Rubenstein (1967) where 94 per

cent of the ideas generated in an R&D laboratory had been triggered
in part by an organisational need, problem or opportunity.

Additional support is provided by the detailed case histories of a
number of important innovations compiled by the Battelle Memorial
Institute (1973). In almost all of these there was the decision to focus

Figure 9.1: Stages of the Search Process

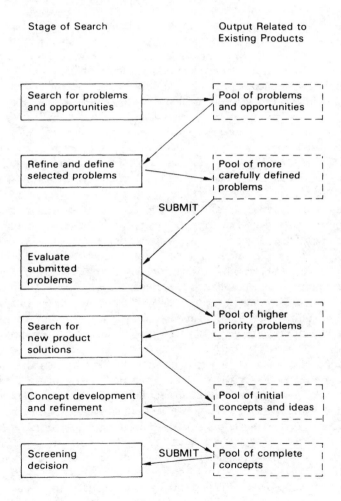

on a particular problem or need that preceded and led to the product that was eventually developed.

In the case of the artificial pacemaker, for instance, New York's Beth David Hospital set up in 1926 a committee to investigate the possibilities of intracardiac therapy. The work of this committee prompted a strong interest in electro-stimulation as a means of resuscitating stopped hearts. The first artificial pacemaker appeared in 1931 but it was not until 1960 that a truly reliable version was developed.

A more dramatic instance of a problem leading to a product concept is provided by the case of birth control pills. No pharmaceutical companies had considered the possibility even though several had much of the necessary technology at hand. Instead the problem arose when two influential women approached the director of a research institute and urged him to find a better method of birth control. His review of the literature led him to conceive the possibility of a pill and his evangelical championing was able to convince drug companies to develop it.

The search for problems and opportunities can be deliberate and purposeful or simply random. During normal operations organisations are always encountering product related problems and opportunities. A special request by a customer, an improvement introduced by a competitor, a suggestion from a supplier, rising costs — all these and many other similar events can stimulate search. It is convenient to think of the output of this early kind of search as resulting in a pool of problems some of which are held quietly in people's minds while others are openly discussed. Most problem items arising from ongoing operations are likely to concern improvements and modifications to existing items. The time horizon associated with these changes is likely to be short and the amount of search required may be minimal. Both the parent and the subsidiary may find themselves making product changes of this sort to meet special needs of their particular markets.

Every once in a while existing products require a complete redesign, or a notion arises that could lead to a completely new product. Such redesigns and innovations give birth to new generation products and often contain technology that is quite new. The time horizon associated with their development is much longer and the search needed to arrive at a feasible concept is liable to be much more extensive. In Figure 9.1, therefore, the pools of problems and opportunities related to existing products and their search requirements for improvements and modifications are shown. However, for potentially new products this process is not known. Subsidiaries are unlikely to be involved with complete redesigns of existing products. But to obtain WPMs they will probably need to search for new products which neither the parent nor the subsidiary currently offers. That kind of search may not arise naturally out of ongoing operations which means that the organisation must get it started in a deliberate, purposeful way.

It is important to note that selectivity operates in the process from the very beginning. The problems and opportunities recognised will be those that seem revelant to what the organisation is trying to accomplish. Recognising that there is a problem is a necessary first step to agreeing to do something about it and sometimes it may take a forceful 'problem champion' or 'opportunity champion' to bring an issue into the foreground of the organisation's concerns. Since potential WPMs are likely to be in areas of low interest to both parent and subsidiary top management, they may be more heavily dependent than other projects on championing activity to get going. Further selectivity is exercised as problems are refined, elaborated and more carefully defined. Much of this refining process may be conducted informally through discussions with peers and supervisors but eventually a problem may need more careful investigation. At this point, if money is to be spent, some kind of formal evaluation may take place. Perhaps a thorough investigation of the market opportunity is required if that is the critical area in the development of the full concept. Or some possibilities may require technical work to determine how the benefits envisioned might best be provided. Again a process of refinement and elaboration takes place. Ultimately, crude prototypes may emerge but that is as far as design should proceed. The more critical output is a fairly comprehensive description of the main attributes of the potential new product along with a clear idea of the technology to be employed. Only then can a well considered screening decision be made on whether or not to go ahead. For clarity the overall process here has been depicted as moving in a linear fashion through a series of stages. In practice that may never be the case. Downstream technical and market investigations, for instance, may call for a major redefinition of the original problem or opportunity. Recycling back to earlier stages may happen at any point. A search project may also sputter out at any stage and be consigned once again to the idle pool of potential projects which the organisation holds in its collective consciousness.

The problem driven nature of the process combined with a heavy dependence on voluntary informal activities by many people may explain why the search for new product concepts in many companies seems haphazard and disorganised. As Little (1974) noted 'firms in this study had little in the way of a systematic routinised set of procedures to generate new product ideas except for those pertaining to planning and budgeting for R&D products'. Another more recent investigation of the innovation processes of nine large US corporations found generally an *ad hoc* approach to generating ideas that made very little use of either market research or R&D (Feldman and Page, 1984). Two of the companies obtained most of their ideas from customers, presumably through direct contact.

There is a tendency to think of messy, badly defined search processes as being ineffective. But that is not necessarily true. The companies that obtained most of their ideas from customers in Feldman and Page's study may have been alertly looking for new possibilities. What seemed *ad hoc* on the surface may have concealed a highly motivated organisational interest in new products that resulted in finding quite a large number of new opportunities. It is usually quite clear to people in an organisation where more formal decisions must be made once problems and opportunities are uncovered. What really count in a problem driven process are two things: the motivation to exert the voluntary effort to find the possibilities and the sense of what is relevant and needed by the organisation. If an organisation can encourage its employees to develop the appropriate state of mind, then its pool of problems and opportunities will be large and attractive enough to stimulate the remainder of the search process in a steady rather than an intermittent way.

How WPMs Emerge

The relatively small amount of theoretical analysis of WPMs says very little about how they emerge or the kinds of products and circumstances that may be most suited to mandating. There seems to be an assumption, however, that the subsidiary may be either not allowed or unable to do much about developing products in Canada that could potentially be mandated. Poynter and Rugman (1982) are not overly clear on this point but their emphasis on the parent's desire to control strategic R&D activity suggests that the subsidiary is restricted from venturing out on its own. Rutenberg (1981) is more clear-cut. His argument rests on the assumption that all significant product development work is carried out by the parent. In his opinion the parent would especially want to control new products because of their negative cash flows and uncertainty of success.

This kind of thinking seems to lead to another assumption — that the products mandated to the subsidiary are fully developed going concerns. Rutenberg (1981) suggests that products in the growth stage of the life cycle may be the best candidates to consider mandating to a subsidiary. At this stage a product is well established, has a fairly secure future and can be safely turned over to the subsidiary. Just why the parent would want to let the subsidiary control a promising growth stage product which may be of importance to the parent in its home market and elsewhere is an important issue which Rutenberg does not explore. Rutenberg does not see much point in mandating mature products to a subsidiary because they are likely to be manufactured at low cost sites around the world leaving the subsidiary to act as the headquarters for a miniature multinational. Regardless of the life cycle stage, however, the overall outlook implicit in these speculations is one that sees mandating as a process whereby the subsidiary acquires a complete and well developed product line from its parent.

It is worth comparing this outlook with the kinds of WPMs that seem to have emerged. Unfortunately there is not a large amount of data available on WPMs and much of what is available was collected by a single study done by the Science Council of Canada (1980). In Table 9.1 the significant features of six WPMs are summarised. Of these six only two were mandated as fully developed and operational product lines which is less than would have been expected from the theoretical research on this subject. A distinguishing feature of the two WPMs mandated as functioning product lines is that the mandate seemed to solve a problem for the parent as much as for the subsidiary. Black and Decker, for instance, was experiencing a shortage of production capacity in the US when it assigned orbital sanders to its Canadian plant. Similarly Garrett Manufacturing was under considerable pressure from an important defence customer, the Canadian government, when it decided to assign responsibility for aircraft temperature control systems to its Canadian subsidiary. This WPM not only aided the relationship between Garrett and the Canadian government but resulted in other important concessions for Garrett too. If the returns to the parent are substantial enough, these two cases indicate that it is possible for the subsidiary to win a healthy, established product line as a WPM.

But of the WPMs outlined in Table 9.1, four of the six cases required the subsidiary to do a large amount of engineering work before the product could be put on the market. Even the Workmate, which was already being sold by Black and Decker's subsidiary in the UK, had to be substantially redesigned to meet North American needs. In the other three of these four cases the subsidiary was able to draw upon its parent's technology as a starting point but still had to do most of the development work itself. It is noteworthy that these products had not already been developed to a satisfactory degree by the various parent organisations. Also significant is the fact that the subsidiaries were able to cope with the engineering work that was required. Foreign subsidiaries in Canada may have greater innovative capabilities than they are sometimes given credit for. This point is reinforced by a study which examined the innovations in five Canadian industries that managers rated as having contributed most to profitability (De Melto, McMullen and Wills, 1980). Of the innovations submitted by foreign owned subsidiaries 48 per cent were original designs and not copied from their parent or any other source. If a substantial proportion of WPMs do in fact require a large amount of development work then the ability of the subsidiary to handle the technical task will be critical.

Most important of all in winning a WPM, though, is the entrepreneurial knack for spotting the opportunity in the first place. In Figure 9.2 the six WPMs have been grouped into four quadrants according to whether or not the parent had a strong strategic interest in the product and whether or not the product was already part of the parent's product charter. The degree of parent's interest in the product was inferred from the case data. All four of the WPMs that required extensive development work fall into the left-hand side of the chart indicating that they were of low interest to the parent. Just why the parent had little interest in these product areas is generally not clear from the case history material. What is apparent, however, is that in each case the subsidiary had the entrepreneurial vision to see market potential which the parent either overlooked or had no interest in developing. Thus, Westinghouse was planning to drop its line of airport lighting controls but its Canadian subsidiary saw interesting potential for a much improved design that turned out to be very successful in markets throughout the world.

Sometimes the market for a mandated product line may be just too small to be of interest to the larger operations of the parent. In other cases one suspects that the parent wishes it had spotted the opportunity first. The Canadian subsidiary of Westinghouse, for instance, became aware of an emerging market for small industrial turbines while its parent was immersed in selling larger turbines to a different market, utilities. And Litton Systems was preoccupied with producing guidance systems for the defence market when its Canadian subsidiary proposed developing a parallel line of products for commercial aircraft. The Black and Decker Workmate, though, provides the most outstanding example of entrepreneurial initiative by a subsidiary. It was only after the parent

Table 9.1: Summary of WPM Data

Company	World Product Mandate	Approximate date of mandate	Initial status of product with parent	Key Canadian factors in decision
Black and Decker	Orbital sander	1968	Well established Mature design Short of production capacity Least market share of all B&D core lines	Subsidiary needed volume to reduce costs
	Workmate (acquired by British subsidiary from inventor)	1974	Parent not interested in acquiring the product	Saw market potential for the North American mandate Redesigned product for North America (used outside personnel)
Westinghouse Canada	Small steam turbines	1973	Parent concentrated on large turbines for the utility market	Had built some turbines already Had production capacity since going out of the waterwheel generator business Saw market potential for industrial turbines
	Airport lighting	?	Poor sales Planning to drop product	Good sales Saw additional market potential

Company	World Product Mandate	Approximate date of mandate	Initial status of product with parent	Key Canadian factors in decision
Garrett Manufacturing Limited	Temperature control systems for aircraft	1961	Strong, high technology	Pressure from federal government to produce defence product in Canada Willingness of the government to treat other Garrett products as 100 per cent Canadian Existence of a Canadian defence market
Litton Systems Limited	Inertial guidance systems for commercial aircraft	1968–1970	Product neglected by parent	Pressure by government in 1960 to produce in Canada Slump in Canadian defence market Subsidiary sees potential for commercial systems Availability of government procurement and investment

Figure 9.2: Categories of WPMs

	Low strategic importance to the parent	Significant strategic importance to the parent
Parent has product charter	Airport lighting Small steam turbines Inertial guidance systems for commercial aircraft	Orbital sanders Temperature control systems
No product charter exists	Workmate	a

Note: a. this quadrant is seemingly not the natural realm of WPMs

had rejected the product because they thought it was not suitable for the North American market that its Canadian subsidiary decided to undertake the extensive market and technical development task that was involved. All three of these WPMs have developed into very successful businesses which the parent organisations might have been glad to have had themselves. Indeed now that the Workmate has become an important product in the US, the parent's home market, there are signs that the parent is moving to impose more direct control (Rutenberg and Jaeger, 1981).

Entrepreneurial search and the willingness to engineer the product seem to have been the crucial ingredients needed by subsidiaries in getting four of the six WPMs started. Moreover the search did not focus on strong products that the parent might have been willing to give up but rather on new opportunities that the parent had not yet developed. In addition, the subsidiaries did not seem to search in areas that were of high strategic interest to their parents. In this small sample, none of the WPMs fell into the lower right-hand quadrant of Figure 9.2. This quadrant represents completely new products that could be of strong interest to the parent and where the parent, therefore, might feel more inclined to dictate where the innovative activity should occur. Instead the search pattern was the nontraditional one of looking for a market which had not already been exploited by their parents and which lay somewhat outside the primary product/market focus of their parents.

The case studies are vague on the subsidiaries' strategic outlook but none of them seems to have had an ongoing policy of searching for

WPMs. Instead the WPMs appear to have arisen out of an *ad hoc* search that was triggered by business difficulties. Westinghouse Canada, for example, had surplus capacity, due in part to its withdrawal from the waterwheel generator market, which led to the pursuit of a mandate for small steam turbines. Similarly, Litton's Canadian subsidiary was experiencing a serious slump in its defence business and Black and Decker of Canada had noncompetitive costs when they sought their respective WPMs.

Subsidiaries that are serious about acquiring more WPMs, however, will need to search in more than just an intermittent way. They must develop a frame of mind and outlook within their organisations so that the search for new products is steady, ongoing and entrepreneurial enough to find opportunities which the parent organisation has not yet spotted. Since this tends to be a nontraditional form of behaviour for most Canadian subsidiaries, it may be a formidable task to get more active search processes established.

Ongoing WPM Development in a Canadian Subsidiary

Litton Canada (LC) was founded in 1960 as a vehicle whereby Litton Industries, a US electronic equipment supplier, would fulfil a 40 per cent Canadian content requirement for the inertial navigation system on a group of Lockheed 104 aircraft being purchased by the Canadian government. After a decade of manufacturing aircraft navigational equipment, often for other than the US and Canadian airforces, LC's business plummeted so steeply that its work force had declined to only slightly above 20 per cent of its mid-1960s size.

As a result of that idle plant capacity and the Canadian management's zeal to have the organisation survive, LC was granted a manufacturing mandate to be the company's sole manufacturing source of commercial navigation systems. It would market these in Canada only while a Californian division would market them to the rest of the world. Therefore, although this mandate created export markets for LC, it did not provide for the all-important general market contact that would provide insight into problem recognition, critical in the search process described earlier.

This situation could have been the net strategic thrust at LC, at least until the commercial navigation business atrophied and another over-capacity crisis arose. There were two intervening variables that prevented these consequences from arising. The first intervening variable was the overall corporate context at Litton. Each of Litton's divisions is expected to be an independent business, and management careers are far more tightly tied to a particular division than they are to any wide corporate notion of Litton Industries. In the Litton context, division managers must recognise the resources they need and acquire or borrow them from wherever they exist (sometimes in other Litton divisions). Because of the corporate dedication to divisional autonomy (and responsibility) there are, in fact, no resources (such as an R&D department) available from corporate headquarters. In place of a centralised technological capability, Litton has deliberately given prominence to technological development and sharing, by and among its divisions. The climate is such that managers who know what they need, why they need it, and where in the multinational network it exists, can often borrow or rent the help needed internally for a time. Although corporate rules are few at Litton, 'do not spend resources solving a technical problem already solved elsewhere in Litton Industries' is a well understood caveat. The corollary to the latter is that technical personnel are expected to share their solutions with others who ask for help.

The second intervening variable was the behaviour of the Canadian management. Under division president Ron Keating's leadership the Canadian division set a course aimed at being as good as (or better than) any division within Litton. To achieve this goal meant converting the cash flows from the commercial navigation mandate toward searching for and solving new problems which allowed an enhancement of both divisional capabilities and market sensitivity. Remembering that LC's original early 1970s worldwide mandate was for manufacturing only, the task of becoming a searching, product developing entity still lay ahead. In recent years and in a number of product areas, LC has been able to develop its own product mandates. Only one example will be briefly explored here.

In 1977, Transport Canada approached LC (based on LC's previous success with product development) with an objective of finding a way to streamline the cumbersome flight inspection systems then in use to test land based equipment for guiding, directing, and informing in-flight aircraft. LC's personnel saw this as a possible additional practical application of its inertial navigation experience and thus as a natural focus for search activity. Under an investment sharing arrangement with Transport Canada, LC developed what may be the most advanced automatic flight inspection system in the world. Taking a prototype of the new system to the international air show at Farnborough (England) in 1978, LC was able to initiate sales to the Netherlands and later to

Britain and China. Interestingly, Transport Canada, the potential customer whose initial interest seemed to dispel the risk of producing a marketless product, did not order the system until 1984.

It is important to realise that while LC was developing its new system, a sister division in the US was also working on the development of a new flight inspection system. The development of a sophisticated working system by LC did not stop the US division from trying to obtain a company mandate for the product. Such natural competition among divisions made LC managers value the role of Ron Keating in going to corporate headquarters as their product champion. They believe he is willing to 'fight for our rights' and highly capable of doing so.

We have only briefly sketched one of what have become many successful new product searches at LC (its 1985 forecast was for $186 million in export sales against only $36 million domestically). Still, it is useful to stop and recapitulate some of the key elements of the new product search process.

(1) The original mandate provided important cash flows but no access to international market information, which is a critical element of search.

(2) The Litton corporate context, based on divisional autonomy and responsibility, demands a certain amount of search activity in order that division management maintains credibility. In addition, the identification of personnel with their divisions rather than with Litton Industries makes the ongoing survival of the division a key ingredient of a successful career.

(3) There are few ideas or resources at headquarters that can form the basis for a mandate — thus, assigned mandates must be reallocated from other divisions.

(4) Unlike the well-known examples reviewed earlier in this chapter, LC did not have to deal in areas that were of low strategic interest in the US. However, it did have to create a rationale as to why Canada was a sensible place for solving the problem and it had to be early in the problem recognition phase. It is clear that had a US division clearly staked out a problem area as its territory and made some significant developments there, the Canadian division should search elsewhere.

(5) Transport Canada's approach provided a rationale for LC's involvement in an area of moderate strategic interest and priority at the corporate level. First, Transport Canada underwrote some of the development costs. More importantly, it created what seemed an

assured customer for a problem solution — such seemed to certify the product as a practical (sellable) application of company experience and technology.

(6) Such independent product development provided for an independent presence in world markets. Thus, LC could search for its own mandates — it did not rely on their being reallocated.

(7) The fact that the product was an extension of corporate capability made it interesting to a US division as well. Note that LC managers believed they had 'rights' within their multinational organisation. Note also that they believed there was a need to champion their products, skills and people within the larger corporate context.

Implications

In summary, for a subsidiary to seek WPMs successfully it must encourage more entrepreneurial searching by its various business units. This, in turn, calls for a shift in the strategic outlook within the subsidiary which may be more possible now that the vogue in North American industry seems to be favouring more innovation and a 'small is beautiful' style of management. Whatever the subsidiary does, however, must reflect to some degree the overall context of the multinational corporation. If an innovative thrust is emerging then the subsidiary may consider the merits of moving in the direction of development work that could lead to WPMs. The entrepreneurial search needed is a difficult and complex activity to encourage, largely because it calls for voluntary initiative and risk taking at lower levels of the organisation. It is a problem or opportunity driven process that at first yields only fragile, nebulous notions that are easily squelched or ignored. To nurture the process, subsidiary management must send clear signals of its seriousness. Among the actions which management could take some of the more important ones relate to (a) evaluating whether existing leadership has the capabilities for the task at hand, (b) specifying carefully the strengths, capabilities and markets in which the subsidiary will try to develop WPMs, (c) demonstrating a willingness to forego some short-term profitability in favour of longer term development, and last, but certainly not least, (d) giving recognition, rewards and promotions to those who show prowess at entrepreneurial endeavours.

Canadian subsidiaries, and any who make policy affecting Canadian subsidiaries, must concentrate upon making the Canadian division a truly worthy competitor for corporate resources and confidence within the multinational organisation. Even if initial product mandate possibilities are only for manufacturing on a worldwide basis and for exclusive marketing in Canada, management'must work in those two domains towards finding solutions that will thrust them into the mainstream of worldwide problem solving. The search model presented in this chapter precludes much new product development without access to market information and interaction. Intensive search for important problems and solutions within the Canadian market may lead to products with worldwide application. Such can lead to the much needed exposure to worldwide market information. Equipped with a sense of what they want to achieve, Canadian managers have access to a great deal of technology and experience within the multinational organisation. Searching out, and being committed to finding, solutions to important problems can make the Canadian subsidiary a source of important products.

The authors are optimistic that more and more multinational corporations are putting higher value on divisional autonomy and initiative. Such, in turn, should lead to the replacement of staid, efficiency minded Canadian subsidiaries' managers and to the flowering of more venturesome managers. If such initiative is not possible within most multinationals, however, it is difficult to recommend any policies aimed at encouraging Canadian subsidiaries, whether those policies are encouragement of WPMs, R&D incentives, or something else.

References

Advisory Committee on Global Product Mandating (1980) *The Report on Global Product Mandating*, Ontario Ministry of Industry and Tourism, Toronto, December

Allen, T.J. (1977) *Managing the Flow of Technology*, MIT Press, Cambridge, Mass.

Allen, T.J., Hyman, D.B. and Pinckney, D.L. (1983) 'Transferring Technology to the Small Manufacturing Firm: A Study of Technology Transfer in Three Countries', *Research Policy*, vol. 12, no. 4, pp. 199–211

Aguilar, F.J. (1967) *Scanning the Business Environment*, Macmillan, New York

Baker, N.R. and Freeland, J.R. (1972) 'Structuring Information Flow to Enhance Innovation', *Management Science*, vol. 19, no. 1, pp. 105–16

Baker, N.R.; Seigman, J. and Rubenstein, A.H. (1967) 'The Effects of Perceived Needs and Means on the Generation of Ideas for Industrial Research and Development Projects', *IEEE Transaction on Engineering Management*, vol. EM–14, no. 4, pp. 156–63

Battelle Memorial Institute (1973) *Interactions of Science and Technology in the Innovative Process*, Report prepared for the National Science Foundation, Contract NSF-C667, Washington, DC

Berg, N.A. (1965) 'Strategic Planning in Conglomerate Companies', *Harvard Business Review*, vol. 43, May-June, pp. 79–92

Bower, J.L. (1970) *Managing the Resource Allocation Process*, Harvard University Press, Boston, Mass.

Chandler, A.D. (1962) *Strategy and Structure*, MIT Press, Cambridge, Mass.

Conway, H.A. (1983) 'The Evolution of the Corporate Office in the Large, Diversified Firm', unpublished PhD dissertation, Harvard Business School, Boston, Mass.

Crawford, C.M. (1983) *New Products Management*, R.D. Irwin, Homewood, Illinois

DeBrentani, U. (1983) 'Evaluation of New Industrial Product Ideas: An Empirical Study of the New Product-Screening Model and an Analysis of Managers' Screening Behaviour', unpublished PhD dissertation, McGill University, Montreal

De Melto, D.P., McMullen, K.E. and Wills, R.M. (1980) *Preliminary Report: Innovation and Technological Change in Five Canadian Industries*, Discussion Paper no. 176, Economic Council of Canada, Ottawa, October

Feldman, L.P. and Page, A.L. (1984) 'Principles Versus Practice in New Product Planning', *The Journal of Product Innovation Management*, vol. 1, no. 1, pp. 43–55

Little, B. (1974) 'New Focus on New Product Ideas' in B. Little (ed.), *The Right Now Product*, School of Business Administration, The University of Western Ontario, London, Ontario

McGuire, E.P. (1972) *Generating New-Product Ideas*, Conference Board Report no. 546, Conference Board, New York

Peters, T.J. and Waterman, R.H., Jr (1982) *In Search of Excellence*, Harper & Row, New York

Poynter, T.A. and Rugman, A.M. (1982) 'World Product Mandates: How Will Multinationals Respond?', *Business Quarterly*, vol. 47, no. 3, pp. 54–61

Rutenberg, D. (1981) 'Global Product Mandating' in K.C. Dhawan, H. Etemad and R.W. Wright (eds.), *International Business: A Canadian Perspective*, Addison-Wesley, Don Mills, Ontario, pp. 588–98

Rutenberg, D. and Jaeger, C.V. (1981) 'Black and Decker Canada Inc. (B): Workmate' in K.C. Dhawan, H. Etemad and R.W. Wright (eds.), *International Business: A Canadian Perspective*, Addison-Wesley, Don Mills, Ontario, pp. 853–60

Science Council of Canada (1980) *Multinationals and Industrial Strategy: The Role of World Product Mandates*, Science Council of Canada, Supply and Services Canada, Ottawa, September

Sloan, A.P. (1963) *My Years with General Motors*, Doubleday, Garden City, New Jersey

Urban, G.L. and Hauser, J.R. (1980) *Design and Marketing of New Products*, Prentice-Hall, Englewood Cliffs, New Jersey

Williamson, O.E. (1970) *Corporate Control and Business Behaviour*, Prentice-Hall, Englewood Cliffs, New Jersey

Wind, Y.J. (1982) *Product Policy: Concepts Methods of Strategy*, Addison-Wesley, Reading, Mass.

PART III

SOME EMPIRICAL AND THEORETICAL EVIDENCE

10 WORLD PRODUCT MANDATES AND FIRMS OPERATING IN QUEBEC

Bernard Bonin and Bruno Perron

World product mandates (WPMs) have now been in use for several decades (Rutenberg, 1981, p. 9). If a sudden interest in the subject seems to have surfaced recently in Canada, it is because it was thought that the acquisition of these exclusive rights to world distribution would become a potentially effective element in this country's industrial policy. This way of thinking was in reaction to the role of subsidiaries of foreign firms, and in response to the trend toward greater freedom in international trade.

The Science Council of Canada (1980) was the first to publish a report on this subject in this country. During the same year, Ontario's Ministry of Industry and Tourism also put out a report on the subject. In the latter report an attempt was made to assess the importance of such arrangements for the Ontario economy. The telephone survey conducted in this study revealed the presence of about 50 world mandates among the foreign firms established in Ontario (Advisory Committee on Global Product Mandating, 1980).

In October 1981, a two-day conference was held in Toronto, providing academics, civil servants and businessmen with an opportunity to exchange views on the subject of mandates. And, although the topic is scarcely mentioned in economic literature, it does come up for discussion more frequently in writings specifically concerned with international management.

What does a typical WPM actually consist of? Basically, it is an agreement between a multinational enterprise's (MNE) parent company and one of its subsidiaries to grant the subsidiary exclusive rights to produce and market a product and, if circumstances warrant, to pursue the necessary research and development (R&D) activity. As a result of such agreements, the firm generally acquires greater managerial autonomy because it has in fact become the international centre for a product (Poynter and Rugman, 1982).

The subsidiary's autonomy is generally increased by such an agreement but the extent of the greater autonomy will vary depending on a number of factors: whether the subsidiary's managers are responsible for a whole product line, a limited number of products or a single product;

whether they are responsible for the product's entire production process, the manufacturing of product components or for the assembly of only those parts in which the subsidiary is most competitive; whether their mandate truly covers the world market or is limited to certain regions (in which case it becomes a regional rather than a world mandate); whether or not they are obliged to use the parent company's distribution channels, etc.

In short, a WPM is granted within the framework of a firm's rationalisation activities. The managers are then able to run the subsidiary on the basis of a specialisation of its operations while giving them greater leeway within this specialisation.

Stating the Problem

Governments may set up a framework for, and even stimulate, the product rationalisation effort. These governmental actions are materialised by the formulation of an industrial policy intended for all production units regardless of their mode of ownership. Thus, corporations can be interested in using the product mandate in order to achieve various objectives such as increasing a subsidiary's profitability by having it specialise in the production of one or more products of the MNE's total product range, increasing productivity and reducing average unit cost. As a corollary effect, the subsidiary would have greater autonomy, and when appropriate, its managers could initiate the expansion of the subsidiary's activities. In principle, the parent company would no longer be expected to control its subsidiary's exports. Finally, the subsidiary would benefit from the marketing effort and the access to distribution channels of the parent company and sister subsidiaries in international markets.[1]

Advocates of WPMs in Canada point to the long-term gains that could be drawn from such arrangements. They argue that these mandates could generate jobs both directly and, indirectly, through a bandwagon effect on local firms. In this view, the subsidiaries would obviously be stimulated to get more supplies from Canadian firms. The proponents of mandates usually call for freer international trade, believing that, with the lowering of tariff and nontariff barriers and increased international trade, Canada's position in the world economy would be strengthened. According to this school of thought, an expanded market would result in increased Canadian exports and an improved balance of payments for Canada. The greater economic integration would take advantage of the

United States' technological lead and stimulate economic growth through specialised production.[2] Wolf (1983) contends that specialisation could even be expected to increase the importance of Canadian R&D activity which would, in turn, have positive effects on Canada's balance of payments. He reasons that the increased R&D activity would lower technological imports and would lead to the development of new processes rendering Canadian products more competitive on world markets.

In these matters, it does seem that government has a role to play, especially since we are told that it has the will to obtain WPMs for Canadian subsidiaries. Canadian industrial policy might be helpful if it does not come into conflict with MNEs' desire for free international trade. In any case, fostering a better spirit of cooperation between government and private enterprise would be a step in the right direction.[3]

But, taking the transnational firm as a whole, where do its interests lie on that matter? Their interests could be motivated by the will to increase the profitability of certain subsidiaries. In that case, this type of agreement will not only be compatible with the corporation's global objectives but might also produce short-term dividends since the subsidiary will become more productive. The corporation will also reap the benefits associated with managing a small flexible organisation as contrasted to a large rigid structure (Rutenberg, 1981). The dynamic company will find advantages in the subsidiary's capacity for product innovation, conception and adaptation following the granting of the mandate (Crookell and Caliendo, 1980). Tensions between government and business will be alleviated since, by granting these mandates, multinational corporations demonstrate their willingness to expand their production activity in Canada. The corporation's image will be enhanced, personnel recruitment and product marketing facilitated and relations with suppliers improved because, assured of long-term contracts, they will be encouraged to improve product quality, and make use of the possible economies of scale (Etemad, 1983).

But, if these mandates are so obviously advantageous to the subsidiaries, to the Canadian governments and to the parent companies of multinational firms, the question then arises: How can one explain that there are not more of them? Is the granting of world mandates easily harmonious with the functioning of an MNE whose management is sufficiently centralised to constitute a single entity especially when the management of financial resources is concerned? Does the MNE face a serious risk in becoming dependent on a single supply source? Might exclusive world distribution rights cause conflicts among the corporation's various subsidiaries, obliging the head office to resolve these conflicts? Would the granting of a mandate threaten the corporation's competitiveness for the mandated product? Will mandates hamper or facilitate communication within the firms? Will hierarchical relations be altered in favour of the subsidiary and to the detriment of the head office? Are all products equally suitable for the granting of mandates?

Apparently, the MNE's openness to requests for mandates formulated by subsidiary managers is not a foregone conclusion. Thus, Etemad (1983) may be right to state that:

> The parent company has very little incentive to grant a WPM to any subsidiary. Doing so defeats the very basic feature of MNEs — that is, flexibility and freedom of choice with regard to source and location of supplies. (p. 117)

To the authors' knowledge, there are only two studies which permitted them to obtain empirical data on the importance and the nature of product mandates in Canada (i.e. the 1980 Science Council of Canada study and the 1980 Ontario Ministry of Industry and Tourism study). The telephone interview methodology employed in the latter study, which usually limits the quantity of information one can hope to obtain, restricted the depth and the scope of the study.

Based on the findings of these two studies, mandated firms seem to exhibit three predominant characteristics: they have technologically advanced production facilities; they are small in size (although a few large corporations have obtained mandates); and they enjoy a dominant market share. In addition, the studies revealed that these firms believe that governmental pressures constitute an important and perhaps decisive factor in the acquisition of mandates. This government action may take various forms:

> (1) the establishment of a favourable climate characterised by consultation and cooperation rather than governmental regulations. From management's viewpoint, this climate should extend to financial aid, subsidies, tax incentives especially earmarked for research.
>
> (2) although world mandates are only conceivable in a context of free trade, the formulation of an appropriate governmental procurement policy can help in obtaining mandates. Concerning this, Wolf (1983, p. 106) says: 'Trade barriers attributable to government procurement policies may assist in the implementation of a world product mandating strategy'.[4]
>
> (3) the rapid depreciation of fixed assets necessary for the granting

or obtaining of the mandate and a tax reduction on profits coming from exports to third parties.
(4) the will to take full advantage of imported technology. Certain restrictive attitudes sometimes show up in international transfers of technology: export restriction, taxation of supply sources integrated in the MNE's network, etc.

When considering the international transfer of technology, the Science Council of Canada would represent the nationalist position and the Economic Council of Canada (1983), the internationalist position. The former considers the following as a possibility: employment may not increase in proportion to the government's effort; current account balances may show a chronic deficit, reflecting structural weaknesses in the Canadian economy; if technology is in large part acquired only through transfer mechanisms of the MNE the result may be an absence of research at the subsidiary level, an inadequate diffusion of technology and a stunting of the Canadian economy's technological capacity; the price of products or techniques imported from the MNE's other units may be exorbitant while the product's local content may prove to be weak; and there may be export limits since many subsidiaries obtain only national mandates, i.e. good only for the Canadian market (Science Council of Canada, 1979; Britton and Gilmour, 1978).

On the other hand, a recent study by the Economic Council of Canada asserts that a large number of Canadian firms obtain technology by imitation and that those companies acquiring technology from their parent companies have an advantage over firms developing their own technology. The advantage would seem to reside in the possibility of reducing the interval between the innovation's introduction elsewhere and its adoption and diffusion in Canada. But even by acquiring new technology, this interval still seems surprisingly long.

Procedure

The research undertaken had two main objectives:

(1) to define the universe of world or regional mandates existing in subsidiaries of foreign companies operating in Quebec, their number, their nature and their scope;
(2) to determine, from a more normative point of view, what conditions would favour the acquisition of a greater number of mandates.

The authors chose to concentrate their research on Quebec firms for several reasons. First of all, there already exists some information on mandates in Ontario. Second, data gathered in Quebec would be a useful complement to the Ontario study. Furthermore, since most of Canada's manufacturing industry is concentrated in these two provinces, the combined data would give a more representative picture of the importance of these mandates in the country as a whole, than otherwise.

With this goal in mind, the authors obtained from Quebec's Centre for Industrial Research[5] a list of 759 firms (both Canadian and subsidiaries of foreign companies), meeting the following criteria:

(1) they carried out production activities in Quebec;
(2) they pursued R&D activity (R&D was very broadly defined so as to include firms with even only one R&D technician);
(3) they exported to markets outside of Canada.

The 'nationality' of parent companies was checked against a Statistics Canada document (Statistics Canada, 1984) based on data drawn from the CALURA (Corporations and Labour Unions Returns Act) report. Subsidiaries with majority control by foreign parent companies were then selected; this supplementary criterion resulted in the choice of 151 firms out of the original list of 759 firms. Further investigation revealed that 16 of these firms were actually under Canadian control, one had shut down and another had no manufacturing operations in Quebec. These firms were then removed from the list, leaving a population of 133 firms whose head office locations were situated in the following pattern: 93 in the United States, 11 in the United Kingdom, 9 in France, 5 in the Federal Republic of Germany, 4 in Switzerland, 3 in the Netherlands, 2 in Sweden, 2 in Luxembourg and one each in Japan, Saudi Arabia, Finland and Bermuda.

The next step involved establishing telephone contact with the firms located in Montreal's metropolitan area (86 of the 133 selected) in order to find out which held mandates and to encourage them to respond to the questionnaire. Thirty of the 86 confirmed that they did hold a regional or world mandate, and 40 said that they held no such mandate. In the other sixteen, the authors were unable to reach anyone capable of answering their questions. The firms thus contacted were requested to answer the questionnaire (pretested by way of long interviews with a number of mandated firms), whether or not they held mandates.

Since certain multinational firms had more than one subsidiary in Quebec, 126 questionnaires were sent out by mail. The recipients (usually the firm's chief executive) were asked to return the completed question-naire by mail. A month after sending out the questionnaires, follow-up letters were forwarded to the same persons. A few weeks later, a telephone reminder was made to the seven mandated firms that were among those who were initially contacted by telephone. This resulted in only two additional responses.

In sum, 42 returned questionnaires were collected resulting in a response rate of 33.3 per cent. Of this number, twelve firms (mostly non-mandated) decided, for various reasons, not to complete the ques-tionnaire. The authors were therefore left with 30 properly completed questionnaires from 30 firms, of which twenty-two are subsidiaries of American corporations and three are British subsidiaries.

Results Obtained

The Number of Mandates

Of the 30 respondents, 19 are mandated firms while eleven are not. These 19 mandated firms hold a total of 21 world and 13 regional mandates which are currently in force.[6] We also have information on eight previously held mandates which have now lapsed (6 world, 2 regional). Our entire universe is thus composed of 42 product mandates (see Table 10.1). When considering the number of mandates, two large sectors of activity stand out clearly from the others in the sample: more than three-quarters of the mandated firms belong either to the electrical and elec-tronic industries or to the machinery industry.

As the authors have already mentioned, product mandates are nothing new. In fact, the oldest mandate can be traced all the way back to 1884 and nine others were granted between 15 and 45 years ago. In contrast, nine mandates originated between 1970 and 1974, 15 between 1975 and 1979 and six between 1980 and 1984. Unfortunately, the authors were not given the date of origin for the two remaining mandates. As can be seen by this more recent series of dates, the mandate seems to be an old type of agreement that has only recently been rediscovered.

Half of the respondents state that they have never made any attempt to acquire a world mandate. Furthermore, when asked whether they knew if their parent company had ever granted product mandates elsewhere, 17 out of 30 firms replied negatively. For those who had information on this subject, the number of firms whose parent company had not granted mandates elsewhere was roughly the same as the number of firms affirming the existence of such mandates (in other subsidiaries of the same MNE). Therefore, it seems difficult to find any systematic predisposition of MNEs upon which Quebec firms might count to obtain more mandates.

Finally, for two-thirds of the respondents, the role of corporate headquarters was judged important or decisive in the search for a mandate; while the subsidiary's role was considered even more important than that of the headquarters. However, the role of the provincial government was judged irrelevant by 18 firms, while only 14 considered that the federal government's contribution in such a search was unimportant. Rarely have the authors' questions achieved such unanimity. Given that half of the firms consider mandates as 'very important' the amazing thing is that they did not undertake any steps to obtain them.

Table 10.1: Current and Terminated Mandates

Studied:	World:	21	
	Regional:	13	
	Total:	34	
Unstudied:	World:	7	
	Regional:	3	
	Total:	10	
			Total: 44
Terminated mandates:			
	World:	6	
	Regional:	2	
	Total:	8	
			Total: 8
			All mandates: 52

The Nature of the Mandates

Of the 34 mandates currently in force 11 firms hold only one, 3 firms hold two, 3 firms hold three and 2 firms hold four (see Table 10.2). Eight of the mandated products have been in existence for at most 5 years, eight for 6 to 10 years, and 13 for 11 years or more. (Not all of the respondents answered this question). Thus, it appears that mandates currently in force concern mostly relatively old products, that have reached some level of maturity. Mandated products are twice as likely to be capital and industrial goods as consumer goods.

When considering both lapsed mandates and those still in force, one finds that, although the mandated products are relatively old, the number of products having undergone important modifications since being introduced on the market is slightly higher than that of products having been only superficially modified. Similarly, there is an almost equal number of products for which the basic technology has been greatly modified to those whose technology has been only slightly modified. In this regard, one notes that the newer or younger a product is the more it tends to go through important modifications and the more its technological base can change significantly. This seems to conform with the product life cycle framework.

Table 10.2: Total Number of Mandates

Number of mandates (Current)	Number of companies	Total
1 mandate	10	10
2 mandates	3	6
3 mandates	2	6
4 mandates	3	12
Total of current mandates studied		34
(Terminated)		
1 mandate	2	2
3 mandates	2	6
Total of terminated mandates studied		8
Total of mandates studied		42
Total of nonrespondent mandated companies		10
Total of all mandates		52

An evaluation of the state of competition for the mandated firms reveals some rather interesting facts. For 20 per cent of the mandates, respondents indicate that they either have only one or two competitors in Canada or none at all; 30 per cent have at most only five competitors on world markets and 80 per cent have 15 competitors at most. In general, the Canadian and American markets are important while the markets of Europe and the rest of the world are much less significant. The most frequent situation that comes up is that more than half of the sales are made on the Canadian market. When considering market share, the mandated products often claim more than half of the entire Canadian market but a much smaller share of the American market (usually less than 10 per cent). Finally, on the subject of government procurement, almost half of the firms replying to the question indicated that governments make up from 25 per cent to 100 per cent of their sales, while only one-quarter said they had no activity at all in this regard.

How do the subsidiaries themselves evaluate the effects of these mandates? First, as regards the subsidiary's margin of autonomy, an equal number of firms judge that a mandate gives greater access to foreign markets as those who feel a mandate has little or no effect on this matter.

In most cases, the acquisition of a mandate did not have any significant effect on the subsidiary's general import or purchasing policies, nor did it clearly modify the subsidiary's autonomy in R&D or make important differences in investment policies. These results can scarcely be considered a confirmation of the hypothesis that world or regional mandates will lead to an increase in the Canadian subsidiary's margin of autonomy. In any case, the mandated subsidiaries concerned do not themselves seem convinced of this outcome.

Most mandated firms replying to the relevant question noted no change in their relations with the federal or provincial governments after the acquisition of a mandate. A slightly higher number of respondents felt that obtaining a mandate brought no change in their relations with other sister subsidiaries than felt that a mandate did make a difference. The latter felt that the change was for the better.

The authors also tried to ascertain whether obtaining a mandate would effect changes in the supply sources for the mandated product or products. On the whole, the answer would seem to be negative. Most respondents affirm that mandates have little effect on: (i) intra-firm trade, (ii) variations in the imports coming from the US or Europe, and (iii) variations in the purchases from Canadian or Quebec subsidiaries or from other MNEs. Any change noted would at most be a slight increase in purchases from local firms.

Finally, for reasons already mentioned, we also tried to find out whether or not the R&D program is changed by the acquisition of one or several mandates. Almost three times as many respondents believe that change does occur as feel that it does not. But when the attempt is made to determine what specific aspect of the R&D program has been modified, the issue becomes cloudy. It seems that there is little, if any, intensification of efforts to develop new technical processes or new products. Among the respondents affirming a change in R&D activity after having obtained mandates, almost as many feel their efforts to adapt technologies or products are reduced as feel they are increased. The same observation is valid as regards the intensification of quality control activity. And, when firms are asked to indicate what they consider the two most significant changes, their responses reveal no discernible trend.

The Economic Impact of Mandates

What place do currently mandated products occupy in Quebec's economy? The total sales figure for the 24 products on which we have information stands at 1.455 billion dollars. Providing an adequate margin to account for mandates on which data are not available, the authors have estimated that mandates currently in force represent about 3 per cent of Quebec's total value of manufacturing shipments and about 1.5 per cent of the total worldwide sales of the multinational corporations that granted mandates to their subsidiaries in Quebec.

Approximately three-fifths of the respondents represent subsidiaries established in Quebec directly by the parent company, while another fifth represent subsidiaries acquired by purchase or takeover of existing firms. Two-thirds of the respondents have been operating in Quebec for more than ten years.

Although MNEs do have a strong impact on the findings, the study's sample also includes small to medium sized companies. Seven out of the 30 firms have fewer than 50 employees in Quebec, 17 fewer than 300, while half of the respondents employ fewer than 500 people. In contrast, six firms (only four of which are mandated) have more than 1,000 employees in Quebec. These four firms alone represent almost 80 per cent of total employment of Quebec's mandated firms. Their employment situation is not very different for Canada as a whole. A little less than half of the respondents are subsidiaries of so-called small MNEs as they employ fewer than 5,000 people worldwide.

Around one-third of the respondents have sales of less than five million dollars in Quebec, less than ten million dollars in Canada and less than 50 million dollars worldwide; and the R&D efforts of a majority of them are between 0 and 4 per cent of sales, which is considered weak or average.

Conditions Favourable in Obtaining Mandates

The universe of product mandates is not yet very well developed in Quebec. The authors attempted to ascertain what conditions could favour the acquisition of a greater number of mandates by Quebec subsidiaries. In so doing, respondents were asked to identify: (i) the factors which facilitated (or could potentially facilitate) the acquisition of more mandates and (ii) the factors which might have favoured (or could potentially favour) Canadian subsidiaries against sister subsidiaries in acquiring mandates. They were also asked to rank a certain number of variables explaining refusals of requests for mandates.

A rather clear consensus emerges regarding the importance of the following factors: the desire to rationalise the firm's activities; the intensification of international competition; and the exploitation of Canada's comparative advantages. A similar consensus also appears as regard the negligible importance of the following factors: decline in the competitive capacity of Canadian operations as perceived by the MNE;

political pressures; and government procurement policies. In contrast, no consensus emerges as to the effect of freer trade between Canada and the United States, the success of previous mandates and the importance of the Canadian market for a particular product.

Similarly, when attempting to discover how certain factors might have favoured (or could favour) Canadian subsidiaries over those in other countries, the authors obtained a clear consensus on the importance of only two factors: the dynamic nature of the Canadian subsidiary and the quality of its human resources. The authors also obtained a clear consensus on the negligible importance of the following distinctive features of the Canadian subsidiary: the will to improve relations with the political authorities from Canada and Quebec; the will to reduce political risks; and the will to affect policies concerning government procurement. No consensus emerged as to the role of taxation; government subsidies for R&D activity; the importance of the Canadian market; the abundance of Canada's raw materials; the expansion of free trade; and the will to improve the Canadian company's image.

The breakdown of answers relating to the reasons cited for refusing mandates to Quebec subsidiaries does not give rise to very many motives applicable to the entire population of firms. It is obvious that the answers do not clearly consider the possibility that the liberalisation of trade between Canada and the United States might be a factor in such refusals. Likewise, a rather strong majority of respondents pointed to several important factors explaining mandate refusals to Quebec subsidiaries: the weight of Quebec and Canada's taxation systems, Quebec's political context and the negative perception of Quebec's labour climate. Yet, there was no precise indication as to how these factors could explain mandate refusals.

However, when questions were raised on variables related to the multinational itself rather than to the environment, the consensus dissolved. Opinions were divided as to the role of certain factors as causes of refusal, factors such as: the problem of reconciling the mandate's decentralising effect with the corporation's centralised management; the MNE's organisational structure; the refusal of dependency on a single subsidiary for the manufacturing of one or several products; the will of the MNE's managers to maintain their negotiatory power; or union pressures exerted in the head office's country.

Division of Tasks within the Multinational

This study on WPMs has also provided some interesting spin-off information as to the role and functioning of Quebec subsidiaries within their multinational firm's structure.

Organisation of the Firm's R&D Function and the Origin of the Technology used. About one-fifth of our respondents currently employ no R&D scientist, engineer or technician; in other words, they do not carry out any R&D. But what is perhaps more surprising is that more than half of the respondents have no more than five scientists and engineers and no more than five R&D technicians in their Quebec subsidiaries. In a series of questions on R&D, more than half the respondents, and sometimes much more than half, evaluated as important or very important the following aspects of their R&D programs: technology development; conception and development of new products; quality control; adaptation of technologies and products; and technical services. Since all these R&D functions were rated as important or very important, one should be very cautious in interpreting these findings.

The need for caution is all the more apparent when the subsidiaries, in response to a question on the origin of their technology, list in order of decreasing importance: the parent company; the Canadian subsidiary; Canadian sources other than sister subsidiaries; non-Canadian subsidiaries; Canadian companies established abroad (only occasionally significant). It should be noted that 24 respondents out of 30 rate the parent company's role in this matter as strong, very strong and even decisive.

Two-thirds of the respondents applied for patents in Canada and in the parent company's country (usually the United States as indicated earlier). Half of the respondents also obtain them elsewhere in the world. Federal government initiatives receive the full support from about half of the respondents; those of the provincial government, the support of one-third. Almost two-thirds of the respondents have already been recipients of government subsidies, most often for the development of new products and technologies. One-third of the respondents have also benefited from subsidies for the expansion and/or modernisation of their production facilities, whether for mandated products or for their other products.

Concerning R&D carried out in Canada, two-thirds of Quebec subsidiaries replying to the question indicate that this research is done principally or totally in Quebec. For the firms in our sample, no trend emerges in the MNE's localisation of R&D functions. Contrary to the widely held opinion, these functions are not often centralised in the parent company.

Other Variables of the Organisation. Two-thirds of the MNEs to which

Quebec subsidiaries belong have undertaken major reorganisation of their operations in the last five years. Such reorganisations resulted as often in a decentralisation of activities as in greater centralisation.

In response to the question: 'Are you authorised to compete with the head office or other subsidiaries in order to obtain a sale?', more than half the respondents say they are never authorised to do this or that they might be, but only in certain cases.

As to who makes investment decisions (whether for expansion and/or modernisation), such decisions are made jointly by the parent company and the subsidiary or by the parent company alone. Only very exceptionally would a subsidiary be authorised to make this decision alone. Decisions concerning market delimitation are also mostly made jointly, but, subsidiaries are more often empowered to make these decisions on their own than in the case of investment. Similarly, subsidiaries seem to enjoy a broader margin of autonomy when introducing a new product on the market: half of the respondents consider that this kind of decision is mainly the domain of the subsidiary's management; the other half said that the decision is taken either in concert with the parent company's management or by the parent company's management alone.

Summary and Conclusions

(1) There does not seem to exist on the part of the multinational any systematic predisposition favouring the granting of WPMs.

(2) The role of government is considered negligible in the acquisition of mandates. It is rather the roles of the head office and the subsidiary that are judged important and even decisive.

(3) Most mandates currently in force involve relatively old products, with a strong bias toward capital (or industrial) goods as compared to consumer products.

(4) By taking the number of producers in Canada and in the rest of the world, it appears clear that mandates tend to be found on markets with only a small number of competitors.

(5) When dealing with mandates, the markets which really count are those of the United States and Canada. Only exceptionally are other world markets of any consequence.

(6) This study did not confirm the hypothesis that the acquisition of a world or regional mandate resulted in increased autonomy for the Canadian subsidiary.

(7) As concerns the conditions favourable to the acquisition of

mandates, the following factors have been judged important: the desire to rationalise the MNEs' activities; the intensification of international competition; and the exploitation of Canada's comparative advantages. In contrast, political pressures, government procurement policies and the desire to enhance a declining subsidiary's competitive stance seem to have negligible importance.

(8) When competing for mandates with sister subsidiaries, it seems that the subsidiary from Quebec and Canada can count only on its own dynamic nature and on the quality of its human resources. The will to improve relations with political authorities from Quebec; the will to reduce political risks; and the role of government procurement policies, are not significant trump cards for the Canadian subsidiary.

Although the findings are not as always as clear as one would have wished, certain fairly strong points do emerge: the absence of any favourable predisposition of multinationals for the granting of mandates; the fact that, all things considered, it is easier to obtain mandates for older products and technologies than for new products and processes which have not gone through a long market test; the restrictions on the Quebec subsidiary's decision-making powers by virtue of the division of tasks within the MNE; and the experience of respondents regarding the supposed tendency of mandates to increase the subsidiary's autonomy. These points incite us to be cautious in evaluating the potential of WPMs as instruments for restructuring Canada's economy on the basis of greater specialisation of the subsidiaries of foreign companies.

Notes

1. Etemad (1982) discusses the advantages of mandates as regards the firm.
2. See on this point Crookell and Caliendo (1980).
3. Etemad (1983) describes the implications of a WPM as viewed by the mandated subsidiary's host country.
4. One should not think that this point of view receives the unanimous support of all those having expressed their opinion on this question. Quite the contrary, several voices have been raised in the Senate hearings to oppose any use of procurement policy which might affect the competitive character of the firm (See Standing Senate Committee on Foreign Relations, 1982).
5. We would like to thank Mr Richard Beaudry from the Centre for having so kindly (and, above all, so promptly) forwarded this directory to us.
6. Our telephone contacts revealed the existence of seven other world mandates and three other regional mandates. However, the firms in question did not respond to our requests for information, and were not counted in this study.

References

Advisory Committee on Global Product Mandating (1980) *The Report of the Advisory Committee on Global Product Mandating*, Ontario Ministry of Industry and Tourism, Toronto, December

Britton, J.N.H. and Gilmour, J. (1978) *The Weakest Link*, Science Council of Canada, Background Study no. 43, Supply and Services Canada, Ottawa

Crookell, H. and Caliendo, J. (1980) 'Competitiveness and the Structure of Secondary Industry', *Business Quarterly*, vol. 45, no. 3, pp. 58–64

Economic Council of Canada (1983) *The Bottom Line: Technology, Trade and Income Growth*, Supply and Services Canada, Ottawa

Etemad, H. (1982) 'World Product Mandating in Perspective' in *Proceedings of the Annual Conference of the Administrative Sciences Association of Canada, International Business Division (ASAC)*, vol. 3, Part 8, Ottawa, pp. 107–19

Etemad, H. (1983) 'World Product Mandates' in A.M. Rugman (ed.), *Multinationals and Technology Transfer: The Canadian Experience*, Praeger, New York, pp. 108–25

Poynter, T.A. and Rugman, A.M. (1982) 'World Product Mandates: How Will Multinationals Respond?', *Business Quarterly*, vol. 47, no. 3, pp. 54–61

Rutenberg, D. (1981) 'World Product Mandating', unpublished paper presented at the Financial Times–Corpus CP Conference on World Product Mandates, Toronto, October 5–6

Science Council of Canada (1979) *Forging the Links: A Technology Policy for Canada*, Science Council of Canada Report no. 29, Supply and Services Canada, Ottawa

Science Council of Canada (1980) *Multinationals and Industrial Strategy: The Role of World Product Mandates*, Science Council of Canada, Supply and Services Canada, Ottawa

Standing Senate Committee on Foreign Relations (1982) *Canada-United States Relations: Canada's Trade Relations with the United States*, vol. 3, Supply and Services Canada, Ottawa

Statistics Canada (1984) *Inter-Corporate Ownership 1982*, Supply and Services Canada, Ottawa

Wolf, B.M. (1983) 'World Product Mandates and Freer Canada-United States Trade' in A.M. Rugman (ed.), *Multinationals and Technology Transfer: The Canadian Experience*, Praeger, New York, pp. 91–107

11 INVENTIVE ACTIVITY IN MNEs AND THEIR WORLD PRODUCT MANDATED SUBSIDIARIES[1]

Hamid Etemad and Louise Séguin Dulude

Introduction

To enhance the competitiveness and performance level of Canada's manufacturing sector, several authors and institutions have proposed various solutions. For example, in a controversial publication entitled *The Weakest Link*, Britton and Gilmour (1978)[2] suggested that the root of most problems in the manufacturing sector could be traced to its lack, or very low levels, of research and development (R&D). Low levels of R&D in Canada, as compared to other industrialised nations, have been a cause for concern for some time. To remedy this situation, or at least to encourage R&D in Canada, the federal government has consistently provided generous R&D assistance in terms of tax exemptions, grants, contracts, and subsidies (Hewitt, 1980; Howe and McFetridge, 1976; McFetridge, 1977; and McFetridge and Warda, 1983). Unfortunately, the evidence is not entirely clear as to the effectiveness of such supports (Lacroix and Séguin Dulude, 1983).

In a highly provocative proposal, the Science Council of Canada (1980) envisioned world product mandates (WPMs) for subsidiaries of multinational enterprises (MNEs) as essential elements of Canada's industrial strategy. There were only a handful of known successful WPMs by 1980. In all of these cases, a WPM operation had been established and a substantial level of R&D activity was already in progress. These cases may have prompted the notion that a transformation from 'miniature replica' and 'truncated' subsidiary operations to a WPM could automatically lead to more R&D activity and hence resolve Canada's R&D deficiencies. Although there are strong opinions along the spectrum, a central question still remains: whether a WPM necessitates high R&D, or at least enhances R&D? There is no substantive empirical evidence in favour of either position.

Therefore, the primary objective of this chapter is to provide an objective view on this question by empirically studying the R&D and patenting characteristics of WPM operations in Canada. This chapter will present:

(1) A background discussion on WPMs related to R&D and the patenting relationship;
(2) A perspective on the forces and pressures that influence the distribution of R&D facilities in MNEs, ranging from highly concentrated cases centralised at corporate headquarters, to decentralised R&D facilities dispersed at subsidiary level;
(3) A statistical analysis of Canadian patent data,[3] supplemented by other publicly available information in order to provide an empirical perspective on the R&D and patenting characteristics of WPM operations in Canada.

Following a discussion of the results, the highlights and the policy implications of the study are presented in the concluding remarks.

Interaction between WPM Production and Associated R&D and Patents

As WPM operations differ from a typical subsidiary's operations, its salient R&D and patenting features must be established at the outset. Specifically:

● Is it necessary that the WPM subsidiary has its own R&D facilities?
● Is it necessary that the WPM subsidiary hold all patents and other associated rights to the innovative aspects of the product, processes, or technologies involved?
● Could WPM related decisions (e.g. production, logistics, etc.) be successfully made at the local level, while the involved product concepts, processes, technologies or innovations are developed elsewhere (e.g. headquarters) and patents are held by yet others than the WPM subsidiary itself (e.g. another subsidiary or headquarters)?

Most subsidiaries of MNEs have successfully started their operations based on the R&D results of the headquarters and/or other subsidiaries. This includes almost all truncated and replica operations. There is no logical reason stopping a WPM subsidiary from starting to operate successfully as a licensee, provided that it can secure access to the ongoing technological improvements through a binding contractual agreement similar to that of a licensee. As a matter of practical convenience, however, it is easier and more efficient (Teece, 1981) for the WPM subsidiary to be in full control of the innovative aspects of its mandated product(s) and associated technology or technologies. But the subsidiary need not start off with the control over its own technology. New technology and innovation are essential to preserve the mandate holder's comparative advantage. Policing and monitoring of such advantages are then necessary to avoid any undue erosion. This can be more easily and efficiently controlled internally by the WPM subsidiary. One way to obtain such control is by patenting.

For preserving the comparative advantage over time (e.g. dynamic comparative advantage) R&D controlled by the subsidiary could be more responsive to market conditions than otherwise. This suggests that WPM operations will be more secure and independent if they have their own R&D facilities and control their patents.

Other traditional arguments in favour of having one's own R&D are not valid for the WPM case. Replication in production and licensing is not a logical occurrence when total world demand is smaller than the capacity of the optimally sized plant. When world demand is larger than the capacity of an optimal plant, either multiple plants in one location or similar optimal plants in multiple locations (and also combinations) could be considered. For multiple locational situations, the headquarters may find it difficult to divorce itself completely from future R&D and patenting aspects of the WPM. Should it do so, either by design or default, the WPM subsidiary becomes *de facto* headquarters for the mandated product and replaces the parent company in that regard. In spite of the possibility and existence of a 'natural' or 'fully developed' mandate — where a subsidiary develops and controls all aspects of its operations (Etemad, 1982a, b) — MNEs are not generally in favour of such developments. One can easily show that WPM production can be successfully carried out, based on a licence for which headquarters, for example, would hold the patents. The outflow of royalties and licence fees for world-scale production may amount to a large sum and may constitute a serious drain on cash flows, but it cannot possibly cripple WPM operations. For many subsidiaries, an arrangement similar to licensing is the rule as opposed to the exception. This is another reason for headquarters to avoid or hold back from initially assigning all rights to a WPM subsidiary.

It may be unnecessary for a WPM subsidiary to have its own R&D facilities or hold all patent and associated rights to the innovative aspects of its operations, but it must be able to decide on the inventive and innovative aspects of its operations. Without such decision-making powers and associated controls, the perceived risk of exposure to remotely located and controlled R&D and patenting activities may not be acceptable. The management of a WPM subsidiary may prefer to minimise or eliminate the exposure to such operational uncertainties as it may entail. Nevertheless, with proper controls in place, WPM operations can go on functioning successfully.

In summary, it is not initially necessary for a WPM subsidiary to own and/or control its R&D and patents as many smaller subsidiaries have successfully made the transition from truncated to WPM operations with very little or no R&D facilities. To ensure functional integrity as well as relevance and competitiveness in the world market over time, a reasonable level of R&D support and control of associated patents and rights become practical and functional necessities in the later stages. It is in this light that we examine descriptively and empirically the factors favouring centralisation and decentralisation of R&D and patenting.

Background on Location of R&D

The presence in many markets has been and still is one of the main features of MNEs. To keep this presence relevant and profitable, MNEs have produced and sold goods and services in these markets. To ensure marketability, the extreme diversity of international markets has generally forced the MNEs to decentralise — even localise — their marketing in most cases. The product(s), being the key feature of a marketing strategy in such markets, is adapted as much as possible to local market needs, environmental requirements and governmental regulations. Although such an extreme decentralisation of the marketing function may not be necessary for some highly advanced industrial goods (e.g. computers), the necessity of adapting consumer goods to local needs in order to obtain long-range success has been very well understood and established (Keegan, 1980, pp. 262–5; Terpstra, 1983, pp. 157–61). Despite the large costs involved in adaptation and coordination, MNEs have responded positively to such market and marketing requirements, mostly through their local 'adaptive R&D' (Creamer, 1976). Although adaptation to local environments through the decentralisation of the R&D and marketing functions has become a *de facto* feature of the MNE's international marketing posture (Terpstra, 1983, pp. 597–9), the picture in manufacturing and general R&D is not as clear.

In fact, the task of comparing and evaluating the respective merits of centralised versus decentralised R&D facilities does not seem to be an easy one. The decisions leading to pure centralisation, pure decentralisation, or some mixed arrangement are influenced by a combination of factors internal and external to a firm, including:

- headquarters' management style;
- organisational culture;
- overall corporate efficiency;
- ease of communication;
- competitive pressures;
- protection and security needs;
- risks involved;
- costs involved;
- economies and/or diseconomies of scale;
- availability of R&D personnel;
- local knowledge;
- local requirements;
- quality of local management;
- host and home countries' demands and pressures;
- time dimension (urgency or lack of it).

These factors will be fully discussed in the following pages. In fact, the completely centralised and fully decentralised cases are the two pure extremes of a spectrum which covers a variety of intermediate combinations. Most real-life situations contain some elements of the two pure extremes. The following pages present some of the documented arguments in favour of centralisation or decentralisation of the R&D facilities.

Arguments in Favour of Decentralisation

In the absence of environmental risks and threats, the following seven arguments favour the decentralisation of R&D facilities:

Upgrading of Local Facilities. MNEs have traditionally transferred technology in order to support or upgrade a subsidiary's operations in response to more advanced competition, or to counter the lower priced imports coming from Third World countries (Creamer, 1976).[4] Such upgrading concerns have resulted in setting up some R&D facilities in the host countries in order to support local operations in two fundamental avenues: R&D activity has mostly been geared to the adaptation of production or process technology to local or market conditions; and in other cases the R&D's main domain has been to redefine and/or to modify products to provide the locally desired quality and quality standard at reasonable costs. In later stages, some of these modest R&D facilities may become fully-fledged R&D centres in response to continued external pressures and local demands (Ronstadt, 1977, 1978).

Taking Advantage of Local Talent, Market Knowledge and Production Skills. The MNE can also take advantage of locally available talent. India is a good example of a country providing highly educated personnel at a fraction of Western costs (Robinson, 1978). Additionally, readily available local market knowledge at the subsidiary level can be used to produce locally desired goods. To avoid losses in time or communication, MNEs have allowed their local R&D facilities to process local information with the technical support of headquarters. In some instances, traditional local products, or locally conceived products have fared well in international markets[5] (Behrman and Fischer, 1980b; Franko, 1976, p. 181).

When basic R&D is conducted in more than one centre, the chance of fruition of innovative ideas leading to the conception of new products or processes increases, as a more diverse R&D personnel brings a wide range of varied ideas and approaches, and different flows of thought from that of any single R&D centre (Thomas, 1983, p. 31). Numerous MNEs view this diversity of ideas (especially when the generation of new ideas has been very slow for the entire industry) as too valuable to ignore.

Increasing Involvement. Although extreme specialisation and concentration of skills in one R&D centre (e.g., headquarters) can theoretically result in superior initial results, it cannot guarantee continued progress and overall efficiency. For example, when new ideas, processes or products are continually brought in from the outside to a subsidiary, local management may not identify with them — in fact the staff may start to resist them and affect them adversely, or may not willingly make the special effort necessary for an innovation's success as compared to when the innovation is locally inspired, developed and supported. Personnel's feelings of attachment and responsibility, combined with their proximity to the local market and knowledge of the local environment in which the innovation is to be introduced, are among the critical and necessary factors for a new innovation's survival, without which a new product or process cannot flourish.[6] Additionally, locally inspired and generated goods or processes can be utilised much more quickly and easily and probably at lower costs than those developed by headquarters. The intensified sense of local responsibility and commitment (combined with local pride and ease of communication, adaptation and implementation) has motivated MNEs to set up local R&D facilities (Hakansson and

Laage-Hellman, 1984, pp. 235-6).

Increasing Specialisation and Division of Labour. To take better advantage of the economics of learning, it might be more efficient for a large and highly diversified MNE to divide the requirements of its R&D activity to fit personnel expertise, production specialisation, etc., of its subsidiaries (Behrman and Wallender, 1976, p. 13; Stobaugh and Telesio, 1983). Such a division would allow for the concentration of similar R&D activity at one centre, which in turn leads to a faster accumulation of learning and experience. The economies of learning due to such concentration may well outweigh the potential costs of decentralisation (or divisionalisation). Although this is a functional division and not a geographical separation, the special environmental requirements of each specialisation may accommodate a geographical separation as well (Terpstra, 1977, p. 390). For example, processes requiring a large amount of natural resources or unskilled labour could be set up in the developing areas; while high technology or processes requiring a large pool of skilled labour may be located in the industrialised countries (Terpstra, 1983, p. 161).

Avoiding Diseconomies of Size. In the case of large MNEs (i.e. most MNEs on the *Fortune* 500 list) and also MNEs in R&D intensive industries, diseconomies of size may cause problems. In such cases, R&D activity and personnel could be logically divided into groups of a more reasonable size in order to sustain a balance between the dynamics of specialisation and group size. Therefore, size may necessitate division and specialisation, and hence force decentralisation, however indirectly. In fact, the scale and the sheer size of some projects are so vast that they exceed the scale and expertise of any single R&D facility. But, for a variety of reasons, including security and ease of communication, only one or a few R&D facilities is or are usually involved (Ronstadt, 1977, pp. 70-3).

Responding to Internal Subsidiary Pressures. Subsidiary staff and management often desire to become fully-fledged members of the MNE — as opposed to being just a marketing, packaging or manufacturing operation. Local management can take pride in having its own complete operations, ranging from basic R&D for product and process innovations at one end to competent and successful marketing activity at the other end of the activity spectrum. In response to such desires, the manager of a subsidiary pressures headquarters to allow him to add R&D

to the range of the subsidiary's activities. Failure to respond to such internally motivated pressures may expose local operations to indirect and costly hazards, i.e. low morale, low productivity, lack of motivation and aggressiveness, etc. (Fuller, 1983, p. 35; Terpstra, 1983, p. 161).

Creating Good Public Relations and Generating Goodwill. By transferring some modest R&D activity to their subsidiaries, MNEs can generate goodwill and improve their public posture to please host country governments (Hewitt, 1980, p. 324; Terpstra, 1983, p. 298). Refusal to transfer any R&D, however, might cause irreparable damage on all fronts or otherwise raise implicitly the actual cost of doing business.

Finally, and in light of all the forces and pressures one would expect to observe increasing trends. But decentralising R&D does not seem to be simple. In reporting the results of a survey, Duerr (1970) summarises the problem very well:

> The research and development function is not one that can be easily decentralized. In spite of their desire to make maximum use of the capabilities of their foreign units, most companies cooperating in the survey make limited use of them for R&D. In spite of pressures to decentralize research activity, most companies carry out the bulk of it in the United States (p. 2).

Arguments in Favour of Centralisation of R&D

In the presence of local environmental uncertainties, competitive pressures and technological threats, a strong position for dealing with such adversities is required. A higher degree of centralisation and control can minimise obstacles in the achievement of such a position. Specifically, seven arguments favour centralisation, and they are mostly in reaction to, or because of, external uncertainties or competitive pressures. They are presented below:

Lacking a Critical Mass. The lack of a critical mass forces a company to keep its R&D staff together in order to benefit from their potential interactions and synergy. For smaller companies or companies with lower levels of R&D this is a practical and economic necessity; although they may have already reached production volumes several times that of optimal plant size. But such companies are not able to respond to the forces and pressures for decentralising R&D, as they find it economically and functionally necessary to keep their R&D at a centralised location (e.g. headquarters). This argument therefore suggests the consideration of the size of R&D activity instead of other measures of size for the centralisation/decentralisation decision (Behrman and Fischer, 1980a, pp. 73–4; Mansfield, Teece and Romeo, 1979, pp. 377–9).

Taking Advantage of Complementarities or Externalities. Conducting R&D in the proximity of other divisions and within a highly sophisticated R&D infrastructure produces advantages that are external to the R&D activity itself. The mere existence of infrastructural support in developed countries (where most MNEs' base operations are located) and the large volume of advanced R&D of others can prevent costly duplication, financial losses and time delays. Being close to others' complementary and competitive R&D in advanced societies may also help to overcome information lags. The centralisation of R&D related information at the headquarters may therefore make decision-making easier and more timely (Ronstadt and Kramer, 1983).

The extreme centralisation in some advanced countries may have drawbacks of its own. Stringent environmental and regulatory provisions of some societies are deterrents. American pharmaceutical companies, for example, are reported to have moved their R&D to other countries because of the Food and Drug Administration's stringent guidelines. Outright cash grants and subsidies of other countries are also externalities which may force movement in the other direction. R&D grants and subsidies of the Canadian government are good examples.

Growing Concern for Security and Protection of Know-how. New ideas leading to new products, new processes, improved technologies, or more efficient operations are among the most valuable assets that a firm can possibly possess. Therefore, it is essential that a firm protects them. The centralisation of basic R&D at one location helps to satisfy concerns for protection, control and security of the assets. Extreme fears of leaks and industrial espionage have transformed the R&D laboratories of high technology firms into small fortresses. For obvious reasons, these have reached their peak in the defence industry. For defence contractors, security and protection of know-how are a prime concern. Any national security related R&D is also required to be done domestically and by personnel with special security clearance. In the light of the large volume of defence related R&D and an increasing level of industrial espionage, both in the areas of commercial and defence related R&D, security minded firms are pushing for exceedingly stringent controls. The centralisation of R&D facilities in one country and preferably in one location makes it easier for implementing the security measures than otherwise.

Increasing Leverage Against External Agents. The need to increase leverage and bargaining power against outside agents (e.g. labour unions, host governments and others outside the MNE) arises from their economically unjustifiable demands or pressures against which the MNE is compelled to fight. The absence of certain sensitive activities like R&D makes the subsidiary and its clientele more dependent on the parent company (which in most cases is beyond the direct reach of host country authorities). This helps to strengthen the MNE's bargaining power and leverage. The benefits derived from increased leverage must however be balanced against the internal side effects of such policies within the subsidiary. For example, it may create a poisonous and hence a costly environment. Not only may such an environment be very damaging internally but it can also cause a deterioration in the external environment, especially in relation to the host country's government. Host country governments have traditionally been sensitive to the parent company's R&D policy and can quickly respond with rewards or penalties,[7] depending upon the merits of the situation, by decreasing or increasing opportunity costs. In fact, R&D policies have been one of the major sources of friction and complaints of developing host nations. These nations appear to feel powerless to retaliate economically when the MNE is perceived to be acting unfairly. Given the uncertain and, at times, unstable business environment in developing countries, MNEs do not usually find it easy to change their pattern of behaviour to provide their developing country subsidiaries with high-powered or sensitive R&D facilities in response to tangible government rewards or penalties[8] (Behrman and Fischer, 1980a, p. 101).

Minimising Miscommunication. Extreme centralisation at a location avoids most — if not all — communication problems. The possibility of personal and oral communication can minimise costly misunderstandings, misinterpretation or time losses. Additionally, privileged and/or commercially valuable information can be conveyed without fear of interception or compromise, and the use of sophisticated measures is unnecessary. Another added advantage is that such ease of communication is bound to enhance coordination and control which in turn means that:

— unnecessary duplications can be avoided;
— ill-conceived projects can be terminated in time; and, finally,
— inadvertent incompatibilities can be corrected.

Minimising Environmental Risks. The fear of unfamiliar environments and the uncertainties they may entail, increases the perceived risk of operations associated with such locations. In contrast, familiarity with the domestic environment and operations results in more favourable conditions. Furthermore, this familiarity gives management a better basis upon which to distinguish between risks associated with environment and those inherent to R&D problems, so that they can decide for or against the further continuation of any particular R&D process. The additional environmental uncertainties of conducting R&D in unfamiliar foreign environments are bound to complicate the R&D's decision processes. These uncertainties compound R&D's inherent, but limited, uncertainties to which the firm is exposed and accustomed.

This is, however, different when MNEs acquire existing national companies with successful R&D facilities. MNEs have in the past kept these facilities in operation since the uncertainty factors have already been discounted and absorbed (Business International, 1971, p. 22; Terpstra, 1983, pp. 304–5).

Achieving Corporate R&D Goals within Specified Time Horizons. Centralised activities stand a higher chance of achieving corporate R&D goals on time or at least at a faster rate. Better communication, coordination and control in centralised R&D provide for a better match between centralised R&D's plan of activities and the corporate goals and time schedules than those of the subsidiary or decentralised activities. Decentralised activities may develop their own priorities, and hence goals, plans and time horizons. These may not necessarily provide the best match with those of the headquarters. Furthermore, corporate evaluation criteria may force local subsidiary management, and by extension decentralised R&D, to respond to shorter horizons, objectives and projects to avoid the adverse effects of budgetary, disciplinary and other corporate control measures (Branscomb, 1983, p. 87; Fuller, 1983, pp. 35–6; Thomas, 1983, p. 32).

The Decision: Centralise, Decentralise, or Combine?

Initially, one tends to expect that a careful trade-off among factors favouring centralisation or decentralisation can lead to a representative weighting of each and easily point to the proper option. Real-life observations point to the contrary.

Environmental conditions — complex and fluid over time — vary dramatically within a country, and from one country to another, as local governmental authorities change their laws and regulations rather frequently in pursuit of their own national goals and objectives which are not necessarily compatible with those of the firm. Cost elements vary from one R&D facility to another for the same firm, and from one firm to another within the same industry. These costs are dependent on many elements including the efficiency of R&D personnel, R&D process, management style, organisational orientation and cultural and environmental conditions.

Depending upon the assessment of the various factors influencing the decision, the perceived degree of importance (or otherwise) of any of the major factors may vary dramatically. Naturally, different assessments lead to different sets of trade-offs, which may lead to varying sets of evaluation criteria. When evaluation criteria are different, even for an identical set of information, the final results are expected to be different.

Furthermore, some dimensions cannot be concretely measured. They include probabilistic and perceptive dimensions such as environmental risks, ease of communication, etc. It must finally be noted that there is no hard evidence to suggest:

— whether different headquarters consider a different or more or less similar list of dimensions and use the same measurements;
— whether the analyses of the same measurements on a nearly identical set of factors leads MNEs of similar profiles to consider comparable countries for R&D locations;
— whether a given company uses identical evaluation criteria for two similar decisions and if the criteria remain static in the short run.

Location of R&D and Patenting Activities: Empirical Analysis and the Results

The above discussion only serves to highlight the complexity of R&D related decisions. The R&D locational decision, in comparison to other critical decisions, seems to possess its own unique complexities and subtleties.

Decisions leading to the protection of R&D results, and the locations for receiving patent and licence revenues present another set of complex but related issues. The analysis of Canadian patent information presented in the next section provides further insight into some of the above issues.

The Data Set

Information on WPM subsidiaries in the provinces of Ontario and Quebec was collected to form the basis of the analysis. Ontario's Ministry of Trade and Tourism provided an initial list of Ontario's WPM subsidiaries. This list was based on telephone interviews. In the case of Quebec, a survey (sponsored by the HEC's Centre for International Business Studies)[9] provided the initial list of WPM subsidiaries. These two lists, after refinement and verification, resulted in 84 subsidiaries in Ontario and Quebec each with at least one mandate. These subsidiaries are related to 80 MNEs. For the 1978–80 period, all patent related information for these subsidiaries and their associated group of MNEs was extracted from 'PATDAT'. 'PATDAT' is an extensive data base on all patents granted by the Government of Canada (called Canadian patents hereafter) and was developed by the Bureau of Intellectual Property of Consumer and Corporate Affairs Canada.

The data base covers patent related information on 12,467 patents granted to 71 parent companies and their foreign and domestic subsidiaries (including Canadian subsidiaries). The remaining nine parent companies had not taken out any Canadian patents over that period. The information related to each patent, among other things, includes the country of residence of the patent holder, and the country of residence of the inventor.

In the absence of supplementary information, two assumptions had to be made. First, all patents granted to an MNE are the results of the MNE's internal R&D and inventive activities; and secondly, 'the country of residence of the inventor' identifies a subsidiary in that country as the origin of the invention. Both assumptions are reasonable and are largely accurate.

Other information in the data base was collected from public sources and includes: employment in Canada, number of scientists and engineers involved in R&D in Canada, MNE's worldwide employment, total number of subsidiaries for each MNE, and total number of countries with subsidiaries for each MNE. (See the detailed list of data sources in the references.)

MNE's Locational Strategies: Extent of Centralisation of R&D Activities and Patent Holdings

The analysis indicates that the concentration of patent holdings by single entities within each MNE is very high. The highest patent holder, called the largest patentee, is not necessarily the headquarters. From the total of 12,467 patents in the sample, 10,028 or 80.4 per cent of all Canadian patents are granted to the largest patentee of each group. In most cases the largest patentee is the headquarters. Headquarters account for 9,581 or 76.9 per cent of total Canadian patents granted to the MNEs in the sample. Even more significant is the heavy concentration of patent holdings at the headquarters' country for patents with inventors residing in the same country. Specifically, 93.8 per cent of patents granted to the 71 headquarters are for inventions originating in the same country. Taken all together, these figures paint a strong picture of the centralisation of R&D and patenting activities at the headquarters or in the home country.

A detailed examination of the top five largest patent holders included in the data sheds further light and is presented in Table 11.1.

These results confirm:

(1) A high concentration of patent holdings at the headquarters of the five MNEs.
(2) A similar but high concentration of R&D activity in the home country (US) of General Electric Corp. and Westinghouse Electric Corp. A relatively large share of R&D and patenting activities at the home country; some 'pooling' of patents to the headquarters for R&D activity and inventions of other countries for IBM Corp. and Xerox Corp.; and finally extensive 'pooling' from other locations to the headquarters for Philips N.V.
(3) The existence of very few key subsidiaries with R&D and patenting activities — all located in the industrialised countries — for the five MNEs.

The reasons for the 'pooling' of patents at headquarters or at very few key subsidiaries are:

(1) complexity of patenting procedures;
(2) availability of legal expertise at headquarters and lack of it at the subsidiaries;
(3) language barriers and lack of local technical expertise;
(4) minimising duplication of costly information and expertise in many locations;
(5) revenue reasons (licensing fees and royalties), and above all;
(6) strategic and planning considerations.[10]

Table 11.1: Distribution of Patents in MNEs with the Highest Number of Patents in the Sample

	Total Number of Patents Granted To:			Total Number of Countries:		
	MNEs	Headquarters	Headquarters for foreign inventions	with subsidiaries active as patentees	as inventors' residence	with foreign subsidiaries
General Electric Corp. (US)	1,136	1,028	6	2 Canada Australia	4	32
Philips N.V. (The Netherlands)	947	839	244	3 US, UK Switzerland	11	69
IBM Corp. (US)	924	920	69	1 Canada	6	33
Westinghouse Electric Corp. (US)	747	716	6	2 Canada Belgium	2	23
Xerox Corp. (US)	711	672	48	1 UK	3	50

Strategic patent planning entails decisions on the location, sequence and timing of patent application. Prudent planning and decision-making in this area require an elaborate data set containing information covering all potential markets on: the patentability of the invention at the location; the degree of legal protection offered by the location; the timing of the introduction of the innovation; and the value of the patent at the given location. When subsidiaries doing R&D fail to collect and hence do not possess such a data set to assist them in making and supporting patenting decisions, or they are not mandated to make such strategically important decisions, headquarters simply 'pools' patents and takes over patenting decisions.

The best example of 'pooling' of subsidiaries' inventions for patenting at headquarters in our data base is the case of Philips N.V. The 'pooling' phenomenon seems to persist for all MNEs in the sample but to a much lesser degree than that of Philips. From the 9,581 patents granted to the 71 headquarters, 598 or 6.2 per cent of them recorded a different country of residence for their inventors than that of the headquarters.

The extent of the 'pooling' phenomenon is limited to 40 MNEs in our sample, and it points to the existence of a systematic policy for patenting. This policy seems to assume a greater degree of importance for large MNEs and especially in technologically oriented sectors.

Diversity of R&D and Patenting Related Characteristics. In spite of a common trend in the centralisation of R&D and patenting activities, in a large number of MNEs, its degree of intensity is rather diverse. Table 11.2 shows selected results that confirm this diversity.

From the total of 71 MNEs in the sample, ten of them are highly active in patent holding. They hold more than 300 patents each. An equal number of MNEs however hold less than 20 patents. The organisational structure of R&D and patenting activities is almost completely centralised at headquarters for the MNEs with more than 300 Canadian patents during the period. For the ten MNEs in this category, 91.4 per cent of all patents are granted to headquarters. This suggests that R&D and patenting strategies are extremely important to these large MNEs — which are also specialised in high technology sectors. In fact these MNEs show the highest concentration ratio of patents at the headquarters (0.93) with the smallest standard deviation (0.073). This is the only group for which the centralisation of patent holding is without any exception at headquarters.

Although the ten MNEs in this group are very large and on average have operating subsidiaries in 43 countries, only one or two subsidiaries

Table 11.2: Concentration of Patents and Total Number of MNEs' Patents

MNEs' Total Number of Patents	300 and over	200-299	100-199	50-99	20-49	1-19
Number of MNEs in the group	10	7	17	13	14	10
MNE's home country						
USA	7	6	15	11	9	7
Europe	3	1	2	2	5	3
Average percentage of patents granted						
to headquarters	91.4	61.0	56.8	57.6	48.7	79.5
to largest patentee	91.4	69.2	66.2	59.3	63.2	89.0
Concentration ratios of patents						
– Headquarters' share						
Average	0.93	0.63	0.59	0.58	0.46	0.89
Standard deviation	(0.07)	(0.33)	(0.35)	(0.30)	(0.37)	(0.23)
– Largest patentee's share						
Average	0.93	0.71	0.69	0.60	0.63	0.94
Standard deviation	(0.07)	(0.23)	(0.25)	(0.28)	(0.22)	(0.09)
Nunber of patentees' countries of residence (excluding headquarters' country)						
Average	1.6	2.3	2.4	1.1	1.2	0.2
Standard deviation	(0.9)	(1.0)	(2.1)	(0.9)	(1.4)	(0.4)
Number of countries in which MNEs have subsidiaries						
Average	43.4	38.1	28.6	27.9	19.3	11.7
Standard deviation	(16.5)	(20.6)	(9.6)	(10.3)	(10.6)	(8.2)

are holders of Canadian patents. The overall picture suggests that these MNEs seem to attach a great deal of importance to the strategic role of technology and innovation as key elements of their international competitiveness, where concerns for efficiency and security favour centralisation at the headquarters (Etemad and Séguin Dulude, 1985).

The 51 MNEs in the mid-categories, from 20 to 299 patents, show strong indications of decentralised patenting. The average ratio of patents granted to headquarters as a percentage of the MNE's total is much lower than of the top category. These MNEs seem to have grown beyond the critical mass and the other centralisation requirements, and have started to take advantage of those factors that favour the decentralisation of their R&D and patent activities. The greater diversity in the concentration ratio of R&D and patents at headquarters suggests that technology and innovation has a lesser strategic importance to these MNEs. In some cases, they have concentrated R&D and patents in a firm different from headquarters. On average, however, they project a more decentralised pattern of R&D and patent activities than the first category (i.e. a somewhat larger number of subsidiaries are involved in R&D and patenting).

For the ten MNEs with less than 20 patents, there are good reasons to believe that the size of their R&D staff is just about or short of the critical mass required for a take-off in inventive activity; hence, they are still highly centralised. These MNEs are either quite small or are in low technology sectors. In the majority of cases, they do not have any active subsidiary in R&D and patenting. On the average 79.5 per cent of patents are granted to the headquarters of the ten MNEs in this category. Small size seems to be the overall explanatory factor. These MNEs are functionally forced to concentrate their R&D and patenting activities in the lowest possible number of locations to minimise the drawback of lack of potential interactions and synergy of their limited R&D staff; and to avoid inaccessibility of the economies of scale in labour and capital in their R&D laboratories. In fact, this is supported by the data.

R&D and Patenting Activities of Canadian WPM Subsidiaries

From the total of 12,467 patents granted to the 71 MNEs, only 222 were granted to Canadian WPM subsidiaries. This represents only 1.8 per cent of the total, and shows the very limited extent of R&D facilities and patenting activities of Canadian WPM subsidiaries. However, the number of patents issued to these MNEs for inventions of Canadian origin is somewhat larger and equals 330. In fact, 'pooling' seems to be a plausible explanation, as the headquarters or other foreign companies have been granted patents in Canada for a number of Canadian inventions. In general, the highly centralised R&D and patenting activities at headquarters or at a very few key subsidiaries do not seem to leave room for a greater possibility for the Canadian subsidiary's participation in those activities. The pattern is not homogeneous, however. There exists an extreme diversity within the 84 WPM subsidiaries.

Based on the R&D and patenting activities of the Canadian WPM subsidiaries and their MNE parents, the 84 WPM subsidiaries fell into four groups:

Group 1. This group consists of 23 WPM subsidiaries with R&D and patenting activities. For this group at least one Canadian patent has been issued to each of the WPM subsidiaries for an invention of Canadian origin (i.e. Canada is the country of residence of the inventor).

Group 2. This group consists of 17 WPM subsidiaries with presumed R&D activity but without patenting activity. For this group at least one Canadian patent has been issued to the parent or some other foreign sister subsidiary for an invention of Canadian origin, but no patent has been issued to any of the WPM subsidiaries.

Group 3. This group consists of 35 Canadian WPM subsidiaries with no R&D and patenting activities in Canada. However, Canadian patents are issued to the parent or other sister subsidiaries, but all are for inventions of non-Canadian origin.

Group 4. This group consists of nine WPM subsidiaries without any R&D and patenting activities. Furthermore, there are no Canadian patents issued to their parent and other foreign or Canadian sister subsidiaries.

Table 11.3 presents a summary of the R&D and patenting characteristics for the 84 WPM subsidiaries and their 80 MNEs. The above division of WPM subsidiaries and Table 11.3 point to a fundamental finding: world product mandating in itself does not seem to generate R&D and patenting activities in the subsidiaries in all cases. In fact, some 40 Canadian WPM subsidiaries are not active in R&D and patenting. What could possibly explain such divergent characteristics? Two rival explanations provide plausible answers.

(1) The MNE's overall strategy in terms of centralisation and decentralisation of R&D and patent holdings. This strategic context directly affects the Canadian WPM subsidiaries' chances for

Table 11.3: R&D and Patenting Characteristics of the WPM Subsidiaries' MNEs

	Group 1[a]	Group 2	Group 3	Group 4
Number of WPMs	23	17	35	9
Locational distribution of WPMs				
Quebec	37%	10%	40%	13%
Ontario	29%	24%	39%	8%
Number of MNEs	23	15	33	9
MNEs' home country				
USA	20	14	22	5
Europe	3	1	11	4
Average number of countries with subsidiaries	31	28	22	10
Average number of patentees' countries with residence (excluding headquarters' country)	2.4	1.5	0.8	0.0
Concentration ratios of patents				
— Headquarters' share				
Average	0.64	0.60	0.67	—
Standard deviation	(0.33)	(0.40)	(0.37)	—
— Largest patentee's share				
Average	0.70	0.69	0.75	—
Standard deviation	(0.23)	(0.29)	(0.28)	—

Note: a. The Quebec and Ontario lists contain respectively 30 and 59 companies. Five WPM subsidiaries are common to both lists.

involvement in R&D and patenting activities.
(2) The structural and behavioural characteristics of the Canadian WPM subsidiaries. Included in these characteristics are the sector of activity, volume of sales, rate of profit and growth rate, as well as production and technology development efficiencies and costs. These characteristics obviously affect the outcome of the decision on whether a WPM subsidiary can be chosen to become a key subsidiary for R&D and patenting activities, or achieving an active role in such activities.

The present data set neither contains definitive information to permit objective discrimination among all factors that are mentioned in the first part of this study, nor does it permit a clear and positive rejection of one of the two above hypotheses. The direction of the variables within the four groups of Canadian WPM subsidiaries, as presented in Table 11.3, however, allows for some general observations.

In general, the R&D and patenting activities of Canadian WPM subsidiaries cannot be entirely explained by the MNE's strategy of centralisation of R&D and patent holdings at headquarters and at a few key subsidiaries. In all four groups, the concentration of patents at headquarters stands at a significantly high ratio, and thus it cannot be the unique factor for explaining the diversity in the R&D and patenting involvement of Canadian WPM subsidiaries. A case by case examination shows that in fact many MNEs have a high degree of centralisation of R&D and patents at headquarters and at a very few key subsidiaries and the Canadian WPM subsidiary does not occupy this key role in most cases. Furthermore, the WPM's own characteristics seem to play a significant role in explaining their R&D and patenting involvement.

The summary of selected characteristics of WPM subsidiaries is presented in Table 11.4. The size and activity level of WPM subsidiaries in Canada appear to be the strong explanatory factor. In fact, literature refers to a relationship between R&D expenditures abroad and the relative size of foreign markets (Behrman and Fischer, 1980b, pp. 57–8; Mansfield, Teece and Romeo, 1979, pp. 376–8; Terpstra, 1983, pp. 304–6). On average, WPM subsidiaries of the first group (with R&D and patent activities) are relatively large subsidiaries. They employ an average of 3,166 employees, and keep a relatively large R&D related staff (33 scientists and engineers); they have also taken out about nine patents for their inventions. Most of them are subsidiaries of large MNEs. Using employment as a comparative measure of their size in the MNEs, these firms perform fairly well. That is, their patents of Canadian origin are, on average, 4.0 per cent of the MNE total while their share of

Table 11.4: Patenting Characteristics of Canadian WPM Subsidiaries

	Group 1[a]	Group 2	Group 3	Group 4
Average number of patents granted to WPMs	6.4	0	0	0
Average number of inventions of Canadian origin among the patents granted to MNEs	8.5	2.6	0	0
Average number of R&D related scientists and engineers in the WPM	33	7	5	2
Average number of patents granted to MNEs	215	226	93	0
Average employment in Canada	3,317	1,249	707	185
Average worldwide employment in the MNEs	100,059	79,867	62,240	22,147
Canadian employment as a percentage of MNEs' total employment	3.3	1.6	1.1	0.8
Canadian origin patents as percentage of MNEs' total patents	4.0	1.2	0	—

Note: a. One WPM subsidiary is excluded in group 1 and another in group 2. See note 1. Two WPM subsidiaries distort the average figures of groups one and two. For this reason, they have been excluded from the table. In the first group, one WPM subsidiary accounts for 37 per cent of the total patents granted to the group. In the second group, on the contrary, one WPM subsidiary is the largest in terms of employment in Canada, yet makes a very limited contribution to the inventive activity.

employment is only 3.2 per cent of the MNE's total employment. The members of this first group appear to be among the key subsidiaries of their MNEs as they are largely involved in R&D and patenting activities. Some of these affiliates have been among the very successful Canadian companies because of their well established natural advantages or unique expertise in their sector of activity. Most members of the first group appear to have capitalised on this expertise or these advantages and have combined them with the WPM's advantage to run a very successful operation. Possession of a WPM may or may not have further enhanced their positions, operation and efficiency. With respect to R&D and patenting, the members of this group of WPM subsidiaries are among Canada's more active corporate citizens and have succeeded in surpassing the average level of inventive activity for Canadian WPM holders — at least in the earlier stages of world product mandating.

In comparing the employment of scientists and engineers with production and administrative employment for the first and second groups of WPM subsidiaries, it is clear that R&D related activities have a higher degree of importance in the first group of subsidiaries. While the general employment level of the first group is only 2.5 times that of the second group, the first group of subsidiaries employs roughly 4.5 times more scientists and engineers than those in the second group. This, combined with higher economies of scale and greater productivity due to synergy, makes it easier to see the much higher R&D involvement of the first group of WPM subsidiaries.

The members of the second group of Canadian WPM subsidiaries are also active in R&D, but they do not hold patents. In fact, the size of their R&D staff is very small. In contrast with the first group, these subsidiaries have small Canadian operations and their share of worldwide employment of the MNEs is also much smaller. In many cases, it seems that their inventive activity is not regular and sustained. Their technical and legal expertise for the processing of patent applications may be generally lacking, and Canada's small domestic market may not have helped the cause of their natural competitive position in the past.

The members of the third group on average are rather small employers and are not active in R&D. Despite the large size of parent MNEs of this group, not a single patent for Canadian inventions is granted to the entire MNE system.

Judging from their employment, most of the MNEs in the third group are large enough to support decentralised R&D and (perhaps) patenting. But there are only some MNEs with rather small global R&D and patenting activities in this group. Requirements of minimum critical mass may have forced highly centralised inventive and patenting activities. This explanation can account for a somewhat higher concentration ratio of patents at headquarters or at the largest patentee of this group. Furthermore, the Canadian operations of the MNEs in the third group are rather small. On average, their subsidiaries employ 749 Canadians. When comparing this group with the first and second groups, one finds many differences but the small size of their operation in Canada could well be responsible for their low R&D involvement.

The fourth group is composed of MNEs which are relatively small in size and whose affiliates are also naturally small. Using the extent of involvement in different countries and the number of subsidiaries as a measure of size indicates that these MNEs are relatively small. These MNEs as a whole have not taken out any Canadian patents and do not seem to have an extensive international patenting activity. Most MNEs of the fourth group and their Canadian subsidiaries seem to be specialised in low technology sectors.

Conclusion

The primary motivation of this chapter was to bring an empirical perspective to the relationship between WPM and inventive activity. On one side of the spectrum, some policymakers and academic writers believe that a WPM and an increase in R&D activity are synonymous. In fact, within this group, some have gone to the extent of suggesting that in-house R&D is a necessary and integral part of a WPM subsidiary's operation, and without it an operation does not qualify and therefore should not be considered as such. It does not satisfy its own operational and economic policy requirements of what is being envisioned as WPM operations.

The other side of the spectrum belongs to the sceptics. For this group, the MNE's strong need for efficiency requires centralised planning, co-ordination and control. These requirements, combined with the strategic importance of inventive activity run very much against the arguments of any subsidiary running its own independent R&D activity. Furthermore, independent or decentralised R&D in one country or in one subsidiary, even with all of its associated benefits (i.e. host government subsidies, research grants, procurement contracts, etc.) reduces an MNE's flexibilities and exposes it to some of the perils that MNEs traditionally have tried to avoid or minimise throughout their operations.

Faced with the diversity, merit and strength of these arguments, this chapter set out to examine the issue objectively and empirically. Unfortunately, the review of literature did not provide a theoretically convincing answer, nor did it show a clear direction for an empirical examination of the relationship or an expectation of the results. Although the findings of this chapter cannot definitively accept or reject one of the above extreme positions, they point to the existence of a direction and a pattern in WPM-R&D relationships, while uncovering some other peripheral, but unexpected, relationships.

To the proponents of the necessity, and hence a strong presence, of R&D and patenting activities in a WPM, the findings of this chapter are rather revealing, while the policy implications of the findings are strikingly disturbing. In sum, a WPM is not categorically synonymous with inventive activity. When a portfolio of patent holdings is used to approximate a WPM's degree of involvement in R&D and patenting activities, the picture is rather bleak. From the total number of patents granted to their parent MNE, sister subsidiaries and other affiliates, the WPM's share of patent holdings amounts to only a meagre 1.78 per cent (i.e. only 222 of the total 12,467 patents). Although a more optimistic interpretation of the facts improves the picture slightly, only 2.6 per cent of the total number of patents show a Canadian origin (330 out of the total of 12,467 patents) and can be presumably attributed to the R&D activity of Canadian WPM subsidiaries. Therefore, it is extremely difficult to conclude categorically that R&D and patenting activities are the joint products, or are necessary ingredients of WPM operations, as a great number of WPM subsidiaries lack such activities. In fact, a detailed examination of 84 WPM operations showed a clear absence of any Canadian inventive activity in more than half of the WPM subsidiaries. This forces one to examine policy implications, and to entertain other positions. From a policy viewpoint, the fact that the WPM has not resulted in any inventive activity in more than half of the cases, is a condemnatory implication for the WPM as a centrepiece of a policy for R&D revitalisation.

The findings of this chapter, however, are consistent with those views suggesting that a WPM can begin to operate successfully without its own R&D facilities, but primarily based on unencumbered access to the inventive and R&D results of its parent and the network of sister subsidiaries and affiliates. Such initial access, combined with other characteristics of WPM operations, may allow the subsidiary to establish its own R&D and patenting activities in time, as its evolution provides and demands for more of them.

On the peripheral relationships, and during the course of research, it became very clear that R&D and patenting activities are highly centralised at the headquarters or at the home country of the MNEs. The size and activity level, however, appear to play an influential role in the pattern of centralisation.

Small MNEs (whose affiliates are also naturally small) faced with the requirements of critical mass and with high risks and costs of R&D, are forced to centralise their R&D and patenting activities. The location of these activities is likely to be at headquarters or in a key subsidiary, i.e. a large active subsidiary in an industrialised country with a large market. Our case by case examination of the data confirms the prevalence of the above pattern.

For the MNEs (and their affiliates) in the moderate size range and activity level (covering the second and third groups of WPM subsidiaries) intervening factors seem to be highly influential. As reviewed above, these factors cover a broad scope of issues ranging from concern for efficiency, costs, local talents, host government pressures, security and protection to management orientation and above all, the policies and procedures set by headquarters for R&D and patenting activities. The present data set does not contain the kind of definitive information which would permit one to discriminate objectively and positively among these factors. The direction of certain variables within the context of the group, however, allowed for the emergence of a mixed picture.

Although the majority of subsidiaries in the second and third groups belong to the mid-range of size and activity, subsidiaries with exceptional profiles defied majority rule and presented interesting cases.

For large MNEs or large affiliates in Canada, a clearer picture developed. These affiliates, in general, enjoy a comparatively advantageous position in the marketplace. Possession of a WPM has further enhanced their position, operation and efficiency. Some of these affiliates would perhaps have been among the very successful Canadian companies in any case because of the natural advantage or unique expertise in their line(s) of activity which they seem to possess. Most members of the first group appear to have capitalised on their expertise and have combined it with the WPM's advantages to run a very successful operation.

Finally, limitations of the data set deter us from making a generalised and yet definitive statement. But based on the strength of associations and directions of this study's indicators, it is not possible to accept the general conclusion that world product mandating would necessarily have a positive effect on R&D and patent holdings. The WPM may have had a stimulative role in R&D but, in the absence of other supportive factors, world product mandating cannot be viewed as the sole instrument of policy for promoting inventive activities.

Notes

1. The authors would like to acknowledge and thank Consumer and Corporate Affairs Canada for its invaluable help in allowing them access to information on patents granted by Canada. The analysis, conclusions and the views expressed in this chapter, however, are solely the authors'; they may not conform and are not related to those of Consumer and Corporate Affairs Canada. Notes of thanks and appreciation are also due to Yves Fortier, Sylvie Laviolette, Andre Levert, Marie Anne Selback and Hassan Taghvai for their assistance in the different phases of research, data collection and computer work.

2. This work of the Science Council was not well received in academic and business circles and was heavily criticised (see Palda, 1979).

3. There is some substantive evidence that patent data are a good measure of inventive activity. Some firms, owing to their own internal policy, or to the requirements of their activity (e.g. defence) do not apply for patents. For these firms, patent statistics do not reflect any R&D activity. Scherer (1965) provides some support for this position:

> In spite of their shortcomings, patent statistics seem to be a useful indicator of inventive activity. They should indicate in which industries the search for new or improved processes is most intense and how this intensity changes over time. They should indicate the relative effort devoted to R&D in different fields and the types of inventions developed. (p. 1098)

4. Of the total R&D budget of US MNEs, 10 per cent was spent abroad. Out of this amount, 89 per cent was allocated to adaptive R&D. This could be viewed as a direct effort in adapting to local conditions the technology that was already developed elsewhere (see Creamer, 1976).

5. India and other countries similar to India seem to be overshadowed by highly industrialised countries. A survey of US MNEs shows that their foreign R&D expenditures are about 10 per cent of domestic R&D expenditures financed from their own funds. The survey reports that more than two-thirds of all foreign R&D of US MNEs is conducted in three countries — Canada, Great Britain and Germany. The remaining one-third is highly concentrated in other Western industrialised countries — France, the Netherlands, Belgium and Italy. Japan constituted about 1 per cent and all developing countries combined accounted for 1.8 per cent in 1966 and 3.3 per cent in 1972. Finally, Canada and the UK have lost some of their share to West Germany in recent years (see Creamer, 1976).

6. The transfer of technology seems to be a two-way street, although the traffic is not equal in both directions. In fact, based on a 1971–72 survey, 25 per cent of foreign affiliates' R&D expenditure was in direct support of the parent companies, which amounted to enriching the MNE's product, process or technology portfolio (see Creamer, 1976).

7. The absolute amount and percentage of these R&D incentives or penalties in financial terms remain still very negligible for the developing world. Incentives, tax breaks, government contracts (e.g., defence contracts) play a substantive role in the Western industrialised countries (e.g. US, UK, France, Germany, and Canada). In 1972 the US government funded 26 to 29 per cent of US MNEs' domestic R&D while host countries only funded 2 per cent of R&D conducted by US affiliates. In terms of absolute size, total US R&D overseas amounts to about 10 per cent of the domestic outlay.

8. McFetridge and Warda's (1983) comparative study of twelve countries' systems of tax incentives and government research contracts and subsidies, shows that Canada offers the most generous package.

9. The authors wish to thank the HEC's Centre for International Business Studies for allowing them access to its information in general, and Professor Bernard Bonin for providing the Quebec list.

10. For a further discussion of 'pooling', see Etemad and Séguin Dulude (1985).

204   *Inventive Activity in MNEs*

References

Behrman, J.N. and Fischer, W.A. (1980a) *Overseas R&D Activities of Transnational Companies*, Oelgeschlager, Gunn and Hain Publishers, Cambridge, Mass.
Behrman, J.N. and Fischer, W.A. (1980b) 'Transnational Corporations: Market Orientations and R&D Abroad', *Columbia Journal of World Business*, vol. 15, no. 3, pp. 55–60 reprinted in V.H. Wortzel and L.H. Wortzel (eds.), (1985) *Strategic Management of Multinational Corporations: The Essentials*, John Wiley and Sons, New York, pp. 375–83
Behrman, J.N. and Wallender, H.W. (1976) *Transfers of Manufacturing Technology within Multinational Enterprises*, Ballinger Publishing Company, Cambridge, Mass.
Branscomb, L.M. (1983) 'Corporate Direction and R&D', in J.K. Brown and L.M. Elvers (eds.), *Research and Development: Key Issues for Management*, Conference Board Report no. 842, The Conference Board, New York, pp. 87–90
Britton, J.H.N. and Gilmour, J. (1978) *The Weakest Link*, Science Council of Canada, Background Study no. 43, Supply and Services Canada, Ottawa
Business International S.A. (1971) *European Business Strategies in the United States, Meeting the Challenge of the World's Largest Market*, Business International, Geneva, September
Creamer, D. (1976) *Overseas Research and Development by United States Multinationals, 1966–1975: Estimates of Expenditures and a Statistical Profile*, The Conference Board, New York
Duerr, M.G. (1970) 'R&D in Multinational Company', *Managing International Business*, National Industrial Conference Board, New York
Etemad, H. (1982a) 'World Product Mandates' in A.M. Rugman (ed.), *Multinationals and Technology Transfer: The Canadian Experience*, Praeger, New York, pp. 108–25
Etemad, H. (1982b) 'World Product Mandating in Perspective' in *Proceedings of the Annual Conference of the Administrative Science Association of Canada, International Business Division (ASAC)*, vol. 3, Part 8, pp. 107–19
Etemad, H. and Séguin Dulude, L. (1985) 'R&D and Patenting Patterns in 25 Large MNEs', in *Proceedings of the Annual Conference of the Administrative Sciences Association of Canada, International Business Division (ASAC)*, vol. 6, Part 8, pp. 21–32
Franko, L. (1976) *The European Multinationals, a Renewed Challenge to American and British Big Business*, Greylock Publishers, Stamford
Fuller, R.A. (1983) 'Decentralized R&D Organization' in J.K. Brown and L.M. Elvers (eds.), *Research and Development: Key Issues for Management*, Conference Board Report no. 842, The Conference Board, New York, pp. 34–7
Hakansson, H. and Laage-Hellman, J. (1984) 'Developing a Network R&D Strategy', *Journal of Product Innovation Management*, vol. 1, no. 4, pp. 224–37
Hewitt, G. (1980) 'Research and Development Performed Abroad by US Manufacturing Multinationals', *Kyklos*, vol. 33, fasc. 2, pp. 308–27
Howe, J.D. and McFetridge, D.G. (1976) 'The Determinants of R&D Expenditures', *Canadian Journal of Economics*, vol. 9, no. 1, pp. 57–71
Keegan, W.J. (1980) *Multinational Marketing Management*, (2nd ed.), Prentice Hall, Englewood Cliffs, New Jersey
Lacroix, R. et Séguin Dulude, L. (1983) *Les disparités internationales et nationales dans les efforts de R-D: une explication de la situation canadienne et québécoise*, FCAC, Quebec
Mansfield, E., Teece, D. and Romeo, A. (1979) 'Overseas Research and Development by US-Based Firms', *Economica*, vol. 46, May, pp. 187–96 reprinted in V.H. Wortzel and L.H. Wortzel (eds.), (1985) *Strategic Management of Multinational Corporations: The Essentials*, John Wiley and Sons, New York, pp. 375–83

McFetridge, D.G. (1977) *Government Support of Scientific Research and Development: An Economic Analysis*, Ontario Economic Council Research Studies, University of Toronto Press, Toronto

McFetridge, D.G. and Warda, J.P. (1983) *Canadian R&D Incentives: Their Adequacy and Impact*, Canadian Tax Paper No. 70, Canadian Tax Foundation, Toronto, February

Palda, K.S. (1979) *The Science Council's Weakest Link: A Critique of the Science Council's Technocratic Industrial Strategy for Canada*, Fraser Institute, Vancouver

Robinson, R.D. (1978) *International Business Management*, (2nd ed.), Dryden Press, Hinsdale, Illinois

Ronstadt, R. (1977) *Research and Development Abroad by US Multinationals*, Praeger, New York

Ronstadt, R. (1978) 'International R&D: The Establishment and Evolution of Research and Development Abroad by Seven US Multinationals', *Journal of International Business Studies*, vol. 9, no. 1, pp. 7–24

Ronstadt, R. and Kramer, R.J. (1983) 'Getting the Most Out of Innovation Abroad', *Harvard Business Review*, March-April, pp. 94–9 reprinted in H.V. Wortzel and L.H. Wortzel (eds.), (1985) *Strategic Management of Multinational Corporations: The Essentials*, John Wiley and Sons, New York, pp. 400–5

Scherer, F.M. (1965) 'Firm Size, Market Structure, Opportunity and Output of Patented Inventions', *American Economic Review*, vol. 55, no. 5, pp. 1097–1125

Science Council of Canada (1980) *Multinationals and Industrial Strategy: The Role of World Product Mandates*, Science Council of Canada, Supply and Services Canada, Ottawa

Stobaugh, R. and Telesio, P. (1983) 'Match Manufacturing Policies and Product Strategy', *Harvard Business Review*, vol. 61, no. 2, pp. 113–20

Teece, D.J. (1981) 'Technology Transfer and R&D Activities of Multinational Firms: Some Theory and Evidence' in R.G. Hawkins and A.J. Prasad (eds.), *Research in International Business and Finance, Technology Transfer and Economic Development*, vol. 2, JAI Press Inc., Greenwich, Conn., pp. 39–74

Terpstra, V. (1977) 'International Product Policy: The Role of Foreign R&D', *Columbia Journal of World Business*, vol. 12, no. 4, pp. 24–32

Terpstra, V. (1983) *International Marketing*, (3rd ed.), Dryden Press, New York

Thomas, L.J. (1983) 'The Centralized Research Organization' in J.K. Brown and L.M. Elvers (eds.), *Research and Development: Key Issues for Management*, Conference Board Report no. 842, The Conference Board, New York, pp. 30–3

Data Sources

Dun and Bradstreet Canada Limited (1983) *Canadian Key Business Directory 1983*, Dun and Bradstreet Canada Limited, Toronto

Dun and Bradstreet International (1983) *Europe's 10,000 Largest Companies 1983*, Dun and Bradstreet International, London

Dun and Bradstreet Limited (1983) *Who Owns Whom 1983 — Continental Europe — Structure of Company Groups*, vol. 1, Dun and Bradstreet Limited, London

———— (1983) *Who Owns Whom 1983 — North America — Structure of Company Groups*, Dun and Bradstreet Limited, London

———— (1983) *Who Owns Whom 1983 — United Kingdom and Republic of Ireland — Structure of Company Groups*, vol. 1, Dun and Bradstreet Limited, London

Dun's Marketing Services (1983) *America's Corporate Families — The Billion Dollar Directory 1982*, Dun and Bradstreet Inc., Parsippany, New Jersey

———— (1984) *Million Dollar Directory 1983*, vols. I, II and III, Dun and Bradstreet Inc., Parsippany, New Jersey

Gouvernement du Canada (1982) *Comptes publics du Canada 1983 Volume II: Details des dépenses et des recettes*, section 36, Approvisionnements et Services Canada, Ottawa

International Directory of Corporate Affiliations 1983–1984: 'Who Owns Whom' (1983)
National Register Publishing Company, Skokie, Illinois

Scott's (1980) *Industrial Directory Atlantic Manufacturers 1983–1985*, (4th ed.) Scott's
Directories, Oakville, Ontario

———— (1982) *Industrial Directory Ontario Manufacturers 1983–1984*, (14th ed.) Scott's
Industrial Directories, Oakville, Ontario

———— (1980) *Quebec Industrial Directory 1980*, (10th ed.) Scott's Industrial Directories,
Oakville, Ontario

———— (1982) *Industrial Directory Western Manufacturers 1982–1983*, (6th ed.) Scott's
Industrial Directories, Oakville, Ontario

Science and Technology Canada (1978) *Directory of Scientific and Technological
Capabilities in Canadian Industry (1977)*, Supply and Services Canada, Ottawa

Statistics Canada (1979) *Inter-Corporate Ownership 1978–1979*, Supply and Services
Canada, Ottawa

———— (1984) *Inter-Corporate Ownership 1982*, Supply and Services Canada, Ottawa

12 WORLD PRODUCT MANDATES AND TRADE

Bernard M. Wolf

Introduction

In its report, the MacDonald Commission came up with the following question: '. . . especially in the event of free trade arrangements, how can Canadian subsidiaries of foreign corporations be encouraged to seek world product mandates (WPMs) from their parent corporations?' (Royal Commission on the Economic Union and Development Prospects for Canada, 1984, p. 38). The question is not whether WPMs are desirable but rather how their acquisition can be encouraged, particularly if Canada follows a freer trade strategy. Encouraging the acquisition of WPMs is clearly a current goal of Canadian economic policy. Elsewhere in its report, the Commission (1984, p. 37) states that 'there is evidence of strong market potential for specialised industries on a world scale'. World product mandating is seen as a method of restructuring and increasing the international competitiveness of Canadian subsidiaries of multinational enterprises, which control well over 40 per cent of manufacturing in Canada. Given the strong policy support for WPMs, the focus of this chapter is to consider the relationship between world product mandating and international trade.

WPMs, international trade, specialisation and freer trade are clearly intertwined. The restructuring of the subsidiaries with a view to increasing productivity is seen as necessary in an environment where, through various GATT multilateral tariff cutting rounds, the effectiveness of tariff protection has been substantially eroded. In the Tokyo Round alone, the average reduction in the Canadian tariff on dutiable industrial products will be about 40 per cent. The tariffs' weighted average will fall to about 9 to 10 per cent by 1987 from the 15 per cent level of 1979 (External Affairs, 1983b, p. 133). When duty-free imports are taken into account, the overall incidence of tariffs falls to between 4 and 5 per cent (External Affairs, 1983a, p. 29).

In its pure form, a WPM involves the assignment to a subsidiary of the total responsibility for all aspects of research and development (R&D), production and marketing of a product line on a worldwide basis.[1] In turn, the subsidiary imports other products from its parent or sister subsidiaries. In practice, a WPM granted to a subsidiary can be restricted either geographically or functionally. The geographical limitation can be in the form of granting exclusive market rights for only part of the world. Functional abbreviations can take the form of importing components, conducting some of the production outside Canada and/or having the marketing handled abroad for the mandated product. With respect to marketing, it may make sense for the Canadian subsidiary to allow the marketing of its mandated product to be carried out by the marketing arms of its sister subsidiaries. However, the subsidiary would still have to do some internal marketing so that the sister subsidiaries would promote its products. In turn, the Canadian subsidiary would act as a wholesaler for the products imported from the parent and other subsidiaries. Components of the mandated product can also be imported leaving the subsidiary with a viable WPM. However, when it comes to R&D, at least some development work must be carried out by the subsidiary, otherwise there really is no true product mandate but only a rationalisation of production. The R&D aspect is integral to mandating. Without it the subsidiary is not really in charge of the product line in terms of its evolution; it would be totally dependent on the parent for keeping it on the technological frontier.

The objective of this chapter is to consider the relationship between world product mandating and international trade, particularly with respect to Canada. Two questions are asked:

(1) What is the theoretical basis for the international trade which results from world product mandating, and how does it differ from the underpinnings of more conventional trade theory?
(2) What are the factors contributing to a change in the trade balance when world product mandating is introduced? To answer this question a simple model is developed. For policy purposes the model emphasises the variables which governments may seek to influence.

The Basis for Trade Resulting from WPMs

Conventional trade theory, often referred to as the Heckscher-Ohlin-Samuelson (HOS) model, emphasises different factor endowments as the basis for trade. To put it simply, countries tend to specialise in the production of goods utilising the relatively abundant (and hence relatively cheap) factor.[2] The emphasis here is on interindustry trade between countries rather than trade between firms. This model has come under strong criticism for not accurately portraying the way in which trade is carried out (Casson, 1984, pp. 15–16). When one looks at trade stemming from world product mandating the shortcomings of the HOS model are obvious.

World product mandating is particularly important for a small country. In small domestic markets, such as Canada's, product specific economies of scale in production (and perhaps to a lesser extent plant specific economies of scale) cannot be attained without exporting. Plants must specialise, and to specialise they must export.[3] Thus, the *raison d'être* for trade stemming from world product mandating is the attempt to realise product specific economies of scale. These economies of scale can be in the form of the production run's length during a specific time period and/or the cumulative length of the production run over time. In the latter case, cost savings are often said to occur by moving along (downward) the experience curve or the learning curve.[4] Different factor endowments are not essential for trade. For example, it is possible that two equal sized small countries, both having the same factor endowments, might find it advantageous to trade by each manufacturing half of the products in twice the quantity required domestically. If each of the products is in the same industry the trade is intra-industry rather than interindustry. In any event, the trade is intra-firm. The transactions utilise the firm's internal market rather than its external market.[5] Above all, the firm rather than the country is the focal point.

While the primary emphasis is on the scale economies attainable by the firm, demand conditions can play a role as well. For example, if a country consumes substantially more of good one than good two, that country is likely to be the location for the good one mandate, *ceteris paribus,* since transportation costs will be minimised.[6] It might be added that product differentiation serves as an inducement to world product mandating. In the absence of differentiated products longer production runs could be achieved in the small domestic markets without resorting to exports.

Although factor endowments are not the key element in explaining trade stemming from WPMs, they are still of significant importance. The factor endowment perceived by the firm, compared to the factor endowment available in another country, will influence whether or not a WPM strategy is followed and this in turn will have an effect on the trade flows resulting from the decision. Production costs are clearly an important consideration in determining which subsidiary will receive a product mandate, and relative factor endowments contribute to cost differences. Government policies of various kinds can alter the factor endowment as seen by the individual firm. As well, the quality of available management needed to carry out a WPM must be considered part of the factor endowment. Furthermore, a WPM often arises out of the situation where a subsidiary has been producing a variety of products all with short production runs, but trade liberalisation makes that output no longer competitive. The decision whether or not to create a WPM then rests in part on the costs of closing the plant compared to the costs which need to be incurred in order to establish a WPM and the costs associated with using that plant compared to the costs of using plants located elsewhere. In some sense the existing plant can be seen as an element in the factor endowment.

Thus, scale economies, demand conditions, product differentiation and factor endowments (broadly defined) together, as viewed by the firm, provide the impetus for the international trade which arises out of a world product mandating strategy. However, the analysis is yet more complicated when one ceases to focus solely on production. As previously indicated, for a subsidiary to hold a WPM some R&D must be conducted there; otherwise one is only dealing with production rationalisation. We now turn to the task of sorting out the interplay between R&D and factor endowments as well as between R&D and scale economies.

First, in deciding to do R&D at a subsidiary level the firm must examine whether the resources are available for the task or, if not, whether they can be easily generated. These resources are, of course, part of the factor endowment. Second, in doing R&D the subsidiary will acquire know-how which will become part of its factor endowment. The innovative and managerial know-how can perhaps be used not only for the initial mandate but subsequent ones which evolve out of the first mandate. Thus, the mandate may actually contribute to changing the factor endowment of the firm; this will potentially have an impact on future trade flows.

When R&D is included, the scale economies associated with that activity must be considered in relation with the production economies of scale. A conflict may arise between the scale economies associated with R&D and those of the production process. For example, the run length resulting from the establishment of a WPM may produce goods at the minimum point on the cost curve but, in contrast, the R&D may be done more cheaply by centrally combining it for several product lines (economies of scope). If so, the trade-off between the two must be examined. Under these circumstances only when the production scale economies exert a stronger impact on cost than do the R&D scale economies is the WPM strategy viable. In the cases where the opposite is true, government aid to R&D could be considered as a tool to tip the balance in favour of mandating (Wolf, 1983, p. 103). Alternatively, it may be possible to divide R&D in such a way that some is done centrally and the rest is conducted by the subsidiary. Aside from having to reconcile the scale economies associated with production and R&D, Rugman (1981, p. 606) has argued that the WPM strategy is often not viable because the decentralisation of R&D can lead to the dissipation of the firm's specific advantage. He argues that the foreign subsidiary may develop a degree of autonomy that the parent would find objectionable. Buckley (1983), in contrast, dismisses Rugman's case by suggesting that decentralisation is not necessarily in basic conflict with internalisation. He indicates that 'it is mistaken to equate the internalization of activities with the centralization of these activities' in the parent firm (Buckley, 1983, p. 44). This chapter's author is also not very persuaded by Rugman's argument and therefore tends to agree with Buckley. Nevertheless, empirical work on the costs of decentralised R&D would be valuable.

Finally, having discussed the relationship between international trade and WPMs, a word should be said about WPMs and trade barriers. For WPMs to exist, trade in the mandated products must be relatively free and transportation costs relatively low. Firms advocating WPMs become spokesmen for trade liberalisation.

While WPMs and free trade generally go hand in hand, the relationship is actually a more complex one. The reason is that nontariff barriers are often used by governments to secure WPMs for subsidiaries. For example, government procurement policies can be used to provide the subsidiary with a ready domestic market. In the foregoing analysis of the relationship between trade flows and WPMs, the emphasis has been on the firm and how it utilises factor endowments and considers scale economies not only in production, but also in R&D. Much more research is needed along these lines to develop both a better theory of international trade and of the multinational enterprise within which trade stemming from world product mandating can fit.

Modelling the Changes in Trade Balance Resulting from WPMs

In this section, a model is developed for the purpose of analysing the change in the merchandise trade balance resulting from the introduction of a WPM by a multinational enterprise's Canadian subsidiary. No attempt is made to include royalties or other service payments or any capital flows. Although it was emphasised earlier that for a true WPM to exist some R&D must be done by the subsidiary, the following analysis looks only at the production process since the R&D aspect does not in the short run critically influence the merchandise trade relationships. In this respect the model would be equally applicable to simple production rationalisation by a subsidiary which does not involve a WPM (such as under the Canada-US Automotive Products Trade Agreement).

The model begins with a typical 'tariff factory' type of subsidiary. The subsidiary produces a wide variety of products, all in very short production runs, at costs which generally would not be viable without tariff or the equivalent nontariff barrier protection (Caves, 1975). Based on data generated by Baldwin and Gorecki (1983), MacCharles (1984) concludes that these short runs stem from efficient size in a small market. To create the necessary volume, a wide variety of goods must be produced. Given its high cost structure, the subsidiary cannot export. It will import, in a wholesaling capacity, the products required to fill out its product line which it finds uneconomical to produce in Canada, as well as the components for the goods it does produce in Canada. Initially, the subsidiary has a high average propensity to import, which is quite typical (Statistics Canada, 1981).

The successive postwar tariff reductions, ending with the current Tokyo Round, have eroded protection. Moreover, a number of low cost newly industrialised countries have entered the Canadian market through imports. These two conditions no longer make the 'tariff factory' viable. One solution is for the subsidiary to specialise by seeking a WPM for one of its product lines. The subsidiary changes the methods by which it produces these goods and lengthens the production run. It now services not only the Canadian market for these goods but also the multinational enterprise's markets in other countries. Meanwhile, it imports from the parent or sister subsidiaries the goods whose production it has phased out. The model examines how such a strategy affects the subsidiary's trade balance.

The Model

It is assumed that the Canadian subsidiary of a multinational enterprise sells three classes of goods in Canada:

Let subscripts
a = final goods initially produced domestically which will become mandated.
b = final goods initially imported which will continue to be imported.

c = final goods initially produced domestically in short production runs which will be imported after the introduction of the WPM.

i = intermediate goods or inputs into any of the above (i.e. *ia* refers to inputs required to produce a).[7]

X = value of exports per annum.

M = value of imports per annum.

P = value of domestic production per annum.

B = value of the balance of trade per annum.

* = period after the WPM's introduction (no * refers to the period before the introduction of the WPM).

Other assumptions are that, compared to the initial period, in the interval after the introduction of the WPM:

● the output of a expands and productivity increases as a result of product specific scale economies.

● the price of a declines thus making a competitive in export markets.

● the value of the domestic consumption of a may be altered as a result of the decline in price.

● the domestic consumptions of b and c do not change.

● the prices of b and c do not change.

● the exchange rate is unaffected.

● the tariffs and nontariff barriers are unaltered. (The trade barriers will have previously fallen enough to make the WPM strategy viable.)

● no allowance is made for one time only imported capital equipment.

With respect to trade, it is assumed that the unrationalised subsidiary has no initial exports ($X_a = 0$). This would be expected in a 'tariff factory' type of subsidiary. With a WPM, it will then export a. Again, as is typical of 'tariff factory' subsidiaries, it is assumed that components or inputs for both a and c are initially imported, (M_{ia} and M_{ic}). For a, some inputs (M_{ia}) continue to be imported after the WPM and their magnitude will be discussed below.

The original trade balance is:

$$B = X_a - (M_b + M_{ia} + M_{ic}) \text{ or} \tag{1}$$

$$B = -(M_b + M_{ia} + M_{ic}) \text{ given that } X_a \text{ is assumed zero.} \tag{2}$$

The new trade balance is:

$$B^* = X_a^* - (M_b^* + M_c^* + M_{ia}^*) \tag{3}$$

The change in the trade balance is (3) minus (2)

$$B^* - B = X_a^* - (M_b^* + M_c^* + M_{ia}^*) + (M_b + M_{ic} + M_{ia}) \tag{4}$$

Given that $M_b = M_b^*$

$$B^* - B = X_a^* - M_c^* - M_{ia}^* + M_{ic} + M_{ia} \quad \text{or} \quad (5)$$

$$B^* - B = X_a^* + (M_{ia} - M_{ia}^*) + (M_{ic} - M_c^*) \quad (6)$$

Each of the elements in the right hand portion of equation (6) will now be considered. A numerical example is given in the Appendix.

(1) The improvement in the trade balance will be greater, the larger the exports of a, X_a^*, resulting from the WPM.

(2) The improvement in the trade balance will be greater, the bigger is $(M_{ia} - M_{ia}^*)$. In most typical 'tariff factories' the percentage of imported inputs is very high so that M_{ia}/P_a would be large. Firms often import components from their parent firms or from their parent firms' suppliers. In the latter case, the suppliers' long production run and the lack of having to assert search behaviour are obvious reasons for such imports (See MacCharles and Wolf, 1982, pp. 605–6). After introducing the WPM there is reason to suggest that this average import propensity might decline. The subsidiary will now have exclusive rights to the production of a. Hence, it is likely to be worthwhile for it to establish its own search for suppliers. Moreover, the tendency toward Japanese style 'on time' deliveries of inputs might give the edge to a local Canadian supplier. On the other hand, the percentage of inputs imported could also decline if the subsidiary itself decided to integrate backwards now that the quantity of inputs would represent a larger production run. However, according to MacCharles (1984) it is more likely that the subsidiary, which no longer has the need to use the capacity of the plant by producing a large variety of goods, may decide to increase its purchased goods to value added ratio by opting out of the production of some components. In so doing it would make a larger market available to suppliers, who again are more likely to be Canadian based. (The fact that the supplier may be Canadian has a particular attraction to policymakers since Canadian owned firms do not have an easy access to foreign markets as do multinational enterprises with sister subsidiaries in place.)

While the relative amount of imported components may thus decline $(M_{ia}^*/P_a^*) < (M_{ia}/P_a)$, the absolute amount may increase because of the greatly increased volume of production $(P_a^* > P_a)$. However, the value of the imported inputs would not increase by as much as the volume increase if there is a fall in the price of inputs resulting from the larger volume utilised. When the value of imported inputs used in the production of a increases, the trade balance is reduced.

(3) The third element in the equation is $(M_{ic} - M_c^*)$. Two factors are important with respect to c. First is the size of the production of c, (P_c), which is displaced by the same value of imports (M_c^*). The smaller P_c is, the smaller M_c^* will be and hence the smaller the deterioration in the trade balance. Second, the higher the average import propensity for inputs into c, (M_{ic}/P_c), the smaller the value added contributed by the subsidiary prior to the implementation of the WPM and, therefore, the smaller negative effect on the trade balance when finished c goods are imported.

The focus placed on X_a^*, $(M_{ia} - M_{ia}^*)$ and $(M_{ic} - M_c^*)$ reveals a number of the crucial aspects affecting a subsidiary's balance of trade when a WPM is introduced. Of course, it should be noted that it is not always desirable to increase the trade balance of the subsidiary. However, in times of high unemployment, a larger trade balance does stimulate the economy. As well, unless the trade balance of the mandated subsidiaries increases, the overall trade balance will worsen as non-mandated plants close and substitute imports for their production.

Aside from the trade balance, much attention has been given to the proportion of sales which are imported (Statistics Canada, 1981) and which are exported. In this model the subsidiary's import propensity (imports/sales) goes from

$$\frac{M_{ia} + M_b + M_{ic}}{P_a + M_b + P_c} \text{ to } \frac{M_{ia}^* + M_b^* + M_c^*}{P_a^* + M_b^* + M_c^*}$$

and the subsidiary's export propensity (exports/sales) goes from X_a which is assumed to be zero to

$$\frac{X_a^*}{P_a^* + M_b^* + M_c^*}$$

Again, the same variables that influence the trade balance are important here.

Implications of the Assumptions

It is not the author's intention to analyse at length the effects of relaxing some of the assumptions made in this model. However, some limited comments are worth pursuing.

If the demand for a is elastic when the price of a declines, more a will be consumed domestically. In the event that P_a^* is fixed, less a will be available for exporting and the trade balance will be reduced.

The price of c may change when the switch is made from domestic production to imports. If it rises and demand is inelastic, the trade balance will be adversely affected compared to what is indicated by the model.

No account has been taken of income changes resulting from the productivity increases attributable to the WPM. The rise in income may lead to increases in the domestic consumption of some goods. If it is in a, then X_a^* will be smaller (assuming again that P_a^* is fixed); if it is in b or c, then M_b^* or M_c^* respectively will be larger. In each of these cases B^*, the new trade balance, will be smaller.

Much will also depend upon what other firms and their subsidiaries do. Thus far the analysis has been restricted to the trade of one subsidiary, ignoring what other firms do. Among the possibilities are that (1) rival firms may also rationalise by establishing a WPM in a, (2) they may rationalise by establishing a WPM in another product such as b or c, (3) they may maintain the *status quo* or (4) they may leave the industry. Any of these changes may affect the initial firm's trade balance and certainly the aggregate trade balance for all the subsidiaries. Although the possibilities are many, only one will be specifically considered here. If several firms rationalise in such a way as to require inputs similar to those used in product line a, the scale factor will provide more incentive for the domestic production of a, thereby reducing M_{ia}^*.

Finally, it should be noted that the model, as is characteristic of comparative static analysis, has assumed a one time only change. However, with a WPM which includes innovative and managerial capacity, the mandated products will evolve over time and additional mandates may be obtained. These aspects are crucial to the longer-run consequences for the trade balance, the import and export propensities. Even in cases where there is simple rationalisation of production and no real WPM, the product mix can change over time as technology, costs, and tastes change.

Increased Intra-Industry and Intra-Firm Trade

It is often suggested that the specialisation integral to a WPM strategy will lead to more intra-industry and intra-firm trade. The intra-industry phenomenon is examined first. Given that the subsidiary was not initially exporting, there could not have been any intra-industry trade at all. If X_a^* is in the same industry class as M_{ia}^*, M_b^* or M_c^*, there will now be intra-industry trade generated. The resulting intra-industry trade can be measured by one of the formulas used for that purpose such as Grubel and Lloyd's formula (1975).

As for intra-firm trade (non-arm's length trade), prior to the introduction of WPM, trade was assumed to be all one way — from parent to subsidiary. If the parent now handles the subsidiary's foreign marketing of a, then X_a^* becomes part of intra-firm trade. There is no change in the trade in b. M_c^* is likely to come from the parent (or sister subsidiaries) and thus is part of intra-firm trade. It is also likely that both M_{ia} and M_{ic} were in part derived from the parent firm. Let us denote shipments from the parent with a superscript δ. Taking the above into account the change in intra-industry trade will be:

$$\Delta \text{ Intra-firm trade } = X_a^* + M_b^{*\delta} + M_c^{*\delta} + M_{ia}^{*\delta} -$$
$$(M_b^{\delta} + M_{ic}^{\delta} + M_{ia}^{\delta})$$

Given that $M_b^{*\delta} = M_b^{\delta}$, then

$$\Delta \text{ Intra-firm trade } = X_a^* + M_c^{*\delta} + M_{ia}^{*\delta} - (M_{ic}^{\delta} + M_{ia}^{\delta})$$

Further Research

The analysis has focused on changes in the trade balance (and changes in both the import and export propensities). However, it would be possible to consider the change in the subsidiary's overall balance of payments. Modelling this situation, of course, would be very much more complicated. One would have to consider, on a multiyear basis, the level of new investment in the subsidiary, the method of financing the investment, the origin of the new capital stock, the royalty payments for R&D, the repatriation of profits, etc. One would be confronted with an analysis reminiscent of Hufbauer and Adler's (1968) classical, anticlassical and reverse classical assumption cases used in trying to define a recoupment period for foreign direct investment. This is clearly beyond the scope of this chapter.

The trade flow model in the second part of this chapter has been developed as a tool in order to analyse the impact of world product mandating on trade relations. Despite the model's shortcomings it does highlight the key variables. Empirical studies utilising the model would provide a good deal of information on international trade stemming from world product mandating.

Appendix 12.1

Numerical Example to Illustrate the WPM Trade Balance Model

Let

X_a	= 0		X_a^*	= 90
M_a	= 0		M_a^*	= 0
M_b	= 20		M_b^*	= 20
M_c	= 0		M_c^*	= 70
M_{ia}	= 5		M_{ia}^*	= 20
M_{ic}	= 35		M_{ic}^*	= 0
P_a	= 10		P_a^*	= 100
P_b	= 0		P_b^*	= 0
P_c	= 70		P_c^*	= 0

$$\frac{M_{ia}}{P_a} = \frac{5}{10} = 50\% \qquad \frac{M_{ia}^*}{P_a^*} = \frac{20}{100} = 20\%$$

$$P_a + P_b + P_c = 10 + 0 + 70 = 80$$

$$P_a^* + P_b^* + P_c^* = 100 + 0 + 0 = 100$$

$$B = -(M_b + M_{ia} + M_{ic}) = -20 - 5 - 35 = -60$$

$$B^* = X_a^* - (M_b^* + M_{ia}^* + M_c^*) = 90 - 20 - 20 - 70 = -20$$

$$B^* - B = -20 - (-60) = -20 + 60 = 40$$

Imports have risen by 50, exports have risen by 90, the trade balance has improved by 40.

Notes

1. This definition of WPM is not universally accepted. D'Cruz (1983), for example distinguishes between WPMs and globally rationalised products based on the degree of decision-making autonomy held by the subsidiary. Some globally rationalised products would then in fact fit the author's definition of a WPM. An example of such a case might be where a subsidiary has the responsibility for a component product used by another subsidiary.
2. The relatively physically abundant factor will be the relatively cheaper factor unless demand conditions are extremely strong for the product using that factor.
3. Changes in technology available from computer assisted manufacturing (CAM) may reduce the product specific economies of scale and hence the need for WPMs.
4. Both types of product specific economies of scale can be important. In the first case the savings arise from not having the downtime associated with changing over to make a slightly different product.
5. When the impact of trade liberalisation is intra-industry and intra-firm, the adjustment is less disruptive than when the change results in interindustry trade.
6. In the case of the HOS model, demand conditions also may play a pivotal role. As already indicated, demand conditions can make the physically abundant factor

economically scarce and its price relatively high compared to another factor. Under such conditions the country will specialise in the product utilising the relatively physically scarce factor.

7. One could consider a fourth class of goods, d, which continues to be produced domestically in short production runs. However, since M_{id} is likely to equal M_{id}^* the results are unaffected.

References

Baldwin, J. and Gorecki, P.A. (1983) *The Relationship Between Plant Scale and Product Diversity in Canadian Manufacturing Industries*, Discussion Paper no. 232, Economic Council of Canada, Ottawa

Buckley, P.J. (1983) 'New Theories of International Business: Some Unresolved Issues' in M. Casson (ed.), *The Growth of International Business*, George Allen and Unwin, London, pp. 34–50

Casson, M. (1984) 'General Theories of the Multinational Enterprise: A Critical Examination', *Discussion Papers in Inter-Investment and Business Studies*, no. 77, University of Reading, Department of Economics, Reading

Caves, R.E. (1975) *Diversification, Foreign Investment and Scale in North American Manufacturing Industries*, Economic Council of Canada, Information Canada, Ottawa

D'Cruz, J.R. (1983) *Strategic Planning in Canadian Subsidiaries of US Multinationals: Current Practice and Public Policy Implications*, Working Paper 83–05, University of Toronto, Faculty of Management Studies, Toronto

External Affairs Canada (1983a) *Canadian Trade Policy for the 1980s: A Discussion Paper*, Supply and Services Canada, Ottawa

External Affairs Canada (1983b) *A Review of Canadian Trade Policy: A Background Document to Canadian Trade Policy for the 1980s*, Supply and Services Canada, Ottawa

Grubel, H.G. and Lloyd, P.J. (1975) *Intra-industry Trade: The Theory and Measurement of International Trade in Differentiated Products*, John Wiley and Sons, New York

Hufbauer, G.C. and F.M. Adler (1968) *Overseas Manufacturing Investment and the Balance of Payments*, Tax Research Study no. 1, US Treasury Department, Washington, DC

MacCharles, D.C. (1984) *Canadian International Intra-industry Trade*, unpublished paper, University of New Brunswick, Saint John

MacCharles, D.C. and Wolf, B.M. (1982) 'Statistics Canada's Flirtation with Mercantilism', *Canadian Public Policy*, vol. 8, no. 4, pp. 603–7

Royal Commission on the Economic Union and Development Prospects for Canada (1984) *Challenges and Choices*, Supply and Services Canada, Ottawa

Rugman, A.M. (1981) 'Research and Development by Multinational and Domestic Firms in Canada', *Canadian Public Policy*, vol. 7, no. 4, pp. 604–16

Statistics Canada (1981) *Canadian Imports by Domestic and Foreign Controlled Enterprises*, Supply and Services Canada, Ottawa

Wolf, B.M. (1983) 'World Product Mandates and Freer Canada-United States Trade' in A.M. Rugman (ed.), *Multinationals and Technology Transfer: The Canadian Experience*, Praeger, New York, pp. 91–107

INDEX